Human Dimensions of Water and Development: Issues and Challenges in Context of Climate Change

Mohinder Slariya, Ph.D.
&
Dai Yeun Jeong, Ph.D.

ISBN-10: 1517674824
ISBN-13: 978-1517674823

Table of Contents

Preface and Acknowledgement

Issues and challenges related to development and environment are of paramount significance in wake of climate change. Development as a concept has been defined in existing literature as a process of desired change and has been focused on value which is being attached by the policy makers and excutors. The concept of development has been there since new-lithic stage of human development and man's desire to make his life more comfortable led him on the road of development. Starting from that period to-date because of many reasons development has been focusing on issues and challenges related to particular water based development. Whole book is not only concerate on water related issues but also with some related issues has been included.

As an outcome of chamba climate meet-2014, the third volume is divided into 18 chapters contributed by different scholars coming from different parts of the globe. The first chapter is contributed by an eminent scholar and Professor of Sociology Prof. OP Monga on development and biodiversity, which is a detailed describption of theoretical framework related to development and biodiversity highlighting existing legislative at global and local level. The second chapter is based on primary data collected and complied by associate professors of chemistry and geography i.e. Dr. Rashmi and Dr. Sanjay working in the department of higher education, govt. of Himachal Pradesh and is an effort to present a picture of social and ecological resilence about the montain hazards like earthquakes, add another aspect. Third chapter contributed by Dr. KL Sharma and the title of his contribution is impacts of climate change on traditional agricultural practices and highlights the concerns of farmers in wake of climate change which compelling them to shift from traditional agricultural practices. The fourth chapter has been contributed by Bhasmati Thakurata and focuses on human-animal confict and exploring the policy, belief and myths of West Bengal in India, while Charvi Mehta in chapter V is contrating on intrepeneurship as a solution for green economy and sustainable development.

The sixth chapter of seri village which adopted sericulture as an alternate source of livelihood and this case study is an answer to enhance livelihood options to the poor farmers of hills. The next chapter i.e. chapter VII is contributed by Dr. Nikhil Kanongo which is a description of tribal use of local flora for Therapeutic in Patalkot area of chhindwara district of Madhaya Pradesh in India, based on

i

traditional knowledge which is being used by them since long time. Contribution of Natasha Sharma on traditional knowledge for medication in Amchis in Himachal Pradesh as a case study of Dharamshala region of Kangra district. Amchi system of medication is similar to Ayurvedic and prominently being practices in Himalayan region where modern medication system is not available and this system believes on Sowa-Regpa which means science of healing and rich accumulation of science, art and philosophy and emphasized on systematically and logically understand the body, disease in relation to the environment. The ninth chapter contributed by R. Subin is based on traditional fishing practices being used by paniya tribes in wayanad district of Kerla southern peninsula of India. Farm water management in wake of climate change highlighting associated problems and solutions thereof in form of case study of Pakpattan. Punjab in Pakistan is the contribution made by Amer Hayat and he tried to put another perspective of water based and requirement for development and it's contribution to enhance the income of farmers.

Botanist Saroj Meena from Rajsthan University has advocated in chapter eleventh and describe morphometric response and germination behavior in arid legumes to salt stress. The 12th chapter is contributed by Rosanne Van Schie, a scholar and economic policy advisor from first nation university, university of Canada and her contribution on the topic Integrating First Nation Traditional Ecological Values (TEV) into Science-Policy Platforms for Sustainable Forest Management in Canada is an eye opener for the scholars who are working on traditional ecological values and it's scientific interpretation and application to understand the traditional knowledge based practices being used since ages. The next chapter contributed by Chintansinh Suratia and Dr. Kewal Krishan on Impacts of temperature variability on rural livelihoods in Kangra, Himachal Pradesh and it is an attempt to see the impacts of temperature variability on livelihood Options. The eminent professor of geography from Pan Grover, University, Chandigarh Prof. Neel Grover, is next contributor who contributed on role of Cultural imperatives to the sustainable development, which is the need of the hour for any developing economy and it is impossible to exclude cultural values from the process of all types of development and it's human dimension cannot be ignored. Shabina Masoodi, a scholar from Kashmir valley and his contribution on the conservation issues andgaps of w has shown the other as orld famous Dal Lake pect which is sometime missing. Neeraj Kumar Sharma, an associate professor has raised the issue of use of traditional floral biosdiversity in context of climate change and highlighted some issues and threat in western Himalayan region of India. Vibhav Mister a has put all environmental legislations focusing on human dimensions of developmental practices in form of title environmental legislations and practical disorientations and provided a detailed description of available legal framework which could be used to understand it's vital application in the process of development. The last chapter has been contributed by PhD scholar from IIT Mumbai, Chandan Kaushal on discourses of cultural landscape and water from anthropological perspective in form of case study of Ravi valley in Chamba district of Himachal Pradesh, India.

As a whole it can be stated that the contribution made by different scholars coming from diverse field worldwide, is a beauty of this academic venture. With a particular stress of human dimension of development and use of water based alternatives is the main thrust of this collection. First of all I would like to put on record the contribution of all scholars who contributed for the volume coming from different parts of the world. And the financial and academic support of Asia Climate Change Education Centre, Jed u, South Korea and it's director Prof. Day Yuen Jeon without whom it was impossible to organize the conference and him believe on me make this historic conference in other part of the world which is relatively very backward and without modern facilities.

I owe this academic contrition to my parents and respected teachers (Dr.RK Kaistha, Prof. SK Sharma and Prof. OP Monga). My parents brings me to this world and my teachers teach me how to make my world of my choice so both are fundamental in shaping me and introduce me in the world.

I am thankful to all my colleagues, friends, students who stood round the clock with me to make the conference possible and get this book published. I am also thankful to the Secretary and director, Higher education, govt. of Himachal Pradesh for believing on me for mega academic event in chamba and Principal of my college who gave me free hand to work and the administrative staff who extended their full cooperation during conference. Last, but not least, my mother, my wife and my kids for their emotional support during conference and at the time I was losing confidence and feel alienated all come to recuse me and help me to come out of it and I could succeed to come over. My daughter Abhidiksha and son Abhishiant and greatest source of emotional support and never fell me down.

I am thankful to almighty who bless me sound mind and kind soul to work and contribute something to the academic world and hoping this little contribution will prove beneficial to all the readers round the globe.

I will be happy to respond to any quarry at mkslariya@gmail.com

Chamba, Himachal Pradesh, India: 23rd of October, 2015

(Dr. Mohinder Kumar Slariya, PD, Ph.D.)

Environmental Sociologist

Chapter-I

Impact of Climate Change Conferences

O P Monga* and Anubhav Monga**

Introduction

Word "climate change" itself shows unpleasant environment to human beings but it has been created by human beings. Change of economy face from traditional economy to industrialized economy, growth in population level and energy security for huge population increased the emissions level many times than it was in the three centuries before and it caused for global warming. Increased emissions resulted in drought, floods, extinction of species, rise in sea level and change in monsoon. The impact of climate change have been started to realise by human society and now trying to remove the footprint of human beings in recent climate changes. So they came up with world conferences for immediate action and it led to creation of treaties and protocols. This paper analysis about international response for climate change, its objectives and challenges faced by the available mechanism. First world climate conference is the first world response towards climate change.

First World Climate Conference

First world climate conference was held on Feb 1979 in Geneva which was organized by World Meteorological Organization. It was one of the major international conferences on climate change. The conference organized four working groups to look into climate scientific data, identification of climate issues, study on impact created by human, research on climate viability and change. The conference led to

---

*Professor of Sociology & Associate Dean, Faculty of Management Sciences and Liberal Arts, Shoolini University of Biotechnology and Management Sciences, Solan (HP).
**Anubhav Monga B.Tech, MBA, Lead Engineer, HCL Technologies, America Inc. Cary, North Carolina, USA

1

establishment of world climate programme and climate research programme and also led to the creation of Intergovernmental Panel on Climate Change (IPCC) by WMO and UNEP in 1988.It urged world's government to forecast the climate change and it mostly focused on how climate change might affect human activities. It examined the possible impacts on special activities such as agriculture, fishing, forestry, hydrology and urban planning. The conclusions were summarized in the Declaration of the world climate conference which highlighted the international community's perception of climate as an essential resource. The Declaration also identified cause of global warming as increased atmospheric concentration of carbon dioxide resulting from the burning of fossil fuels, deforestation, and changes in land use.

Impact of Conferences

This first world climate conference led to signing of convention on Long range transboundary air pollution by 34 governments and EU and this led to commitment towards reduction of reducing sulphur emissions (1985) and reducing nitrogen oxide (1988).

IPCC working structure is given below:

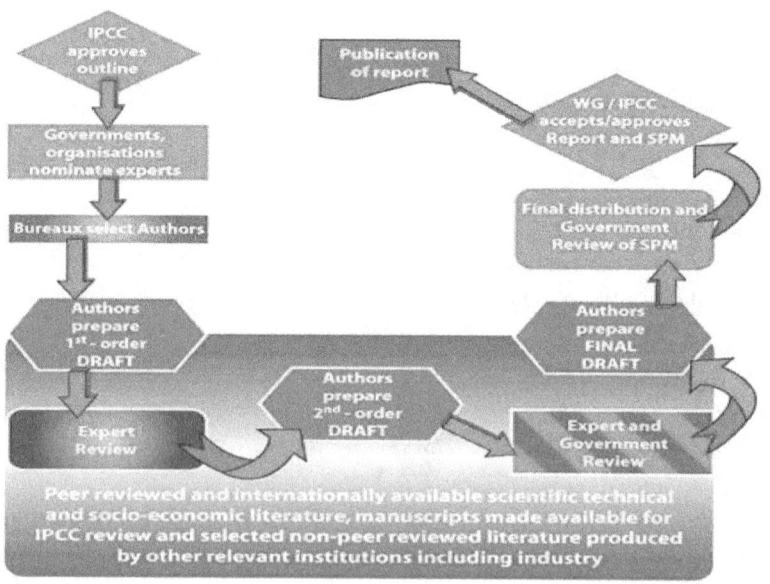

Source-IPCC official site (http://www.ipcc.ch/)

Intergovernmental Panel on Climate Change (IPCC)

IPCC is a scientific intergovernmental body was established in 1988 by World Meteorological Organization (WMO) and United Nations Environment Programme (UNEP). The IPCC is tasked with reviewing and assessing the most recent scientific, technical and socio-economic information and provides world with a clear scientific view on the current state of climate change and its potential environmental and socio economical consequences. The IPCC does not carry out any of its own research work. Main activity of IPCC is publishing special reports on topics relevant to the implementation of the UNFCCC. Thousands of scientists from all over the world contribute to the work of the IPCC on a voluntary basis as authors, contributors and reviewers. None of them is paid by the IPCC. IPCC is only open to member states of the WMO and UNEP. The IPCC reports are cited in almost any debate related to climate change. IPCC is currently organized in 3 working groups and task force. They are assisted by Technical support units (TSU), which are hosted and financially supported by Government of the developed countries. The IPCC work is supported by a central secretariat, whose role is to plan, coordinate and oversee all IPCC activities. The IPCC Bureau comprises the IPCC Chair, the IPCC Vice-Chairs, the Co-Chairs and Vice-Chairs of the Working Groups and the Co-chairs of the Task Force. The Panel meets in Plenary Sessions at the level of Government Representatives for all member countries. Major decisions are taken by the Panel during the Plenary Session.

Second World Climate Conference

The world climate conference was held on 29th October to 7th November 1990 in Geneva. IPCC first assessment report was completed for this conference and this conference was more political than first world climate conference. The main task of this conference was to review the world climate programme set up by the first conference such that to review the world climate programme, IPCC first assessment report. The scientist and experts emphasized on risk of climate change but ministerial declaration was not showing the high level commitment and disappointed the participated scientists. The conference statement emphasized on additional international observational and research efforts would be necessary to strengthen the knowledge base of climate process and human interactions.

SWCC encouraged these streams international activities

- o Future structure of the world climate programme

- o Requirement of developing countries to meet the energy security and build up their capability

- o Cooperation in International Research through the WCRP, IGBP and other related international programmes IPCC First assessment report The IPCC First Assessment Report was completed in 1990 and served as basis of the UNFCCC.

Highlights of First Assessment Report

- ❖ Emissions resulting from human activities increase CO_2, methane, CFC and nitrous oxide. This enhances green house effect and results to global warming

- ❖ Long living gases requires immediate reduction in emissions from human activities to reduce the concentration 60% at present level

- ❖ Based on current model, estimated increase in global mean temperature would be 0.3°C per decade

- ❖ Average rate of global mean sea level rise of about 6cm per decade due to thermal expansion of the oceans and melting of some land ice

United Nations Framework Convention on Climate Change (UNFCCC)

UNFCC is an international environmental treaty submitted at the United Nations Conference on Environment and Development (UNCED) and also it known as earth summit held in Rio de Janeiro from June 3 to 14, 1992. Its objective is to stabilize the greenhouse gas concentrations in the atmosphere at the level of prevent dangerous and reduce anthropogenic (man-made changes) with climate system. Kyoto protocol is part of the UNFCCC. The UNFCCC opened for signature on May 9, 1992 but it came to force on March 21, 1994. At June 1992 UNFCCC treaty signed by 152 countries including voluntary countries and December 2009 it had 192 parties. The UNFCC first task is removal of green house gas inventories which were used to create bench mark level for level1 countries and for the commitment of those countries green house gas reductions.

UNFCCC classified countries into three categories:

Annex1- industrialized countries and economies in transition. There are 40 Annex 1 countries and European Union also a member. These countries are classified as classified and economies in transition. These countries have committed to reduce emission level of green house gases (GHG) to below the 1990 specified level i.e. benchmarking set by UNFCCC according to 1990 emission level which has to be quantified value to achieve the below 1990 emission level. They may implement through allocating the reduced allowances according to emission level for major players. They can exceed their allocations by buying emission allowances or offset their exceeded quantity through accepted mechanism by all the UNFCCC countries.

Annex1 countries: Some of the countries-US, UK, Australia, Canada, France, Germany, Italy, Japan, Newzland, Denmark

Annex 2-Developed countries which pay for costs of developing countries. There are 23 Annex 2 countries and European Union. It is a subgroup of Annex1 countries and it comprises OECD countries but it excluded the transition in economy countries.

Annex-2 countries: Some of the countries-US, UK, Australia, Canada, France, Germany, Italy, Japan

Developing Countries

Developing countries not required to reduce the emission levels unless they are getting fund and technology from developed countries

Reasons for no restriction on emissions level:

1. Emission control adverse link with development of country.
2. Developed nations have contributed for more for the present level concentration
3. Developing countries per capita income is still very low

4. Share of developing countries in emission level likely to increase in future
5. They can sell carbon credit to emission reduction committed countries
6. They can get funds and technology from Annex2 countries developing countries may volunteer to become Annex1 country when they have sufficient economy level.

Conferences of the Parties (COP)

Since UNFCCC came in to force, there has been annual meeting for their parties called Conference of the Parties (COP) to assess the climate change activities progress of those countries. From 2005 onwards COP meeting held along with Meetings of Parties of the Kyoto Protocol (MOP), and parties to the Convention that are not parties to the Protocol can participate in protocol related meetings as observer.

IPCC Second Assessment Report

Working group I, II & III committed itself to completing its Second Assessment in 1995, not only updating the information on the same range of topics as in the First Assessment, but also including the new subject area of technical issues related to the socio-economic aspects of climate change. The IPCC Second Assessment Report was completed in on time and WGI reported on the science of climate change, WGII reported on the scientific-technical analyses of impacts, adaptations, and mitigation and WGIII reported on the economic and social dimensions.

Major conclusions of working group I

- Greenhouse gas concentrations have continued to increase
- Anthropogenic aerosols (tiny particles that are major contributors to smog and haze) tend to produce negative radioactive forcing
- Climate has changed over the past century
- The balance of evidence suggests a discernible human influence on global climate
- Climate is expected to continue to change in the future

- There are still many uncertainties There is evidence of an emerging pattern of climate response to forcing by greenhouse gases and sulphate aerosols in the observed climate record.

WG-II provided several conclusions

- Models project that a substantial fraction of the existing forested areas will undergo major changes in broad vegetation types and deserts are likely to become more extreme

- Productivity of agriculture and forestry will increase in some areas and decrease in others

- Developing countries will be more seriously affected and may have fewer adaptation options.

WG-III found that a sensible way to deal with climate change is through a portfolio of actions, which will differ according to country

Impact

First and second world climate conferences were tried to prepare scientific data, impact assessment, and preparing treaties to the countries. So there were no considerable action taken place towards reduce the emissions. Kyoto protocol was the first successful protocol for emission reduction. Fig shows apparently that there were no symptoms of controlling the emissions even Kyoto protocol came into force in 2005 due to unsolved issues between countries.

Kyoto Protocol

Kyoto protocol is a protocol, part of the UNFCCC treaty aimed to reduce the green house gas emissions caused by humans to fight against global warming. The protocol initially was adopted by COP3 parties on 11th December 1997 in Kyoto, Japan and came to force on 16th December 2005. The protocol has been signed by 191 countries among these 39 Annex1 countries committed to reduce the green house gas emissions (GHG) and two group gases hydro fluorocarbons, perflurocarbons by specified level and chlorofluorocarbon to avoid depletion ozone layer. The Kyoto protocol came into force on 16th February 2005.

Principle concepts of Kyoto protocol

- Legal commitment for Annex1 countries to reduce the GHG emission reduction

- In order to reduce GHG emissions, Annex1 countries required to prepare polices and measure for the reduction of GHG for that they are required to utilise all the available mechanisms such as joint implementation, clean development mechanism(CDM) and emissions trading by carbon credits

- Reduced impacts on developing countries by adaption fund for climate change

- Accounting, review of process and reporting of integrity of Kyoto protocol

Mechanisms for Emission reduction:

- International Emissions Trading (IET)

- Clean Development Mechanism (CDM)

- Joint Implementation (JI) CDM and JI are called project based mechanisms because emission reduction can be achieved by implementing projects. It is based on idea of "production" of emission reductions and it is formulized to encourage reduction on GHG in non-Annex-1 countries. IET based on setting up of quantitative restriction on emission reduction and JI encourages emission reduction in developed countries.

The emission reductions achieved by CDM are called certified emission reductions (CERs) and reductions achieved by JI called emission reduction units (ERUs). These reductions are called in credits.

Commitments towards reduction

- Industrialized countries committed to reduce their collective emissions by 5.2% EU committed to reduce by 8%

- US-7%, Japan-6%, Russia-0% committed reduce the emissions COP6 attempted to solve the issues between EU(wanted stronger agreement) and US, Canada, Japan, Australia (wanted less demanding agreement) but it was unable to reach the solution.COP7 was held on 2001 to establish the final details of the protocol. The first meeting of the parties to the Kyoto protocol (MOP1) was held in 2005 along with COP11 of UNFCCC.

Impact

Kyoto protocol is major initiative taken by UNFCCC to reduce the emissions, even though it was created on 1997 but it came to force on 2005 due to dissolved disputes between countries. Around 190 countries have signed for emission reduction and the Kyoto protocol provided various mechanisms to reduce the emissions. It came up with carbon credits and trading those credits between countries. It has created awareness among industries and society and derived considerable investment to energy conservation and energy efficiency.

But emission reduction lies only in the paper and it does not provided any quantitative production. It has shown clearly in below figure. Carbon dioxide, nitrous oxide and methane are increasing at same rate which had before 1990. Only CFC has come down due to restriction from governments to save ozone layer from depletion.

High rate economic growth of developing countries (China, India, and Brazil) and increase in per capita consumption of those countries are the reasons for increase in emissions of those countries and expected to be major contributors for emissions in future.

Third Assessment report (TAR)

IPCC third assessment report was completed on 2001 and it focuses on environmental, social, economic consequences of climate change and potential adoption responses. It consists of sensitivity, adaptive capacity, vulnerability of natural and human systems to climate change and the potential impacts.

Major conclusions of TAR

1. Average global temperature have increased 0.6°C over 20th century and temperature have risen over past 4 decades in lower 8KM circle and resulted in decrease of snow cover and ice extent.

2. Emissions due to human activities continue to alter atmosphere and produces negative radiative forcing.
3. Ability of simulation models to project the future has increased due to demonstrated performance on a range of space and time scales.
4. There is new and stronger evidence of global warming for last 50years derived by human activities • Human contribution towards climate change will continue throughout the 21st century
5. Special report on emission scenarios, the projected concentration on CO^2 in the year 2100 will be in the range of 540-970 ppm, compared to 280 ppm in pre industrial era and 368 ppm in year 2000
6. Projections using SERS models results in increase of global temperature from 1.4 to 5.8°C
7. Global sea level projected to rise by 0.09 to 0.88m between years 1990 and 2100.
8. Climate change projected to increase threats to human health especially for low income people who are living in tropical/subtropical countries

Bali climate conference (COP13)

COP13 held on December 2007 in Bali, Indonesia, it is famously known as Bali conference. The meeting had 10000 participants including 180 countries representatives and observers from intergovernmental and nongovernmental organizations. The COP13 conference led to final agreement known as Bali road map. This Bali conference outlined a new negotiation process for path of post Kyoto protocol (after 2012). This included adaptation fund for developing countries, technology import from industrialised countries, emission reduction to achieve specified level and solution for deforestation.

1. But there were more controversy between countries especially between U.S and India, China
2. U.S position was not aligned with other countries
3. Restriction on developing countries (china, India) while developed countries was not able to reduce the emissions below specified level expressed their dissatisfaction in the conference itself.

IPCC Fourth Assessment report

IPCC fourth assessment was completed on 2nd February 2007. Three working groups compiled reports on physical science, impacts, adaptation, vulnerability and mitigation of climate change

Working group I: The physical science basis Changes in atmosphere:

1. Carbon dioxide, methane, and nitrous oxide are long lived gases increased rapidly due to human activities
2. Amount of CO_2 in atmosphere in 2005 (379ppm) reached the highest mark in 650000years
3. Amount of methane in atmosphere in 2005 (1774ppb) reached the highest mark in 650000years
4. Primary source of increase in CO_2 due to fossil fuels
5. Primary source of increase in methane is combination human agricultural activities and fossil fuels

Warming of the Planet

1. Global average temperature increased about 0.74°C for last 100 years (which is 0.6°C in third assessment report)
2. Ocean has been absorbing more than 80% of the heat added to the climate system
3. Average arctic temperature increase in almost double the global average rate in the past 100 years
4. Ice, snow, rain and the oceans
5. Mountain glaciers and snow cover have declined on average in both hemispheres
6. Greenland and Antarctica land based ice sheets melting have mostly contributed (>90%) for sea level rise
7. No clear trend in number of hurricanes i.e. increase in hurricanes
8. For increase in hurricane intensity above caused by the human activities

Factors for warm or cool the Planet

1. Sulphate aerosols from fossil fuels combustion have a cooling impact on climate and which partially counteracts the global warming caused by CO^2

2. Radiative forcing from the sun from all human activities is about +1.6watts/sq.mt
3. Radiative forcing from increase in solar intensity is about +0.12watts/sq.mt
4. Radiative forcing from CO2, methane and nitrous oxide increasing at faster rate than past 10000years
5. Projections using SERS models results in increase of global temperature from 2 to 4.5°C and best estimate about 3°C

Radiative forcing is altering the incoming and outgoing energy in atmosphere. Positive index shows the negative impact on climate and *vice- versa.*

Working group II

Impacts, Adaptation and Vulnerability

Major conclusions of working group II

1. Changes in arctic and Antarctic eco systems
2. Increase in rock avalanches in mountain regions
3. Changes in spring events unfolding leaves, laying eggs, migration, etc.
4. More and larger glacier lakes
5. Increasing ground instability in permafrost region
6. Increase in water temperature affects algae, fish, etc and leads change in water circulation, oxygen, ice cover

Working group III: Mitigation of climate change

Mitigation in the short term and medium term:

Sector	Key mitigation technologies and practices currently available	Key mitigation technologies and practices projected to be commercialized before 2030
Energy supply	Improved supply and fuel efficiency-fuel switching from coal to gas, nuclear and renewable power	Carbon capture and storage(CCS) for coal, gas and biomass based electricity and advanced nuclear, tidal and renewable energy

Transport	Fuel efficient vehicles-hybrid vehicles, cleaner diesel vehicles, usage of public transport, usage of cycles and transport planning	Advanced electric and hybrid vehicles, efficient aircrafts and second generation bio fuels
Buildings	Efficient lighting, usage of day lighting, efficient electrical appliances, promoting green building, alternative refrigeration fluids	Integrated design of commercial buildings such as intelligent meters and solar PV integrated in buildings
Industry	More efficient electrical equipment usage, heat and power recovery, material recycling and control of non-CO^2 gas emissions	Advanced energy efficiency, CCS for cement, ammonia and iron manufacture
Agriculture	Improved cropping system Improved rice cultivation techniques Management to reduce methane emission Improved nitrogen fertilizer	Improved crop yields
Forestry	Reduced deforestation, forest management, reforestation and use of forestry products for bio-energy to replace fossil fuels	Improved remote sensing technologies for analysis of vegetation/soil carbon sequestration and land usage. Tree species improvement to increase biomass productivity and biomass sequestration
Waste	Land fill methane recovery, controlled waste treatment, recycling and waste minimization	Biocovers and biofilters to optimize CH4 oxidization

IPCC estimates

1. Stabilizing green house gases between 445-535ppm CO2 equivalent would result in reduction of 0.12% annual GDP
2. Stabilizing green house gases between 535-590ppm CO2 equivalent would result in reduction of 0.1% annual GDP
3. Stabilizing green house gases between 590-710ppm CO2 equivalent would result in reduction of 0.06% annual GDP

Copenhagen climate conference

Copenhagen is a global collaboration between international business and science founded in 2007 by leading independent think tank in Scandinavia, Denmark. The Copenhagen climate meet (COP15) was to provide technical, public support and assistance to the decision makers about creating new treaty to replace Kyoto protocol (after 2012). The Bali conference provided the road map for post Kyoto protocol treaty. The Copenhagen council comprises 30 global leaders classified as business leaders, scientists and policy makers.

Key points of the Accord:

1. Politics – acknowledgement of seriousness of problem and need for immediate emergency action by all the parties
2. Science – global average temperature increase kept below 2°C
3. Developed countries need to provide financial, technical and support for capacity build up.
4. Developed countries will commit to quantified emission reduction by 2020
5. Developing countries will implement emission reduction that are monitored, reported and verified
6. Financial – developed countries committed to provide $30billion between 2010 to 2012 and $100 billion per annum by 2020. This will be from both public and private participation and this fund will be used to provide financial, technical and support for capacity build up
7. REDD plus – provide funds to reduce emissions from deforestation and degradation

Positive bits

1. US, china, India and other developing countries signed agreement for first time
2. All the countries are committed to reduce the emissions

3. Limiting global average temperature increase below 2°C

4. Monitoring, reporting and verification for developing country emission reduction

5. Developed countries committed to provide $100billion per annum

Missing bits

1. No clarity over CDM and other market based mechanisms

2. Lack of long term reduction goal such as 2050

3. No timetable for legally binding agreement

Copenhagen climate summit criticised by many experts and scientists and considered as failure by many countries but its failed to replace Kyoto protocol and controversial in emission reduction commitment between US and developing countries (India & china).

UK calculated its carbon footprint as 1.2billion tonnes of green house gas and Annual CO_2 emissions for top 5 countries as follows:

Country	Annual CO_2 emissions (metric tonnes)	% of global total
China	6538367	22.30%
United States	5838381	19.91%
European Union	4177817	14.04%
India	1612362	5.50%
Russia	1537357 5	24%
World	29321302	100%

Two Asian developing countries listed in the top5 emitters, so consensus of developing countries will lead to effective implementation.

Commitments of countries

India has committed to reduce carbon emissions intensity by 20-25% below 2005 levels by 2020 China has committed to reduce carbon emissions intensity by 40-45% below 2005 levels by 2020 Japan has committed to reduce green house gas emissions by 25% below 1990 levels by 2020 US has committed to reduce green house gas emissions by 25% below 1990 levels by 2020 COP16 to be hosted by Cancun, Mexico and COP17 expected to be held in Durban, South Africa. These two conferences believed to provide a suitable protocol to cut down the emissions while having consensus of all the countries.

References

1. http://en.wikipedia.org/wiki/United_Nations_Framework_Con vention_on_Climate_Changehttp://pubs.acs.org/doi /abs/10. 1021/es60150a606

2. http://www.wmo.int/wcc3/history_en.php   http://unfccc.int/ essential_background/library/items/3599.php?such =j&meeting=%22The+First+World+Climate+Conf erence,+12-23+   February   +1979,+Geneva,+ Switzerland%22#beghttp://

3. www.iisd.ca/vol12/1226006e.html http://www.wmo.int/pages/ themes/climate/partnerships.phphttp://envfor.nic.in/ cc/india_unfccc.htmhttp://www5.imo.org/Share Point/mainframe.asp? topic_id=233

Chapter-II

Mountain Hazards: Social and Ecological resilience with special reference to Earthquakes- A Case Study of Lahaul and Udaipur Division of Lahaul- Spiti, Himachal Pradesh

Rashmi Ramaul & Sanjay Singh Pathania*

Abstract

Disasters signal the failure of a society because such happening are beyond the coping capacity of a society cause severe setback to major development project as construction of building and other infrastructure hapazardly/unscientifically e.g. Chamera Hydel-I which has been constructed on the main boundary fault to face major catastrophes and cause severe setbacks to major developmental projects. Thus attention needs to be paid to mitigating and tackling vulnerability. Earthquakes, landslides, snow avalanches, floods, debris flows, epidemics and fires, among other processes, have caused injury, death, damage and destruction in the mountains. The combination of a dynamic bio- geophysical environment and intensified human use has increased the vulnerability of mountain social–ecological systems to risk from hazards. The ability of social–ecological systems to build resilience in the context of hazards is an important factor in their long-term sustainability. Lahaul and Udaipur division of Lahaul - Spiti is situated in Trans Himalayan zone of Western Himalayas, which is still unstable and makes it vulnerable to earthquakes. The district falls in seismic zone 4 and 5. Due to the accumulation of stress along the Indian and Eurasian Plate over the years there is strong possibility of a major earthquake in this region of the Himalayas. The community is neither prepared nor aware to deal with various hazards. The present paper discusses the efforts made by the researchers to create awareness and preparedness, among the local community and teachers about earthquakes and structural and non- structural issues in the Lahaul and Udaipur Division of Lahaul –Spiti.

Key words: Earthquakes, Risk, Vulnerability, Hazards, Awareness

*Associate Professors, Govt. College of Teacher Education, Dharamshala

Introduction

Hazard is a dangerous condition or event occurring in nature that could cause injuries, loss of life or damage to property, livelihood and environment. Natural hazards like earthquakes, landslides, floods, droughts, cyclones, forest fires, volcanic eruptions, epidemics and major accidents are quite common in different parts of the world. These lead to loss of life, property damage and socio-economic disruption and affects necessary services like water supply, sewerage, communication, transport and power supply etc. Such losses have grown over the years due to increase in population and physical resources. These losses are not evenly distributed and are more prevalent in the developing countries due to higher population concentration and low levels of economic growth. Earthquake is one of the most destructive of all the natural hazards. It occurs due to sudden movement of the ground as a result of release of elastic energy in a matter of few seconds. The impact of the event is traumatic because it covers large area and occurs suddenly and is not predictable. Earthquakes not only destroy the human settlements and its structures but also destabilize the economic and social structure of the country. (R.P.Tiwari, 1999). In any mountainous area the community may be more prone to multiple hazards due to earthquakes, because it causes rock falls which block the roads and affect the transportation system and also landslides can occur which obstruct the flow of the rivers causing severe floods in the lower areas. Like any other natural hazard, it is not possible to prevent earthquakes from occurring. The disastrous effects can be minimized through scientific understanding of their nature, causes, frequency, magnitude and areas of influence. Earthquake disaster mitigation and preparedness strategies are the need of the hour to reduce its miseries to mankind. Mitigation, preparedness and planning includes avoiding hazards for instance, by providing warning to enable evacuation preceding the hazard, determining the location and nature of the earthquake hazard, identifying the population and structures vulnerable for hazards and adopting strategies to combat the menace. (Ravi Sinha etal, 2008).

Earthquakes in India

Our sub-continent is highly prone to various natural hazards including earthquakes, which has a capacity to inflict huge loss of life and property. It poses a real threat to our country with 59 percent of its geographical area vulnerable to seismic disturbances of different intensities. The entire Northeast region, Northern Bihar, Himachal Pradesh, Uttaranchal, Jammu & Kashmir, some part of Kutch and Rajasthan and the Gangetic plain are in the seismic zone V and IV. The occurrence of earthquakes can be explained with the "Plate Tectonic Theory" and most of the earthquakes in the (HFA) Himalayan Frontal Arc occur due to continuous subduction/ collision between the Indian Plate and the Eurasian Plate. This arc is about 2,500 km long and extends from Kashmir in the west to Assam in the east. (Acharrya, 1999 & South Asia Disaster Report, 2010).

India has suffered the most disastrous earthquakes in the world. It is seen that between 1897 to 2005 an average of three earthquakes of intensity 6.0, or more than 6.0 on the Richter scale occured in our country, which shows a high degree of seismic vulnerability in India and pose a real threat to its citizen. (R.P.Tiwari, 1999). Out of the total geographical area of India 59 % of the land is vulnerable to earthquakes. 10.9 % of the land is vulnerable to severe earthquakes and lies in zone V, 17.3 % of the land falls in zone IV, 30.4 % of the land falls in zone III and 41.40% of the land falls in zone II. (Bureau of Indian Standards, 2002).

The 26th January 2001 Bhuj Earthquake and 8th October 2005 Kashmir Earthquake were the most disastrous and very high in terms of loss of life and property. The Bhuj (Gujarat 23°40′N 70°28′E) (D.R.Kullar, 2005) earthquake measured 7.8 on Richter Scale and the death toll was 20,005 people,   63, 21,812 were affected and the estimated damage was 2326 million dollars. The Kashmir (PoK Muzaffarabad 34°25′N,73°30′E) (D.R.Kullar, 2005) earthquake measured 7.4 on the Richter Scale in PoK and 6.8 in India and the death toll was 73,338 persons in PoK and 1,309 persons in India. Total affected people was 51,28,309 in PoK and 1,56,622 in India and the estimated damage was 5,200 million dollars in PoK and the estimated damage was 1,000 million dollars in India.(as recorded by EMDAT on 31 Dec 2010, South Asia Disaster Report, 2010). It was found that due to earthquakes the casualties occurred due to the collapse of buildings however, similar high intensity earthquakes in the developed countries do not lead to huge loss of lives, because structures in these countries are built in structural mitigation measures and earthquakes resistant features. As such there is need for strict compliance of structural codes and mitigation features, proper sensitization programmes and awareness among the masses. (N.D.M. Guidlines, April, 2007).

The past century have witnessed an increase in the number of damaging earthquakes in India, earthquakes which occured during the last two decades showed that there was very little knowledge regarding the earthquakes among the masses. The vast extent of the damage and the consequent loss of life associated with these events reflect the poor construction practices in our country. Before the 2001 Bhuj earthquake, constructions with poor seismic resistance were assumed to be a feature of rural areas, and urban structures were considered to be safer due to the use of engineering knowledge and modern construction materials, but this earthquake shattered the myth of urban seismic safety because of widespread damage to modern buildings. It was seen that there is low awareness among the general masses towards structural safety and the inability of regulatory bodies and technical experts in maintaining quality standards in constructions, whether in rural or urban areas. (Sinha, R. and Goyal, A.2003). So there is need to educate, make aware and prepare the masses about the consequences of earthquakes.

The unpredictability of nature can cause disasters of such high intensity that it becomes impossible to respond unless the community is prepared to cope with the effect in the pre-disaster and post disaster period. Preparedness is foremost in order to mitigate the effects of any calamity and to reduce the loss of life and property. The Disaster Management Act was enacted on 23rd December, 2005 by the Government of India, to adopt a holistic and integrated approach to Disaster Management. Keeping in view the aims of the Disaster Management Act, the present work was conducted to shift the response of the community from relief-centric to a proactive prevention, mitigation and preparedness-driven approach.

Earthquakes in Himalayan Region

Earthquakes pose a great threat to the environmental stability and human life in the Himalayan region because the whole area is prone to high seismic risk. The Indian plate continues to push the Asian plate northward at the rate of about 2cm per year and this colliding force builds up pressure which is released in the form of earthquakes. The entire Himalayan Region is considered to be vulnerable to high intensity earthquakes of a magnitude exceeding 8.0 on the Richter Scale, and in a relatively short span of about 50 years, four such earthquakes have occurred: Shillong, 1897 (M8.7); Kangra, 1905

21

(M.8.0); Bihar–Nepal, 1934 (M8.3); and Assam–Tibet, 1950 (M 8.6). (Biham, R.2004). The 1905 Kangra earthquakes is one of the deadliest earthquakes in the history of India. This earthquake resulted in the death of 20,000 people, destruction of around 1.0 lakh houses, perishing of around 53,000 animals and was felt in an area of around 4,16,000 square kilometres. Scientific publications have warned that very severe earthquakes are likely to occur anytime and the constructions of buildings in high seismic zone are also not much familiar with the earthquake-resistant features specified in the building codes. Indigenous earthquake-resistant houses like the bhongas in the Kutch Region of Gujarat, dhajji diwari buildings in Jammu & Kashmir, brick-nogged wood frame constructions in Himachal Pradesh and ekra constructions made of bamboo in Assam are increasingly being replaced with modern Reinforced Cement Concrete (RCC) buildings without incorporating earthquake resistant features and without compliance to building codes and bye-laws. (Sinha et al., 2001 & 2003). However, it is essential to ensure the earthquake safety of non-engineered construction in the rural areas because more than 61 percent of the buildings in rural areas are built with mud and clay, stone and brick compared to 26.7 percent buildings in urban areas. So the large number of causalities in rural areas in the past earthquakes shows that there is need to give special attention to the earthquake safety of buildings in rural areas. (N.D.M.Guidlines, April, 2007).

Study Area

Himachal Pradesh is a mountainous state located in North–West India. It shares an international border with China. The State has highly dissected mountain ranges interspersed with deep gorges and valleys. It is also characterized by diverse climate that varies from semi tropical in lower hills, to semi arctic in the cold deserts areas of Spiti and Kinnaur. Its altitude ranges from 350 meters to 6975 meters above mean sea level. It is located between Latitude 30° 22′40″ N lat. to 33° 12′20″ N lat. and Longitude 75° 45′55″ E long to 79° 04′20″ E long. Himachal with its complex geological structures presents a complicated topography with intricate mosaic of mountains ranges, hills and valleys. The seismic sensitivity of Himachal is very high as over the previous years about 250 earthquakes with magnitude 4 and 62 earthquakes having magnitude of 5 and above have struck state. Himachal is not only highly sensitive from the earthquake point of view but the risk has also grown manifold as the population and

22

infrastructure have increased considerably over the last 20 years. The Earthquake Hazard Map of BMTPC, 2006 shows that Himachal Pradesh lies in one of the highest risk zone areas of the state (Zone IV & V).

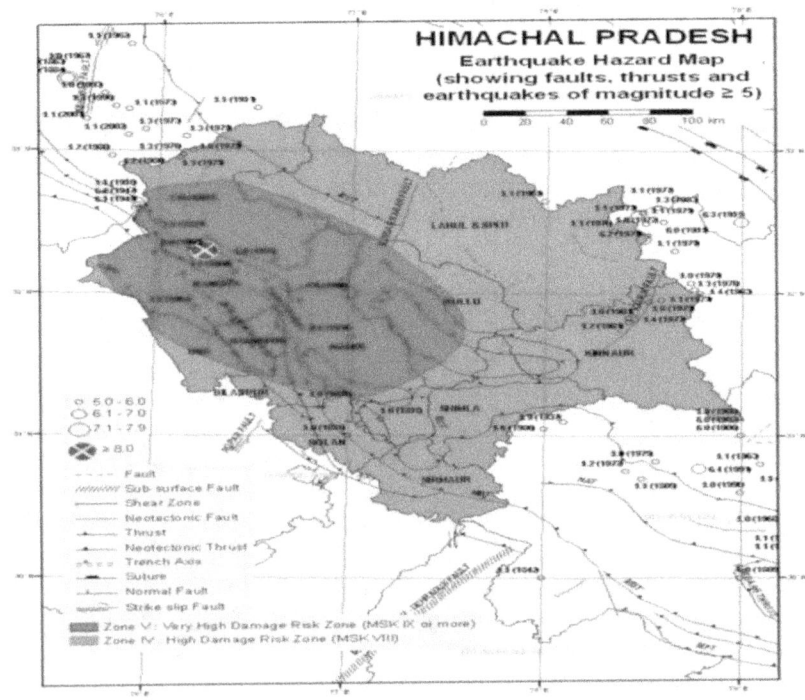

Earthquake Hazard Map of Himachal Pradesh
(Source: BMTPC Atlas of India)

Chamba, Kullu, Kangra, Una, Hamirpur, Mandi and Bilaspur Districts lie in the very high damage risk zone V and the area falling in this zone may expect an earthquake of intensity MSK IX. The remaining districts of Lahaul and Spiti, Kinnaur, Shimla, Solan and Sirmour lie in zone IV and the areas in this zone are in high damage risk with expected intensity of MSK VIII.

District-wise occurrence of Earthquakes from 1800-2008

Sr. No.	District	Number of Earthquakes	Percent in Total
1	Chamba	186	33.63
2	Lahaul-Spiti	99	17.90
3	Kinnaur	93	16.82
4	Mandi	53	9.58
5	Shimla	49	8.86
6	Kangra	39	7.05
7	Kullu	19	3.44
8	Sirmour	8	1.45
9	Solan	4	0.72
10	Hamirpur	2	0.36
11	Bilaspur	1	0.18
12	Una	0	0.00
	Himachal Pradesh	553	100

Source Source: Oldham (1883), Bilham (2004), Chandra (1992), Quittmeyer and Jacob (1979), IMD, ANSS, and NEIC

Keylong is the head quarter of Lahaul-Spiti district. The altitude of Lahaul-Spiti is between 4480 metres to 6400 metres above the mean sea level. According to 2011-2012 Census report there are 521 villages and 41 Panchayats, 03 development blocks, 03 sub divisions Udaipur, Lahaul, and Spiti, 02 tehsil Lahaul, and Spiti and 01 sub tehsil Udaipur in the district. The density of population is 2 persons per sq km which is probably the thinnest in the world. It is the third least populous district of the India out of 640 districts. According to 2011-2012 Census report the total population of Lahaul-Spiti district is 31,528 persons, males; 16,455 and females15, 073 and the sex ratio is 916. The total literacy rate of Lahaul-Spiti district is 77.34 percent, male 86.97 and female 66.50 percent. Agriculture is the main occupation of the population and river Chandra, Bhaga and Spiti develops the main valley which originates from a glacier in the district (Singh, G, 1994).

The district of Lahaul-Spiti in the Indian state of Himachal Pradesh consists of the two formerly separate districts of Lahaul and Spiti. The present administrative centre is Keylong in Lahaul. Before the two districts were merged, Kardang was the capital of Lahaul, and Dhankar the capital of Spiti. Lahaul & Spiti is a big district having international boundary with China. It attained the status of a district in the year 1960. Earlier, it was merely a Tehsil of Kullu Sub-division. The total geographical area of Lahaul-Spiti district is 13,833 sq. kilometres. The valleys, mountains, glaciers, rivers, forests, pastures, *Gompas* (monasteries) and ancient buildings of the former ruling dynasty are the important features of this district. Lahaul-Spiti is situated in Trans Himalayan zone of Himalayas having high mountain ranges considered to be a sedimentary wedge between colliding plate margins enclosing deep narrow valleys/gorges of River Chandra Bhaga and Spiti and its numerous tributaries. Winters are severe with heavy snowfall and summers are mild with rainy season in most of the Lahaul and Udaipur Sub-Divisions of the district. These climatic conditions make it vulnerable to different kinds of natural hazards which have increased due to human activity and intensified human use.

Objectives

1. To sensitize, make aware and prepare the teachers, students and the community   about the earthquakes.
2. Capacity enhancement by training teachers and educating community about earthquakes.
3. To develop emergency response with in the community immediately after an earthquake.
4. The main objective of this study is to prevent loss of life and property through preparedness, prevention, mitigation and quick response.

Significance of Study

The significance of the study is to create understanding and awareness that would help to educate, prepare the community at large and to draw the attention of masses to structural and non- structural issues in the public buildings, homes and work places, medical preparedness and conducting mock drills in government offices and institutions.

To develop Social and Ecological resilience with in the community related to Earthquakes:

The present study i.e. Udaipur and Lahaul sub division are highly prone to earthquakes, floods and landslides. These area lie in the western part of young folded mountains of Himalayas, which is still unstable. The whole district falls in the seismic zone IV & V. A majority of the buildings constructed in this area are non-engineered and built without adhering to earthquake construction principles. In the study it was seen that a lot of wood is used in the construction of houses, hence the houses are also vulnerable to fire hazards due to the earthquakes. The high mountain and steep slopes could result in landslides in the event of an earthquake and result in delaying any kind of outside response. The houses are built of mud unburnt brick walls or fieldstone walls as such the level of damage risk is very high. Due to the accumulation of stress along the Indian and Eurasion plate over the years, there is a strong possibility of a major earthquake in this region of the Himalayas. It was found by the researchers that the community of the area is quite oblivious of any kind of threat due to an earthquake. The people in this region are neither prepared nor aware of any major catastrophe. It was seen that connectivity and terrain of the area would make it impossible for any kind of outside help to reach the area. There was a lack of awareness at all levels whether Government employees, elected representatives or the general public. Hospitals and schools are not prepared to deal with any such causalities. The existing construction is not hazard resistant and public awareness is very low, schools do not have any Disaster Management plan, and have not conducted any mock drills for enhancing preparedness. There is no medical preparedness in schools for effective earthquake response. Preparedness about earthquakes has a direct bearing on the structural and non-structural issues and socio-economic development. The ability of socio-ecological system to build resilience in the context of hazards is an important factor in their long term sustainability. (Berkes etal 2003) identify resilient social-ecological systems as those that enable livelihood sustainability in the pace of change through self-organization, re-organization and learning. Self-organization refers to the ability of a social-ecological system to establish agencies, arrangements and institutions to mitigate the effects of hazards. Self – organization is useful in forecasting and publicizing hazard events, reacting in an organized and effective way in the face of an emergency. The key qualities in building resilience are the ability to learn i.e. to acquire knowledge and the ability to apply it to a situation or anticipated situation i.e. to adapt. Adaptation requires that the knowledge is used to purposefully adjust the characteristics of the socio-ecological system and alter the characteristics of the physical environment. Thus adaptation or adaptability is central to resilience (J.S.Gordner, 2006).

Hazards such as earthquakes not only cause immediate damage to infrastructure of all sorts but also have secondary effects. Due to the inherent vulnerability in mountain terrain, such as Lahaul and Udaipur sub divisions that areas are more susceptible to blockage by landslides and snow avalanches. The interruption of any kind of outside help, communication, fuel, electricity and water supply hampers the rescue and recovery operations and delays medical and other services which can cause the spread of infectious diseases. Keeping the above facts in mind it was felt that communities are not only the first to be affected in disasters but also are first responders. Building community leadership and a chain of trained community cadres through participatory approach can help harness the resilience and resourcefulness of the community to cope up with exigencies. Involvement of students, teachers and the local people will ensure a coordinated and collected action during any emergency. Community participation ensures local ownership, volunteerism and mutual help to prevent and mitigate the effects of any disaster. During the course of the present study public awareness is being created on various aspects of Disaster Management. Initially training, orientation and capacity building of school teachers and students of the district was done, because, it is well known that educating students and teachers is educating the community. Since schools are our universal institutions for sharing knowledge and skills, the expectations for schools to be role models in disaster mitigation is high. The awareness preparedness and mitigation efforts were started by conducting a one day advocacy programme for Principals and Headmasters of Government schools at Udaipur in the month of August 2013. The programme was to sensitize the institutional heads about the basic concept of hazards, disasters, vulnerability, risks, mitigation, prevention, preparedness, relief and reconstruction. It was an effort to describe the roles and responsibilities of the concerned officials and their team members in the wake of a disaster. The training outlined the process by which the school authorities should manage the disaster and to tap human and material resources in the aftermath of an earthquake. The time, year or month of any seismic event cannot be predicted but it is possible to minimize the impact of an earthquake and reduce the loss of life and property if adequate preparations are made at the school and household level. A three days capacity building training was conducted for school teachers of the area.

The frame work of the training was built around four pillars.

[1] Awareness: Awareness was generated by conducting sessions on basic concepts of hazards, disaster, vulnerability, mitigation, prevention, preparedness, relief and reconstruction. Awareness in the community was to be generated by the trainees by organizing rallies, street plays, various competitions in schools, like painting competitions etc. Meeting with key persons of the area like elected representatives, members of youth clubs, women organizations and NGOs to motivate the community to work for a safer living. Structural and non-structural measures of disaster mitigation were discussed. Structural mitigation refers to any physical construction to reduce or avoid possible impacts of hazards which include engineering measures and construction of hazard-resistant and protective structures and infrastructure damage, collapse of structural buildings or infrastructure are common consequences of disasters. Training was given about structural mitigation, which refers to training people to reduce hazards, for example, falling objects during earthquakes. It involves tie-downs, anchors, brackets and others support systems and identification of hazards such as cluttered halls or stairways, jammed windows or exit doors inflammable liquids, suspended ceilings etc. Potential hazards outside the school such as power lines, trees, routes were to be identified.

[2] Preparation of School Disaster Management Plan [SDMP]: Preparation of school disaster management plan would entail the physical location and demographic details of the school building and its surrounding environs. Number of classrooms in the school, staff rooms, laboratories and play grounds or open space within the school premises. While preparing SDMP resource mapping was to be done, which includes human skills and material resources available in the school, and the coping mechanisms for the hazards were to be identified and listed. A building evacuation plan was to be prepared, to identify the safe places where children and staff members could take shelter and the evacuation routes, exit routes should be marked properly. The plan was to be disseminated to the school authorities and students.

[3] Skill Training: Apart from providing knowledge for preparing a plan, certain practical inputs are also needed to implement the plan on the field. This aims at imparting skills so that the participants are well equipped to respond to the disaster effectively. Disaster management

teams would be constructed in the pre-disaster phase which would include awareness team, search team, rescue team and medical first-aid team.

[4] Mock Drills: Efficacy of Disaster Management Plan's are tested and refined through mock drills. Involvement of all the stakeholders and community at large ensures a better and coordinated response during a disaster by making everyone aware of their roles and responsibilities. Mock drill also helps in preparing responding agencies to determine the kind and number of resources required and also helps them to carry out a capacity/resource assessment. A mock drill was conducted by the researchers at Govt. Sr. Sec School, Udaipur, staff members and students of the school participated in the drill. Before the drill was conducted the participants were divided into four groups i.e. awareness team, search team, rescue team, and medical first-aid team. The awareness team gave the basic tips to the students about drop, cover and hold during an earthquake, evacuation route and buddy system etc. The search team identified the casualties room-wise and reported them to the head of the institution. The rescue team evacuated the causalities after assessing the seriousness of the injuries, and the injured were treated by the medical first–aid team. A media report was prepared by the awareness team. The mock drill was a demonstration to the participants so that they could conduct such drills in their schools at regular intervals, making the students and staff proficient to respond to any kind of emergency situation.

In the course of the present work public awareness material like brochures, manuals, booklets and DVDs prepared by National Disaster Management Division, Ministry of Home Affairs were distributed to the teachers in the schools. Community level teams and teams in the schools were given basic training in search and rescue operations. Interaction was done with small groups of people on various issues of earthquakes relating to awareness, preparedness and mitigation in Kukumseri village, Upper and Lower Salpat and at Trilokinath village.

Summary & Conclusion

The inference drawn during the present work from interaction with the local community and school was that the community at large was not much aware about the sensitive issues related to the earthquakes. They had a superficial knowledge about the earthquakes and this too was interspersed with various myths.

Concluding the paper we would like to state that one of the most challenging tasks in earthquake preparedness and mitigation is the sensitization of all members involved i.e. community as a whole, to the prevalent seismic risk, and educating and training them to participate in earthquake preparedness and mitigation efforts. If the community recognizes the importance of incorporating seismic safety measures in the construction of residential buildings and adhering to non-structural safety measures in homes, tremendous gains can be achieved in earthquake mitigation. We have made efforts to mobilize communities especially teachers and students to carry out mitigation efforts. Disaster Management plans in schools, search and rescue drill, fire safety drill and medical and first aid training will go a long way in mitigating the effects in an unforeseen calamity. The above mentioned initiatives are only an indicative list of actions, which require attention. Every person involved needs to contribute his/her bit in order to ensure that the increasing hazards and risks and the vulnerabilities get addressed in a planned and systematic manner, thereby increasing the coping capacities of community at large and making them resilient to the impacts of disasters.

References

[1] Tiwari, R.P. 1999. Disaster management- the utmost need of Mizoram. Proceeding of Seminar on Science & Technology in Mizoram for 21st Century organized by Mizoram Science Society, Aizawl, pp. 139-146.

[2] Ravi Sinha, K.S.P. Aditya and Achin Gupta, GIS-based urban seismic risk assessment using risk.iitb iset *Journal of Earthquake Technology, Paper No.* 497, Vol. 45, No. 3-4, Sept.-Dec. 2008, pp. 41–63

[3] Acharrya, S.K. 1999. Natural Hazards: Earthquakes and Landslides in India during the nineties and mitigation strategy. Proceeding of Seminar on Earthquakes & landslides: Natural disaster mitigation, Calcutta, pp. 5-13

[4] South Asia Disaster Report 2010, May 2011, New Delhi, pp-

[5] Bureau of Indian Standards (2002). "Criteria for Earthquake Resistant Design of Structures." IS 1893 (Part I):2002, New Delhi, India.

[6] Khullar, D.R. 2005, India A Comprehensive Geography Kalyani Publishers, New Delhi, pp-190-195

[7] Disaster Management Guidelines; Management of Earthquakes, (2007), NDMA, Government of India. Pp-

[8] Biham, R. (2004) Earthquakes in India and the Himalaya: tectonics, geodesy and history, Annals of Geophysics, 47 (2), 839-858.

[9] Sinha, R., Shaw, R., Goyal, A., Choudhary, M.D., Jaiswal, K., Saita, J., Arai, H., Pribadi K. and Arya, A.S.(2001)."The Bhuj Earthquake of January 26, 2001." Indian Institute of Technology Bombay and Earthquake Disaster Mitigation Research Centre, Miki, Japan.

[10] Sinha, R. and Goyal, A. (2003). "A national policy for seismic vulnerability assessment of buildings and procedure for rapid visual screening of buildings for potential seismic vulnerability." Report to Ministry of Home Affairs, Government of India.

[11] Singh, G (1994), Himachal Pradesh History, Culture and Economy. Minerva Book House, Shimla

[12] Berkes, F. Colding,J. Folke,C. (eds) 2003Narrating Social-
        Ecological System: Building Resilience for Complexity
        and Change. Cambridge University Press, Cambridge.
[13] James, S.Gordner, Julie Dekens., 2006 Springer Science and
        Business Media B.V. National Hazards.
[14]2http://www.censusindia.gov.in/2011-prov-
        results/prov_data_products_ himachal.html
[15]http://hpsdma.nic.in/DisasterManagement/HPSDMPfinalindex.pdf
        # page mode=bookmarks

Chapter-III

Impact of Climate change on Traditional Agriculture Practices

Kishori Lal Sharma

Abstract

This paper reviews the knowledge on impact of climate change on traditional agricultural practices. Warming is expected to lead to a northward expansion of suitable cropping areas and a reduction of the growing period of determinate crops (e.g. cereals), but an increase for indeterminate crops (e.g. root crops). Increasing atmospheric CO_2 concentrations will directly enhance plant productivity and also increase resource use efficiencies. In northern areas climate change may produce positive effects on agriculture through introduction of new crop species and varieties, higher crop production and expansion of suitable areas for crop cultivation. Disadvantages may be an increase in the need for plant protection, the risk of nutrient leaching and the turnover of soil organic matter. In southern areas the disadvantages will predominate. The possible increase in water shortage and extreme weather events may cause lower harvestable yields, higher yield variability and a reduction in suitable areas for traditional crops. These effects may reinforce the current trends of intensification of agriculture. Research will have further to deal with the effect on secondary factors of agricultural production, on the quality of crop and animal production, of changes in frequency of isolated and extreme weather events on agricultural production, and the interaction with the surrounding natural ecosystems. There is also a need to study combined effects of adaptation and mitigation strategies, and include assessments of the consequences on current efforts in agricultural policy to develop a sustainable agriculture that also preserves environmental and social values in the rural society.

.

Key words: Global warming, Climate change, Crops, agriculture.

*Lecturer-in-Commerce, Govt. Sr. Sec. School Behdala Distt. Una H.P.

Introduction

Man's relentless pursuit of material comfort and 'happiness' has engendered an irreversible harm to the environment. In a country like India where seventy percent of the population is dependent on agriculture, it is imperative that the effects of drastic changes in environment are studied. Also, it is equally important that we rely more on scientifically proven facts about global climate changes rather than mere conjectures and exaggerations. In northern areas climate change may produce positive effects on agriculture through introduction of new crop species and varieties, higher crop production and expansion of suitable areas for crop cultivation. Disadvantages may be an increase in the need for plant protection, the risk of nutrient leaching and the turnover of soil organic matter. In southern areas the disadvantages will predominate. The possible increase in water shortage and extreme weather events may cause lower harvestable yields, higher yield variability and a reduction in suitable areas for traditional crops. Policy will have to support the adaptation of agriculture to climate change by encouraging the flexibility of land use, crop production, farming systems etc. In doing so, it is necessary to consider the multifunctional role of agriculture, and to strike a variable balance between economic, environmental and social functions in different European regions. Policy will also need to be concerned with agricultural strategies to mitigate climate change through a reduction in emissions of methane and nitrous oxide, an increase in carbon sequestration in agricultural soils and the growing of energy crops to substitute fossil energy use. The policies to support adaptation and mitigation to climate change will need to be linked closely to the development of agri-environmental schemes.

Importance of Climate

Importance of climate can be realized due to following reasons;

Climate Stability

Carbon dioxide, methane and other greenhouse gases occur naturally, trapping heat in the atmosphere and keeping Earth's climate stable. But human activities over the last few centuries have released greenhouse gases at levels that are destabilizing the climate — far too quickly for human institutions, and the species they rely on, to keep up. In 2013,

34

CO^2 concentrations in the atmosphere hit 400 parts per million -the highest they've been in 3 million years.

Protection from Storms

From big cities to small communities, 50% of the global population lives near the coast—and they are all at risk from destructive storms, which will become more frequent with the changing climate and sea level rise, which will cause more storm surges.

Water We Drink

Everyone deserves access to fresh water. But climate change puts that access at risk. A warmer world means that some areas will become too dry, causing prolonged droughts. By one estimate, climate impacts will cause up to a 50% decline in water availability in many areas, causing irreparable losses to livelihoods and ways of life and potentially causing conflicts over water use. Other areas will be too wet — and could face increased incidence of devastating floods.

Food We Eat

Scientists estimate that, by 2050, global demand for food will nearly double. Yet the latest research shows that climate change is already disrupting growing seasons in many parts of the world, and the situation will only get worse. We need to use our water and land more efficiently — and support the farmers whose livelihoods are at risk — if we are going to rise to the challenge of feeding everyone who lives on a warming planet.

Climate Change

Evidence is gathering that human activities are changing the climate. This climate change could have a huge impact on our lives. Here are some grim aspects of climate change. Sea levels are expected to rise by at least 40 cm by 2100, inundating vast areas, including some of the most densely populated cities.

What has already happened?

Global temperatures has rise by 0.60C in the last 130 years. This rise in global temperatures lead to huge impacts on a wide range of climate related factor. Levels of carbon dioxide, methane and nitrous oxide gases are rising, mainly as a result of human activities Carbon dioxide is being dumped in the atmosphere at an alarming rate. Since the industrial revolution, humans have been pumping out huge quantities of carbon dioxide, raising carbon dioxide concentrations by 30%. The burning of fossil fuels is partly responsible for this huge increase. Similarly, methane levels in the atmosphere have increased by 145% since the industrial revolution. This increase is a result of gas produced by livestock and paddy fields.The increase in quantity of these gases leads to what is known as the green house effect.

The Green House Effect

Under normal circumstances the sun's rays hit the earth and are reflected back into space. However, gases in the atmosphere such as carbon dioxide and methane form a barrier for sun light. Because of this property of these gases the reflected rays of the sun are trapped in the atmosphere. The sun rays cannot escape from the earth's atmosphere, and the earth heats up. This is called the green house effect.

Global Warming

Global temperatures have risen by 0.50C over the 140 years, since records began. The decade 1990-2000 was the warmest for 300 years and 0.50c warmer than the mean 1961-1990 climate. Warm winters have reduced the number of frosts, and the warmer summer has included record hot spells and high sunshine totals.

Main Reasons of Climate Change

Dependence on fossil fuels

The burning of fossil fuels is the source of human-caused greenhouse gas emissions. If emissions continue to rise, we'll be locked in to devastating rises in temperature. Moving toward a more diversified, cleaner energy portfolio and scaling up energy efficiency lessen our dependence on fossil fuels — and are critical steps toward reducing our emissions.

Vulnerable coasts

From big cities to small communities, 50% of the global population lives near the coast. But this way of life is deeply imperiled by rising seas, coastal erosion and storms that are intensified by climate change. Habitat destruction and land use changes are degrading and destroying natural buffers — wetlands and coastal forests — that help protect against storm surges and rising sea levels.

Deforestation and land use change

Massive amounts of carbon are locked away in tropical forests. When we destroy these forests to clear land for ranches or farms, that carbon gets released into the atmosphere and accelerates climate change. The effects are felt globally: Studies have found that deforestation accounts for 11% of all human-caused greenhouse gas emissions, and land use change is responsible for an additional 5%.

Insufficient funding

It will take an estimated US$ 70 billion per year — less than 0.1% of global GDP — to make the changes humanity needs to adapt to a warming world. Effective and innovative financing from a range of sources is needed to reduce deforestation and support technologies that will reduce emissions. Unfortunately, global contributions to climate finance fall severely short of this need.

Impact of Global Climatic Changes on Traditional Agriculture

It is known that climate change is affecting agriculture in many ways. A lot of studies have been carried out by agriculturalists, scientists and economists on the adverse effects of climate change. In India, agriculture and allied activities constitute the single largest component of Gross Domestic Product (GDP) contributing nearly 25% of the total. The tremendous importance of this sector to the Indian economy can be ganged by the fact that it provides employment to to-thirds of the total workforce. The share of agricultural products in exports is also substantial, with agriculture accounting for 15% of export earnings.

37

Agricultural growth also has a direct impact on poverty eradication, and is an important factor in employment generation. Further, Indian agriculture is fundamentally dependent on weather for higher productivity. The proof of this has been the increasing in agricultural production, owing to good monsoons over the last few years. A few conclusions on the effect of climate change on agriculture from different studies are listed below:

1. Sinha and Swaminathan (1991) – showed that an increase of 20C in temperature could decrease the rice yield by about 0.75 ton/ha (hectares) in the high yield areas; and 0.50C increase in winter temperature would reduce wheat yield by 0.45 tons/ha.
2. Rao and Shina (1994)-showed that wheat yields could decrease between 28-68% without considering the CO2 fertilization effects.
3. Agarwal and Sinha (1993) showed that a 20C temperature rise would decrease wheat yields in most places.
4. Saseendran et al. (2000) showed that for every one degree rise in temperature the decline in rice yield would be about 6%.

The above facts emphasize the need to not only study in detail the climate change vulnerability of agriculture but also the methods of improving the adaptive capacity of agriculture to climate variability and extremes. Climate Change will affect Agriculture in following ways:

Soil Processes

The potential for soils to support agriculture and distribution of land use will be influenced by changes in soil water balance. Increase in soil water deficits i.e. dry soils become drier, therefore increased need for irrigation but; could improve soil workability in wetter regions and diminish poaching and erosion risk.

Crops

The effect of increased temperature and CO2 levels on arable crops will be broadly neutral: Horticultural crops are more susceptible to changing conditions than arable crops, Field vegetables will be particularly affected by temperature changes and Water deficits will directly affect fruit and vegetable production

Grasslands and Live stocks

Poultry and pigs could be exposed to higher incidences of heat stress influencing productivity Increase in disease transmission by faster growth rates of pathogens in the environment.

Table Showing Predicted effects of Climate change on agriculture over the next 50 years

Climatic element	Expected change by 2050	Confidence in prediction	Effect on agriculture
CO_2	Increase from 360 ppm to 450-600 ppm	very high	• good for crops • increased photosynthesis • reduced water use
Sea Level Rise	Rise by 10-15 cm	very high	• loss of land • coastal erosion • flooding • Stalinization of ground water
Temperature	Rise by 1-2°c increased frequency of heat waves	high	• faster, shorter earlier growing seasons • heat stress risk
Storminess	Increased wind speeds, especially in north. more intense rainfall events	very low	• lodging • soil erosion • reduced infiltration of rainfall

Improving Adaptive Capability of Agriculture:

1. The following actions can be helpful in improving the adaptive capability of agriculture;
2. Improved training and general education of populations dependent on agriculture

3. Agricultural research to develop new crop varieties
4. Identification of the present vulnerabilities of agricultural systems
5. Food programs and other social security programs to provide insurance against supply changes
6. Transportation, distribution and market integration to provide the infrastructure to supply food during crop short falls.
7. Creating policies that address climate change
8. Climate change puts us in a food fix.

On the one hand, some land use practices contribute to global emissions. On the other, people and communities depend on agriculture for their income and sustenance. One solution to this challenge: sustainable agriculture. CI works to find new ways of farming that support a healthy environment, minimize climate impacts and create a better quality of life for farmers.

1. Promoting sustainable agriculture practices
2. One of the best ways to reduce greenhouse gas emissions is Rely on nature. CI has been a pioneer in finding ways to help keep carbon stored in natural ecosystems. For example, we're discovering new ways to protect places like tropical rainforests and mangroves — not just for their climate value, but also for the benefits they give to people.

How we can contribute to reduce the effect of climate change on agriculture?

We can contribute to reduce the effect of climate change on agriculture in the following ways:

Reduce your energy consumption

Look for energy efficient appliances, like ENERGY STAR products, that are independently certified to save energy.

Take the pledge

Join thousands of others who have already committed to help protect the planet that provides every breath, every drop and every bite.

Spread the word

Tell the world that the fate of the only planet we've ever called home is in our hands by sharing on face book and tweet on twitter.

Donate to CI

Donate to CI to fight climate change and protect all the parts of nature we can't live without.

In addition to the above improvements, it is imperative that the developed countries and the rapidly developing countries formulate strategies to curb green house gas emissions. Countries on the fast track of economic growth should also look at adopting new energy-saving technologies and planting of more trees. The emphasis should also be laid on increasing the use of renewable energy sources like solar and wind. It is high time for leading emitters of CO^2 to formulate national programs to address climate change. Only then the effect of climate change on agriculture can be reduced. Some more

Conclusions

This paper is complementarities between improving agricultural production, adapting to climate change, and reducing poverty are likely to increase with climate change. Thus, the worse you believe the effects of climate change will be the more valuable it will be to invest in sustainable agriculture and poverty reduction. Agriculture will better support climate goals to the extent that externalities are internalized by market participants through a set of policies termed full-costing. Even though global full-costing may be out of reach for technical, practical and political reasons.

References:

1. Shah, Anup. "Climate Change and Global Warming Introduction." *Global Issues*. 11 Nov. 2013. Web. 11 Aug. 2014.
2. Carbon Dioxide and Ozone on Crop Yields." *Climate Change and Food Security* Advances in Global Change Research 37(Part II), 109–30. DOI:10.1007/978-90-481-2953-9_7.
3. Auffhammer, M., Ramanathan, V. and Vincent, J.R. (2011). "Climate change, the monsoon, and rice yield in India." *Climatic Change* 111(2), 411–24.DOI:10.1007/s10584-011-0208-4.
4. Barnett, T.P., Adam, J.C. and Lettenmaier, D.P. (2005). "Potential impacts of a warming climate on water availability in snow-dominated regions." *Nature* 438, 303–9. DOI: 10.1038/nature04141.
5. Barnett, T.P., Pierce, D.W., Hidalgo, H.G., et al. (2008). "Human-Induced Changes in the Hydrology of the Western United States." *Science* 319(5866), 1080–83. DOI:10.1126/science.1152538.
6. Biasutti, M. and Sobel, A.H. (2009). "Delayed Sahel rainfall and global seasonal cycle in a warmer climate." *Geophysical Research Letters* 36(23). DOI: 10.1029/2009GL041303.
7. Christensen, N.S. and Lettenmaier, D.P. (2007). "A multimodel ensemble approach to assessment of climate change impacts on the hydrology and water resources of the Colorado River Basin." *Hydrology and Earth System Sciences Discussions* 11(4), 1417–34. DOI: 10.5194/hess-11-1417-2007.
8. Chu, J.T., Xia, J., Xu, C.-Y. and Singh, V.P. (2009). "Statistical downscaling of daily mean temperature, pan evaporation and precipitation for climate change scenarios in Haihe River, China." *Theoretical and Applied Climatology* 99(1-2), 149–61.DOI:10.1007/s00704-009-0129-6.
9. Ciscar, J.-C., Iglesias, A., Feyen, L., et al. (2011). "Physical and economic consequences of climate change in Europe." *Proceedings of the National Academy of*

Sciences 108(7), 2678–83. DOI:10.1073/pnas.1011612108.

10. Cline, W.R. (2007). *Global Warming and Agriculture: Impact Estimates by Country*. Washington, DC: Center for Global Development & Peterson Institute forInternational Economics.

11. https://www.youtube.com/watch?v=fl4OdHGQI0&feature=player.

Chapter-IV

Human Animal Conflicts: Exploring The Policy, Belief and Myth in the Bankura district of West Bengal

Bhaswati Thakurta*

Abstract

In the recent years the debate concerning the suitable approach to biodiversity conservation in different location throughout the world can be found in an explosive manner. The venerable protectionist model of forest conservation has been replaced by community based conservation (CBC). There are major two critiques behind it. This method fails to achieve substantial conservation and its implication within neoliberal ideology. In this theoretical ground, the conflict between Human Elephant, Wild Boar and Spotted Deer in South Bengal can be analyzed. The interaction with elephant is widely known and well researched but the conflict with Wild Boar and Spotted Deer is not that deeply understood due to its location, limited to a particular area of South Bengal. The local narrative of the wild boar population was varies person to person. The spotted deer was introduced by the Forest department in the local forest.

Key words: *Community based Conservation (CBC), Forest Conservation, Neoliberalism, Forest Department, Traditional belief, Local narrative, Human animal conflict.*

---

*Women's Studies Research Centre, University of Calcutta, India

Introduction

The spotted deer which is commonly known as 'Cheetal Horin' was released in forest as an initiative of forest department. Villages are located near forest or amidst the forest affected that is why there are conflicts with these three animals are at different levels. This paper will try to analyze the conflict with these three animals in Bankura district of West Bengal with a different level of context. The forest of the plateau was full of elephant. There are religious believes still sustained among tribal as well as non tribal people. The wild boar was not common to the region; the oral narrative analysis helps to trace its path. The Forest Department initiative to introduce spotted deer as a plan of conservation and ecotourism was effective indeed but the growing conflict with spotted deer is making a kind of resistance in the region against this animal. This study will try to explore the different level of conflict between human and these three animals in the Bankura district of West Bengal.

During 1970s and increasingly in 1980s, there was a growing feeling globally that animal life and consequently biodiversity were dwindling fast, particularly in the forests of developing countries and in the global common grounds such as oceans. There was a growing opinion during this period that as forest habitats for larger animals were getting destroyed and large forest blocks were getting fragmented, the ensuing shortage of forest food were reducing the prey base for the carnivores[1]. It was felt together with the increasing space crunch, was compelling animals to encroach upon agricultural and homestead lands to inflict vast damage on human life and property. An increasingly popular view that started prevailing was that these factors were resulting in the growing conflict between local populations and forests animals with the latter often becoming victims of harassment and killing, resulting in the further depletion of animal life. The Indian government response to this depletion was twofold;

First, it worked on the premise that the major depredations were happenings outside the government forestland and that there was no legislation to punish the offenders. The wildlife protection act, 1972 was enacted and later amended three times that brought all lands including non forest private lands under its ambit. The term 'Wild Life' in the Act, includes both animals and plants under its umbrella. The second immediate response of the government was to reserve additional forest as protection reserves such as Biosphere Reserves, National Parks and Sanctuaries etc.

Highlighting the major event of reserving the forest and conserving the wildlife in these zones slowly generated the lacunas of the policy that is emerging human animal interaction which leads to conflict. This paper attempts to unfold the situation of growing animal and human conflict in the degraded forest of Bankura. The initial phase of the protection of wild animal with a changing nature of forest management policy in India actually affected highly the habitat of the wild animal. The wild life act creates a space indeed for the animal but at the same time the pressure of increasing population also invading their space. The discourse on invading spaces in a created zone especially for animal also displaced forest dwellers. The forest dwellers define the human animal interaction from a very different dimension compare to the people who lives in villages located at the periphery of forests. The forest dwellers are mainly tribal population. They co habited or shared the space with animal from a long time. They worship some animals and they have a ritual of hunting. Animal has a different influence in their culture and social life. There is an interaction between villagers of forest fringe and animal in the forest, evidently that is very different from the tribal population.

The research is based on Bankura a district of West Bengal which is located at the eastern part of the state connecting link between the plains of Bengal on the east and Chota Nagpur plateau on the west. The areas to the east and north-east are low lying alluvial plains. To the west the surface gradually rises, giving way to undulating country, interspersed with rocky hillocks. It is known as land of red soil. Forest of Bankura is mainly dry and deciduous in nature. The dominance of dipterocarpeaceae can be observed. This forestland was habitat of many animals. The field work has been done on 2010 for study of forest management and thus as a part of the questionnaire the qualitative data emerged in this regard. The conflict with three animals like elephant, wild boar and deer is indeed a serious problem of the region. The damage done by elephant is massive compare to wild boar or deer. The elephant conflict was widely known but wild boar and deer are also emerged as a damage maker.

Methodology

The method used here for the research is qualitative method in a threefold way. These are Group Discussion, Focus Group Discussion and Interview. During a forest management study as a partial data these information actually emerged up. The study was done in three forest divisions of Bankura. The reaction was recorded from Bankura North and Panchet division. Bankura North was prone to elephant and panchet is prone to elephant deer and wild boar. Based on the some encounters within the villages and the r experience of villagers are the material for analysis. The data were taken from men and women whoever wants to share this information. Both the experience of men and women of tribal villages as well as forest fringe villages were documented. The interviews with forest officials and the literature survey of the divisional forest office also helped for the background study.

Theoretical Framework

Research into Neoliberal Conservation is one of the most useful theories to work on the issue of conservation. Neoliberal conservation refers to an approach in which capitalist expansion and protection of the environment are not only as essentially compatible activities, but mutually compatible ones [2]. Interventions informed by this assumption have proliferated significantly in recent years. They have changed both the ways in which we imagine the world, and the ways that the world actually is. Neoliberal conservation makes natures that are at once symbolic and material. As a result of this argument in the context of the wild life conservation and creating a space for wild animals which is a space for tourism actually creates a severe threat to the animal itself. In this study the conservation of spotted deer in a created plantation that is enough dense but surrounded by villages and agricultural lands become a major problem for the locals. The tourism industry actually benefitted by it but the forest fringe people is very less in number is a part of this tourism and income.

The reappearance of elephant in south west Bengal started beyond mid 1980s probably coinciding with revival of forest cover as a result of participatory forest protection initiatives with local communities [3]. But recreating the forest actually helps the community to survive and also to welcome the old habitant of the forest that is elephants. The issue of wild boar is completely based on the oral narrative. The reason behind the appearance of wild boar at certain extent is same like elephant. But the reason of its reappearance was described by the villagers in a narrative style. All of them causing damage to the harvest as well as killing people and become obstacles of the pace of mundane life. This study actually focusing that the neoliberal attempt to create a tourism as well as conservation actually threat the existence of animal that is spotted deer and the creating forest space actually facilitate the path of old habitant of the forest that is elephant and wild boar which are again creating a conflict with local people.

The Policy

In 1956, forests reserved especially for wild life protection were negligible[4]. By 1961 a Plan was laid out to carve out 18 national parks or wild life sanctuaries from the country's forested areas[4]. By 2000, World Resource India reported that 493 forest areas had been isolated and declared as protected areas (IUCN management categories, I-IV) [5]. Managed by specialized staff, they covered an area of 14.3 million hector which comprised about 4.4% of the land area and more than 20% of the forest areas of the country. By law, the use of these areas by the local people had been officially restricted. No forest management practices were allowed except those that kept the animals well fed and protected and the vegetation undisturbed.

In some areas, for example in Tiger Reserves, The Gir National Park (Lion), The Jaldapara Sanctuary (Rhinoceros) and in some other protected reserves, the census of big animals has been carried out at regular intervals. Many forest officials have also been specially trained in Protection Reserve Management. During this period, various aspects of biodiversity conservation had caught the special attention of the international ecologists and also of Indian foresters. People in the forest fringes and in the biodiversity and protected area reserves were relocated as much as possible. Funds also came in from the Global Environment Facility (GEF) for example as of January 1998, the World Bank, a contributor to GEF reports an allocation of us $ 142.38 million for the preparation of a biodiversity action Plan for India [6]. Further funds were programmed and used for National Parks in India particularly the Tiger Reserves to strengthen the infrastructure staffing and the training of technical staff.

The forest Institution also saw a change to accommodate the attention require to preserve the wild life. In most states and in the centre, special wild life wings were established. The government selected special officers as provided in the wild life Protection Act and entrusted them with the duties and responsibilities of enforcing the provisions of the Act. In addition a new concept called Eco development was introduced in the late 1990s to attract the forest fringe people to participate in biological protection. Eco development offered rural development by investing funds in all villages that were adjacent to certain selected reserves, which had earlier depended on these reserves for their subsistence. The idea behind the investment was to open new avenues of income for the people so that they could become independent of the produce that had hitherto been flowing out of these reserved forests.

The Forest of Bankura

The plateau district of West Bengal is located in the western part of the state comprising of Purulia district and western part of Midnapur, Bankura, Burdwan and Birbhum districts.   It is interesting that extensive part of the plateau has been buried under the thick alluvium, particularly the eastern and southern parts of the region. The western part of the plateau districts is the extension of Chota Nagpur plateau. This plateau area of Bengal gets heavy seasonal rainfall and plenty of sunlight. The soil is also congenial for forest growth. During the past few decades of last century the forests owned by private individuals, suffered wide spread damage by illegal cutting and disintegration. So those forest areas lost their compactness. Change in land use pattern, growth and migration of population in the different periods of history and deforestation have influenced the spatial distribution of forest in the region. Even the forests which have managed to survive after prolonged exploitation, show signs of degeneration. Moreover, gradual progress of agriculture on the forest lands has enhanced the problem and changes the residual vegetation to scrubs. Yet these forests provide the major requirement of fuel, fodder and constructional materials for thousands of people living in this area. In Bankura forests covers about one fifth of the total area of the district. The forests form fairly compact zones in south and east. The important centres are Bishnupur, Ranibandh, Taldangra, Gangajalghati and Sonamukhi. As per classification of Champion and Seth (1968) the forests of this region belong to Northern Tropical Dry and Moist Deciduous Forest Zones[7]. The dry deciduous zone occurs in the western part of the plateau districts. The moist deciduous type, on the other hand occurs at the eastern part. Bankura district falls under this part. This zone can be divided into five types:

1. Moist mixed deciduous
2. Dry Sal (_Shorea robusta_) forest
3. Moist low level peninsular Sal (_Shorea robusta_)
4. Dry deciduous scrub
5. Riparian vegetation.

According to the forest types and nature the forest of Bankura divided into

1. Coppice forest
2. Plantation forest
3. Blank and scrub area

The eastern part of the district forms land for the rice plains of West Bengal. The land under rice cultivation contains the usual marsh weeds of Gangetic Plain. Aquatic plants and water weeds are found in ponds, ditches and still streams. Around human habitations there are shrub species such as _Glycosmis, Polyalthia suberosa, Clerodenaron infortunatum, Solanum torvum_, and various other species of the same genus, besides _Trema, Streblus_ and _Ficus hispida_. The larger trees are different species of _Ficus, Bombax malabaricum, Mangifera indica, Odina wodier, Phoenix dactylifera_, and _Borassus flabellifer_. Other plants found include _Jatropha gossypifolia, Urena lobata, Heliotropium indicum_. Forests or scrub jungles contain _Wendlandia exserta, Gmelina arborea, Adina Cordifolia, Holarrhena antidysenterica, Wrightia tomentosa, Vitex negundo_ and _Stephegyne parvifolia_.

The western part of the district is higher. The uplands either bare or are covered with scrub jungle of _Zizyphus_ and other thorny shrubs. This thorny forest gradually merges into Sal (_Shorea robusta_) forest. Low hills are covered with _Miliusa, Schleichera, Diospyros_ and other trees. Some of the common trees of economic interest found in the district are: Alkushi (_Mucuna pruriens_), Amaltas (_Cassia Fistula_), Asan (_Terminalia tomentosa_), Babul (_Acacia Arabica_), Bair (_Zizyphus Jujube_), Bael (_Aegle Marmelos_), Bag Bherenda (_Jatropha curcas_), Bichuti (_Tragia involucrate_), Bahera (_Terminalia belerica_), Dhatura (_Datura stramonium_), Dhaman (_Cordia Macleoidii_), Gab (_Diospyros

Embyopteris), Harra (*Terminalia chebula*), Imli (*Tamarindus indica*), Kuchila (Strychnos Nux vomica), Mahua (*Madhuca latifolia*), Palas (*Butea frondosa*), Sajina (*Moringa pterygosperma*), Kend (*Diospyros melanoxylon*), etc.

Animal of the Forest

In a degraded condition it is indeed hard to get any animal. The existence of elephant, rabbit, peacock, snakes of different variety were common to this region. There are some variety of migratory birds in specific villages of the districts can be observed. From the description of forest dwellers during the hunting rituals their ancestors have killed wild boar. This is clearly documenting the early existence of this animal in the forest of Bankura. But no one mentioned about spotted deer.

Human Elephant Conflict

Area of Study

The area of study is North and Panchet division of Bankura forest. The information regarding elephant was dominant in both the division. The Dharashole village is a tribal village. They were displaced when Mukutmanipur water dam were constructed. Their ancestral village of Kusumkumandihi was fertile and plenty of water. These displaced people were allowed to live inside the Baramashiya forest of Bankura North division. Under the Join Forest Management (JFM) Programme they were given a patch of forest for conservation apart from the scrub land which was kept for cultivation. The agriculture of the region is based on seasonal rainfall at monsoon. This forest is prone to elephant. When elephant groups pass by the forest they love to take rest at the day time in the forest and at night in the village. They generally eat the harvest directly from the cultivated field. This is indeed a major loss for the villagers. The village of Basudevpur is a part of elephant corridor affected heavily by both elephant herds and residential elephants. The village of Dharashole the elephant menace is done by residential elephant only.

Elephant and the Region

The forest resource was economically viable even from ancient time and hunting was also a part of royal entertainment. The resource are not only botanical it includes faunas too. The main animal resource

51

was elephant to create an army. The lion, tigers and cheetah were also considered as an important animal resource. It is a matter of prime importance for us to note that in Ancient India, people of this country used to think in terms of eight forest divisions which were obviously the more important ones and covered large areas. Since elephants were to be found in all of them, they were styled *gaja-vanas*, 'elephant forests', or in other words, dense forests. Among the kings who own the forest full of beasts evidently becomes the most powerful of the area [8]. The Mughal Kings were offered elephant as a tax for their royal army from Bengal. The history of elephant in this region was very dominant. Perhaps the most important article which the forest provided to the Mughal ruling class was elephants, which were much sought after as war animals and as beasts of burden. The demand for elephants seemed insatiable. Five thousand of them were kept in Emperor Akbar's establishment alone. The statistics of zamindars forces given by Abu'l Fazl, for various provinces of the empire estimate a total of nearly 2000 elephants with the zamindars, the highest number (1,170) belonging to the zamindars of Bengal [9]. It was not only timber, honey and such animals as elephants which made essential for the forest to remain within the domain of the king. Dr. Hunters Annals of rural Bengal depicts after the death of the aboriginal king the royal elephant choose the new king for the region by seizing him from the plebeian and approached to the empty throne. Thus the founder of the dynasty of Bishnupur (ancient capital of the region) Raghunath Singh was selected[10].

Visiting of Elephant herd in the crop field during early 1990s was considered to be a great blessing to the local villagers. They believed that it has a direct relation with the yield. People were eager to see elephant heard near their cultivation areas. Even the common believe of Bengal is if goddess Durga return to Kailash after Dashami by elephant it will be a boon for the earth to produce maximum hasvest.There were no data regarding damage of agricultural crop done by elephant heard in the forest department available of those periods. The barren red soil were start greening with Akashmani (*Accacia auriculiformis*) and *Eucalytus spp* and much and sudden change in the floral diversity as a result of Joint forest Management in the region.

This re forestation invites the elephant to dwell again in the forest.

South Bengal Elephants

It was known to us that from Dolma hills of Jharkhand elephants came to the southern districts. They went back to Jharkhand after a short stay. The recent trend is due to increased population the heard of mega fauna are now staying in the south districts of Bankura, Purulia and Medinipur. The foresters are now calling them as South Bengal elephants. Every year now 25-30 adult elephants out of 90 actually went back to Dolma and the rest are staying in south Bengal. The elephant from Dolma can came back anytime.

Population

During early 1990s the Elephant herd was about 20 numbers only, but the recent nature of elephant hard is beyond the territorial capacity as far as forest has been concerned. The forest without grass land and absence of large water bodies cannot accommodate this increasing population of mega fauna which is creating conflict with the existing species and forest fringe people. It is true that in Bengal the human population can be considered as one of the important co existing species with elephant. Here, the problem is mostly to the local villagers where the economic condition is very critical and their livelihood is only agriculture.

Food Habit

Absence of proper grassland making the mega fauna insisted to eat commercial cash crop to find out its calorific demand. The elephant herd have extended its habitat from inside forest into outside forest and changed its food habits from agricultural crop (Paddy and wheat) in to juicy and palatable Horticultural crops (vegetable and fruit crops) like Cucurbits, cabbage and cauliflower, Potato, Brinjal, Colacacia , Tender Jack fruit etc. These crops are vital to the local village level economy. Elephant generally love to ram in the village at night and thus villagers were extremely agitated by them. Not only that the herd love to visit at night when all the villagers are resting after a heavy physical labour at the day time.

Route

Earlier elephant herd used to come up to Paschim Medinipur from Dolma Hills of Jharkhand and goes back to Dolma. After some time their route extended up to Bankura. Now their route further extended and they have started to go till Burdwan. So the importance of Mayurjharna the elephant reserve of south west Bengal is literally nothing. It is empty right now. There are two groups 'of elephants herds regarding their route they are following:

      1. Bankura Medinipur Group
      2. Purulia Group

This study focused on the Bankura Medinipur Group only.

Bankura-Medinipur Group

The Broader and common Elephant Entry Route in South Bengal was:

Dolma hills⟶ Shilda ⟶ Lalgarh ⟶ Katabari ⟶Hoomgarh ⟶ Roskunda Mandalpushkarani⟶Kolabagan ⟶ Bankadaha ⟶ Kanabari Basudevpur ⟶ Pokasghot ⟶Sonamukhi ⟶ Beliatore ⟶Barjora.

The Broader and common Elephant Exit Route in South Bengal was:

Barjora ⟶Brindabanpur/Panchal ⟶ Onda ⟶Katabari ⟶ Harapathi Rajpur⟶ Piardanga ⟶Dhadhika ⟶ Roskunda ⟶Hoomgarh ⟶ Katabari Lalgarh ⟶ Shilda Dolma hills (Forest Department, West Bengal)

Now, the elephants are moving very differently and also creating new routes and going to the unseen places to find out their food. In Bankura, places like Mejia and even Barjora was not known place for elephant herd menace but now the herd keep on going and staying for longer period and making much difficulties to the local villagers and administration.

Earlier Dolma Elephants was coming to Medinipur- Bankura districts before Durga Puja season (September-October) particularly during the period when the agricultural crops are near to maturity (milky stage) and stays for about three to four months and leave around February

54

end. Now, there is no fixed time, season and place to come and create devastation. All those seasonally moving elephants are started staying permanently and creating nightmare to the local villagers and forest administration.

Damage

Earlier that during 1990s and early 2000s the common damages caused by Elephants was crop damage particularly milky stage paddy crop and very few places house damages was reported. Now the volume of damage has been increased like killing poor villagers, cattle crushing the mud house and granaries of the households. The damage of commercial cash crop was discussed earlier. In addition to that it damages pipelines, small canals, Bore wells, Ring wells, village water bodies and in nutshell; at this region nothing is left beyond the purview of Elephant damage. Why this change in the damage component? because earlier periods these elephants were seasonal rider to the paddy crop field but in the recent time it has started staying almost throughout the year, particularly during off season when there is no crop left in the field but for their own survival, elephants are regularly visiting the villages and lifting food grains by damaging mud houses and killing cattle and eating the fodder left at the cattle shed and also killing the defending poor villagers. Really, now a days living at villages where the elephants are visiting regularly is not better than hell. They are losing life, livelihood and peace. The greatest pain is that existence of mental trauma where you don't know but the elephants may come any time and does anything against you and this is the reality at many villagers mind in Bankura, Medinipur and Purulia Districts.

Villagers and Elephant

Earlier, the local villagers used to come and put their effort to take away the elephants from the villages and they get some wages or with social service by good coordination of forest department and JFMCs members. Now, most of the villagers are violent against the elephant visit and creating much challenge to the department. This is not a simple issue but much more in to it. This is due to large scale damage to many families and because of that they have lost their life, livelihood and peace; the issue becomes long lasting and without addressed; elephants are day to day trouble and also permanent to the local villagers.

Villager and Residential Elephant

We all know that residential elephants living at those three districts of South West Bengal are periodic rejection from the larger herd. Generally it won't have any future but it does complete many human futures within no time at those villages. One of the most dangerous wild lives in these regions is considered to be the residential elephants. Altogether the present population of Residential Elephants in south west Bengal is about 30 numbers but their effect at the field is much more than the herd elephants. They are the main human killer and also destroyer of houses and house hold food grain and other edibles. Earlier only very few numbers of residential elephant in the form of either 'Makna' or old tuskers but now we are seeing even sub-adult male and female elephants are become residential. Whenever the herd elephants enter in to a territory where the residential elephants are habituating, it starts moves away (repelling each other) from those areas and creates much damage to life and property. During those periods, it remains violent and dangerous to villagers. Whenever a residential elephant kills a human being, within no time it disappears from that spot/region. The elephant moves away very long distance and behaves as such it is not known to that event (accident). Really the villagers are lost their patient due to this elephant and very often forest staffs are badly treated by the affected villagers.

Hullah- Driving Elephants

Driving of elephants is nothing but driving without steering. You have lots of plan, Hullah and Hullah parties and hired labourer but you never know that how much it will be effective and successful. Every village have Hullah parties but no one can predict elephant behaviour. Many time during the driving operation, when it looks that the elephants are moving very well for few hours but all of sudden it can be noticed thousands of villagers standing in front of the elephant herd with much more strength of hullahs. The forest fringe villager hates elephants. They generally attack elephant more aggressively and then within few minutes all those elephants either will split in too many more unmanageable micro-group and returned to their original place where from the driving was started.

The Conflict

Elephant menaces in these districts have become regular and the local damage caused by those elephants particularly residential elephants make the life of forest staff and administration very tough. Due to elephant's problems at the field level, villagers are challenging the forest administration and threatening them openly telling the staff that they will create trouble when the elephants will come to their areas. Whenever the elephant goes to the village side they are asking the forest department to 'take your elephant'. The forest is mosaic like patches in south Bengal and no one knows where to take and how to keep those elephants inside the forest. Almost all the local villagers particularly in Barjora areas they are demanding to eliminate the human killing residential elephants and they want peace. Recently, it has been told from the department that few of the sub-adults from the herd will be captured and taken to north Bengal. The news has reached the local villagers and they are also expecting that something will be done by the forest department but due to non-implementation of the same, the local villagers are more disappointed and now convincing them is very difficult during elephant depredation days. The local villagers at the elephant prone areas need permanent solution against the elephant menace,

Now there are thirty resident elephants and they are causing huge damage to life and property of Bankura region. The issue is larger, it needs great attention because many villagers have lost their life and this is not because of the elephant factor alone, there is also considerable amount of lacuna from the administrative part as well. It is the high time to think about the future management by understanding the situation of local poor villager, field staff and also for the mega fauna too. Fodder planting, creation of permanent and large size water hole, more incentive to villagers, involving them by giving more empowerment, scientific training of staff and villagers, culling of futureless trouble shooting residential elephants and shifting of those excess elephant population from South Bengal to some other place or state.

The description of human and elephant conflict in the region has its own tradition. In the village of Dharashole the agricultural part is the most damaged area by the elephant. The tribal village is having many other problems but elephant is a major threat. They especially aware of the residential elephant that some time keep coming to the village. The everyday collection of Sal (*Shorea robusta*) leaves and other NTFP and dry twigs cannot be collected with peace. The women member of the Forest Protection Committee (FPC) Patumoni Hansda told that her daily dried wood collection and the sal leaves collection is heavily hampered by the elephant. For their daily need of household the sal plate stitching is a source of income. But they are not able to collect it from the forest regularly. It is impossible for her to run everyday expenditure of the family. Due to less working opportunity men folk are migrating to the nearby town so automatically women are more visible in forest management and also with their conflict with elephant. One of the old male members of the FPC's told us that our ancestors lived in the forest with elephant. But now there is no forest so where these elephants will roam around? The forest, the place for their grazing is replaced by human settlements. This conflict is inevitable. He opined "if we do not disturb elephant they will not harm us." The local villagers group of Hullah were more concern about it. They are very efficient in this context. The forest department pay them on the basis of their activity. One of the member of hullah told me now a day's another group of men outside are coming to the village when this elephant driving operation is going on and when they are able to drive the group to the forest then suddenly some other people came and try to distract the herd movement so they were divided into small groups and become dangerous. This group of people actually want to be the part of the hullah operation and thus the days of the driving can be prolonged and they can earn for the operation wage basis. The abject poverty is the reason behind this kind of rise of self interested group in the region.

The climate change factor actually reduces the rainfall of this moist deciduous forest. The less rainfall and rain fed agriculture in the small patch of land is a major source of staple food for consumption and also for income. The herd of elephants damages the crop and also ate a huge part of it. So the rest of the small quantity actually cannot feed the family of farmers for longer and they are not able to sale the harvest in the market. The money one spend for the agriculture, starting from buying seeds, fertilizers and arranging submersion pump some time the compensation from the government is nothing. Government pays Rs30.00/Shotok (33Shotok = 1 Bigha, 1 Hector= 15.5 Bigha). One of the villagers told me how his small grocery shop was smashed by elephant and he will never get any compensation from

58

government. His condition was indescribable, but his tribal instinct made him work again and accept the fact of the nature that if one captured unwontedly some ones space they have to pay. There is no electricity in the village. The situation of drinking water is horrible. Patumani said that "we are living in a pathetic condition moreover the elephant menace is an addition which is actually challenging our existence in this village amidst the forest. Youth cannot stay here anymore, they are going out from here. The nights are sleepless for this elephant."

Basudevpur Forest Protection Committee members also told me about the situation of their village. The village is very old for the vaishanava influence of the region. The village population is mostly schedule caste and two families of Brahmins as priest of the temple. The old temple of lord Krishna is one of the major attractions of the village. The old people said to me that elephant was common to this area but they never damage anything. But now a day they are try to damage our crop, house and kill men too. One of the young women of the group asks me "we want our children to be educated but due to the elephant situation we cannot send them to school. That is major threat to our future generation."

Bimala's house was smashed by the elephant and now in the hard cold winter days she is homeless. She asked the forest department for just a tripal (tent material) but the lengthy process will deprived her to get the warmth inside the tripal house. The Sal leaf collection also hampers by the resident elephant and the elephant herd. The regular duties of FPC cannot be done if elephants are roaming nearby. Even after the felling the new Sal plantation cannot be saved from them. They will love to reside near those plantations and slowly destroy it. The felling is major source of earning of FPC Members from JFM programme.

The government intervention in this conflict is nothing but providing a hullah group and pay them in the time of elephant driving and repay for the agricultural loss which nothing but a tokenism. Only in death through forest department, the family will get one lakh rupees which is another long time taking process through protocols.

Human Wild Boar Conflict

Area of Study

The area for the study of wild boar is located in the panchet division of the Bankura forest. In that division the village of Basudevpur is located amidst the forest near the beat office. Thus the animal encounters were recorded properly. The road from the village towards the main bus road is inside the forest but along with Kangshabati canal. The forest area was prone to resident elephants and in the forest the death incident with wild boar was happened. The damage of the crop was reported from another two villages under the same forest division these are Kolaidanga and Tribanka.

The Wild Boar

This part of the wild boar is more influenced by the paper presented by Dr. Radhika Govindrajan titled Pigs Gone Wild: Human-wildlife conflict and the production of wildness in Uttarakhand. In her paper she described that how the wild boars are attacking locals and destroying the harvest. But no one knows from where they came. There are some stories behind it. One was that the local animal research station the boars were run away to the forest and they started growing very fast in numbers and thus they are doing enough damages to the harvest. But it was quite clear that no one knows about the early existence if wild boar in the region. In Bankura it was not uncommon that on the forest stretch there is no wild boar. Actually at the time of deforestation in colonial and post colonial phases there number decreased and the hunting rituals of the tribal's also decreased their population. So the last two generation of the people are unaware of the existence of this animal. The story regarding the appearance of wild boar collected from Basudevpur village. A traveller arrived with two wild boars. The wild boars able to escape from the traveller and went to the jungle and reproduced very fast. Thus the number of wild bar increased in the region.

The population, Food habit, Route

The population of wild boar increased a lot but it was limited in panchet forest division of Bankura. They generally stay inside the forest at the day time but at night they come to the agricultural land and eat the vegetables. Since the encounters were reported in this division we can say for the time being there population is located in panchet division. Due to decreasing forest vegetative resource it was quiet evident that the wild bar is eating harvest and making damage to the crops. Since their numbers are increasing thus they will be found quiet a lot in number in the forest.

Damage

Till date the damage was reported damaging vegetables and one incident of death.

The Conflict

One of the villagers of Tribanka told that 'one can easily understand that who ate the potato tubers. One can find small tunnels in the field as a mark of wild boar damage. Now they are potential threat for our vegetable like potato, tomato or any vegetable. There is no token compensation are available from the government for the damage of the crop done by wild boar. It was quiet evident that they were afraid of it. They kill men also. There is a true story from the Basudevpur village. A wild boar actually attacked a person by its long curved tooth penetrated in the stomach. Thus they killed people.There are some cases of human death caused by wild boar. Forest department help them from a different fund because there is no fund from the government in the region except elephant death compensation.

The population of the village of Kolaidanga is mainly scheduled caste. The name of the village was derived from the major agriculture product that is urad which is kolai or Biuli in Bengali. The village has a Forest Protection Committee. They told me in our side there is no elephant but wild boar are damaging our crop.

Human Spotted Deer Conflict

The area of Study

The area of study is same like wild boar but there is an addition because in that region officially Deer was released for the conservation and a part of tourism. These villages are Kolaidanga and Tribonko. They have reported about the conflict with spotted deer.

Spotted Deer

At the beginning of the study the discussions on neoliberal conservation were noted and that was only related to the case of spotted deer conservation in the region. After the massive re forestation in the area to develop a touristic place the state government released spotted deer in the wilderness. The local people were very much enthusiast at that time for their work of reforestation as a result animal was re located in the wilderness and thus tourism was developed.

Damage

The damage they did is eating grains and pulses from the cultivated land and fodder of cattle.

The Conflict

The idea of conservation was not bad at all if the forest were not surrounded by small villages. The village have their agricultural land and that is place for the damage done by the deer. There is a lack of wide grazing place inside the forest. Thus automatically a crop filled land for them is a rich source of food. Deer loves to eat the grains and pulses from the cultivated land. They come in a group at night and start eating. They are destroying the staple food so the villagers now a day are not taking them enthusiastically. There is no compensation given from the government for the damage caused by spotted deer. Many times they came with the cow and buffalo herd and killed by people for the market value of their skin

Conclusion

With severe restrictions placed on foraging for forest produce in the Protection Areas, these forests became more or less off limits to the local people. When the people did use the forests to graze their cattle or to collect forest produce for subsistence, they were deemed an offence under forest laws. While these restrictions seemed to be the right answer to save the wild life, experience showed that one cannot protect an area from the depredations made by the smugglers and foraging poverty-stricken locals unless the latter participated in protection of the forests and their subsistence needs were ensured. The experience has been that local people participate willingly to protect the wild life if they are involved in the protection area management and get a fair share of the benefits that accrue from the resource. The government did not ease the stringent use restriction but tried to make the people economically better off by investing on eco-development in an effort to assist them to become independent of forest produce.

The government policy of wild life conservation and forest protection both are important but one of the critique of these policies are completely focused other developmental issue like tourism but indirectly that is creating a conflict with the true conservation process. The local forest is a result of policy and human interference inside the forest and the other function of village like agriculture is also important. This created wilderness is not the proper environment for spotted deer. That is why conflict is increasing day by day since they are eating the crop. The neoliberal policy of conservation dominantly describing the idea itself. That is, what we want and what the rule of nature itself. The most known incident of elephant encounters in south Bengal actually describes as a result of re forestation of the region and displaced elephant again love to find their own habitat. But the habitat itself is infested by humans. Another interpretation from the locals was due to massive deforestation elephant were displaced now they are become fatal to human and destroying the yield. But till today tribals are accepting the reality that they have to face elephants. As a forest dweller the co existence with animals is not old but still the changing time and the shifting definition of coexistence actually deteriorating human animal relation. The conflict with wild boar is slowly increasing in the region. According to santals their forefather have killed wild boar in the hunting festival but after the wildlife act there is no more hunting but the existence of the animal was very much here. Due to deforestation and hunting they were finished from the region. The story of a traveler with a wild boar from also interesting that depicts the return of the species in its place. Since the place has been changed a lot the interaction with human also changes as well. The changing environment and the changing relation of human and animal now are creating a conflict because their spaces are overlapping. This study aims to discuss the neoliberal conservation and these case studies actually depicting the point again without taking proper step it cannot be possible to conserve but taking step is again problematic to change the course of their natural habit and habitat.

References

1. Ajit Kumar Banerjee Eds. *Footprints in the Forest; History and Origins of Forestry and Wild Life in India* (Dehradun: Natraj Publishers, 2010), pp. 286

2. Jim Igoe & Dan Brockington, Neoliberal Conservation: A brief Introduction, *Conservation and Society* (special issue), 2014, pp. 432-447

3. Anil Kumar Singh, Rina R Singh, & Sushant Chowdhury Human Elephant Conflicts in changed Landscapes of South West Bengal, *Wildlife Institute of India,* Dehradun, 2002, pp 1119-11130

4. Forest Survey of India, *100 Years of Indian Forestry* 1961, Vol. 1, GOI, New Delhi

5. World Resource India Report, *World resources: People and Ecosystems*: 2000-2001 WRI, Washington, D.C, pp 271-321

6. Nalini Kumar, Naresh Saxena, Yoginder Alag, and Kingshuk Mitra, *India: Alleviating poverty through Forest Development* (Washington: The World Bank, D.C, 2000)

7. Anita Roy Mukherjee, *Forest Resources Conservation and regeneration; A study of West Bengal* (New Delhi; Concept Publishing Company, 1995) pp. 45

8. C.D Chatterjee, Forestry in Ancient India in Ajit Kumar Banerjee (Ed.) *Footprints in the Forest; History and Origins of Forestry and Wild Life in India*, 2 (Dehradun: Natraj Publishers, 2010) pp. 42-86

9. Shireen Moosvi History of forests in the Mughal Empire in Ajit Kumar Banerjee, Eds. *Footprints in the Forest; History and Origins of Forestry and Wild Life in India*, 4 (Dehradun: Natraj Publishers, 2010) pp. 121-146

10. R.C Majumdar, *History of Ancient Bengal.* (Calcutta: G. Bhardwag, 1971)

11. Forest department documents from Bankura North division and Panchet Division.

Chapter-V

Entrepreneurship: A Solution for Green Economy and Sustainable Development of Organizations

Charvi Mehta, Puja Gupta*

Abstract

Twenty first century is witnessing the era of sustainable development. However, sustainability of organisations is not only about following the green standards or addressing corporate social responsibility. Its global application and acceptance owes to the balance it endeavors to establish between the environment and economic development (of economies and organisations). This research paper proposes that sustainable organisations can only be created if senior management adopts a holistic view and amends current policies and practices to nurture the future heroes – the Entrepreneurs.

This research paper validates the potential prerequisites to entrepreneurship and their outcomes. Encouragement by Management and Organization, Individual Motivation, Transparency, Openness and Communality, Individual Competence, Enabling Working Environment, Encouragement to Innovations, Development was confirmed as the essential prerequisites to entrepreneurship. The outcome of implementing the above mentioned prerequisites in an organisation includes Work Appreciation and satisfaction. Results indicate a high correlation between the outcomes of entrepreneurship and the prerequisites to entrepreneurship. Therefore, more an organization will encourage the prerequisites the more likely are the corporate entrepreneurs to appreciate their work and experience job satisfaction. Committed and satisfied workforce works to their full potential for holistic development – social, economic and environmental- of its organisation.

Keywords -Entrepreneurship, Sustainable Development, Green Economy, Prerequisites to entrepreneurship, outcomes of entrepreneurship

*Department of Resource Management and Design Application, Lady Irwin College, Delhi University, New Delhi, India

Introduction

People across the world are facing social, economic, political and environmental issues. Increasing population, poverty, lack of housing and food, environmental destruction, depletion of ozone layer, global warming have become a serious threat to mankind. Ecological footprint data indicates that with the current western lifestyle people would require four or five planets similar to earth [1].

Human exploitation of earth has been substantial and is ever increasing. Human beings don't consider themselves as a part of the larger interconnected social-ecological system. "Humans today extract and use around 50% more natural resources than only 30 years ago, at about 60 billion tons of raw materials a year"[2]. Human's utilize, consume and abandon resources to produce goods that will improve the standard to living of a few people at the cost of all the others on earth. This is popularly labeled as consumerism. Evidently, these practices are not sustainable in the longer term.

The above situation initiated the development of a new philosophy called Communitarianism [3]. Communitarianism highlights the relation between the individual and the community [4]. It acknowledges the larger society and ecosystem as one whole [5] and the economy as its sub system; consuming environmental resources [6]. With the growing awareness and interest, government and other national and international bodies are amending detrimental policies and practices. People now strive for environment friendly approaches and products. And at organisational level, employees are seeking a more open and sustainable organisational culture from their employers.

Few organisations', in spite of social and political pressure, are yet not ready to embrace the idea of sustainability [7]. Wong, L. & Avery, G.C. stated that the reasons for this resistance are, firstly, lack of a common definition of sustainability; secondly, changing existing management systems seems tedious and costly; and thirdly, greater emphasis on profit rather than human and environmental resources. However, slowly and steadily the philosophy of sustainable organisation is receiving its due importance. "During the last 20 years, a relatively small but growing number of companies have voluntarily integrated social and environmental issues in their business models and daily operations (i.e. their strategy) through the adoption of related corporate policies" [8].

66

Sustainability

Often, sustainability is considered and alternate term for environment friendly and socially responsible attitude. But aforementioned understanding of sustainability w.r.t. social, financial and environmental parameter is insufficient. Sustainability is not only about implementing green standards but is about the intent of the entire existence of an enterprise [9]. Wong and Avery stated that the intent should be to:

1. Include practices that ensure a sustainable relation with all stake holders. It is not merely generating profits for them.

2. To be careful about the impact of our everyday decisions on the delicate balance of ecology, social and economic systems.

3. A number of traditional malpractices that are not sustainable will be challenged and amended. Organisations should act proactively by forestalling change in the surroundings. These changes should not depend on outside factors but should be inherent to individuals and organisations. Innovative work approach will inspire employees and organisations to craft a sustainable future.

Sustainability: An Organizational Strategy

With globalization and competition most exiting business models will be irrelevant soon. Superior management of organisations that formulate and successfully implement innovative solutions to these challenges will rapidly have an edge over their competitors in the long term [10].

A sustainable organisation is not merely driven by its moral conduct to meet the social or environmental parameters. It should include sustainability in the soul of their strategy formulation and functioning. A sustainable approach is holistic; it encompasses capturing market share and financial goals as well as crafting a management culture that will establish the core values which will act as a guideline for decision making towards a sustainable future. Consequently, "a sustainable business strategy will try to balance the general object of economic prosperity, economic responsibility and environmental stewardship for all its stakeholders and itself" [11].

To develop a sustainable strategy that uses fewer resources and enhances both shareholder and stakeholder's value as compared to conventional intensive profit making (at all costs) strategies requires corporate entrepreneurship or entrepreneurship.

An organisation encouraging entrepreneurship has an entrepreneurial attitude in its style of functioning. Entrepreneurship is a sub-field of entrepreneurship although it has been lately included in management literature as well [12]. Various researchers have described entrepreneurship as:

- Corporate entrepreneurship is "to which new products/ new markets are developed" [13].

- Gifford Pinchot stated that entrepreneurs are people who dream beyond their regular and mundane work [14].

When employees are given the responsibility to implement their innovations they cease to behave as regular employees and start behaving like entrepreneurs. For the same, they are often expected to create an entrepreneurial team to realize their goal. Also, they are financed by the organisation and have no personal financial risk. However, they work as if they have established a new enterprise. Consequently, they are rewarded with promotions or bonuses [15].

Stevenson & Jarillo stated that organisational support also included training and trusting of employees to identify lucrative opportunities [16]. Lumpkin and Dess focused on organisational factors - firm size, culture and management team characteristics – in nurturing entrepreneurship and organisational performance [17].

Antoncic & Hisrich categorized previously researched factors into four dimensions. He stated that new business venturing, innovativeness, self-renewal and pro-activeness are essential dimensions of entrepreneurship. He further, stressed on organisational factors like management support, commitment and style, as well as the staffing and rewarding of venture activities [18].

The perquisites: potential elements for entrepreneurship were brought up by Heinonen as seven factors namely: encouragement by management; individual motivation; transparency, openness and communality; individual competence; enabling working environment; encouragement to innovations; and development. For the present study aforementioned prerequisites to entrepreneurship and outcomes were utilized [19].

Corporate entrepreneurship for sustainable development of organisations

If the enterprises of the world are to survive intense competition and thrive in a globalized economy, they need to go beyond importing technologies and management models of innovation [20]. Today's marketplace is characterized by fast-paced and unremitting competition on a global scale. To compete in this environment, organizations need a level of innovation and entrepreneurship that was unheard of even a decade ago. As competition becomes more global and time-based, corporations must develop effective trade operations and deliver new and superior products in less time. The challenge for modern corporate organizations is to revitalize them so they can successfully and continuously develop new products and new businesses. They must not only improve their procedures for new product and new business development, but must also improve their management practices. It is not enough that a company has an effective innovation process; it must also have innovative management practices as well. Thus, organizations require a special culture that is much different from the traditional culture of businesses.

The concept of corporate culture, also labeled as organizational culture, has become popular since the early 1980s. Basically, corporate culture can be defined as "the personality of the organization that is comprised of the assumptions, values, norms and tangible signs (artifacts) of organizational members and their behaviors" [21]. It is a way by which people in the organization accomplish their work, relate to one another, and solve the problems that confront them on a daily basis. To be most effective, three essential elements for success (culture, innovation, and entrepreneurship) must be well matched and integrated [22].

Entrepreneurship is the practice of entrepreneurial skills and approaches by or within an organization. Employees perhaps engaged in global trade operations within a large firm are supposed to behave as entrepreneurs, even though they have the resources and capabilities of the larger firm to draw upon (Wikipedia). The concept apparently of entrepreneurship dates back to 1976. The term itself dates to the 1983 PhD dissertation by Burgelman and later defined in a 1985 book by

Gifford Pinchot, "entrepreneuring". Pinchot defined entrepreneurship as entrepreneurship occurring within the setting of an established organization. Synonyms used for the same are, corporate entrepreneurship or corporate venturing.

An entrepreneur is the person who focuses on innovation and creativity and who transforms a dream or an idea into a profitable venture, by operating within the organizational environment. An intrapreneur's success will hinge largely on his ability first to plan and then to empower other people to implement the plans. What makes an organization grow and survive in the competitive world, is its innovative intent [23]. Gifford Pinchot observed that entrepreneurs are people who dream beyond their mundane domain of something usual. Thus, today organizations require Entrepreneurs who can ensure success by their innovative management practices [24].

This is only possible if the organizations provide employees a home away from home (i.e. an environment where they are given independence to take decisions) as employees spend more time at their workplace rather than their home. Gifford Pinchot III stated that these problems can be resolved by setting up a system allowing selected employees a status within the corporation akin to that of the entrepreneur within the larger society. This new status, of an intrapreneur, will provide them the independence of the entrepreneur while still holding over them the technological, financial, and perhaps most significant, the informational umbrella of the corporation [25]. Expatriates will then be willing to take moderate risks and will be more concerned with achieving results for organizations development.

Thus, a strong and effective corporate culture lays a lot of stress on its human resources. They promote a work culture that fosters individual growth, team spirit and creativity to overcome challenges and attain goals. To achieve this, varied and diverse ideas, talent and value systems of the employees should be encouraged.

Increasing interest of academia and industry in the phenomenon of entrepreneurship is reflected in the need of introducing and cultivating entrepreneurship in established organisations. In 1980's Drucker, highlighted that "today's businesses, especially the large ones, simply will not survive in this period of rapid change and innovation unless they acquire entrepreneurial competence" [26]. His observation seems relevant for present and future organisations as well. Large organisations are turning towards entrepreneurship, in the era of globalization and merging markets, as they are unable to manage their past continual growth, innovation and value creation [27].

For sustainable development of organisations, study of factors affecting the same is thought to be essential. For the purpose of the study, prerequisites given by Henione & Korvela from the study 'How About Measuring Entrepreneurship' were used [28]. Based on literature review and data analysis the study identified the following seven factors, referred as Prerequisites to Entrepreneurship:

- Encouragement by Management and Organisation – stresses on actions of management, work culture or environment. It also focuses on organisation's approach towards entrepreneurial activities.

- Individual Motivation – refers to employees' capability and willingness towards meaningful work as well as ability to tolerate uncertainty.

- Transparency, Openness and Communality - represents openness and communality in functioning of an organisation.

- Individual Competence – discusses the ability to develop actively and present new ideas.

- Enabling Working Environment – refers to the authority and opportunities offered to employees by organisation's work environment.

- Encouragement to Innovations – demonstrates the organisation's willingness and encouragement to take risks and innovate.

Development – is attached to overall development in an organisation

For the purpose of the study, selected outcomes of entrepreneurship include the following:

Appreciation of work and job satisfaction– refers to performing varied tasks at work, feeling significant at workplace, feeling happy about ones work and valuing it. Also when others value your work.

External satisfaction in work – is attached to good work atmosphere and suitable work load.

The present paper is a part of a larger study. The object of the present paper is to study the perception of the respondents regarding the Prerequisites to entrepreneurship and its outcome.

Methodology

The present study was confined to the region of Delhi & NCR. Over the last few decades there has been a rapid development of National Capital Region (NCR). This has resulted in an increase the corporate sector in this region. Massive corporate and industrial activities have triggered the need for office space which has compelled companies to locate their offices in NCR. After Delhi, NCR has emerged as the biggest hub for the corporate sector which is not only providing the required space but also good communication and infrastructural facilities.

Six organisations were randomly selected from a list prepared purely on the basis of acceptance of the request. Further, from each organisation ten respondents were selected using purposive random sampling technique. The selected sample included employees who have exceeded the expectations of the organization in at least three consecutive performance appraisals. Exceeding expectations grade in performance appraisal's ensured the sample to be entrepreneurial & outperforming and the condition of getting such grade in 3 consecutive years had taken care of biases if any. It also ascertained that employees were well aware about the work culture of the organization. The study constituted a total sample of 60 entrepreneurs.

A structured interview schedule was prepared for the study. The tool included a mixture of structured, scaled, open ended and opinion seeking questions. This facilitated the researcher to gain an insight into the concept of Entrepreneurship. Profile, Organizational environment from the employees' perspective, Factors affecting entrepreneurship, Motivations, Challenges and perceptions were certain aspects which were studied using the interview schedule. A questionnaire on Prerequisites to entrepreneurship [29] was administered by the researcher to determine the potential prerequisites and outcomes of entrepreneurship. Prerequisites were studied under the following factors:

- Encouragement by management and organization
- Individual motivation
- Transparency, openness and communality
- individual competence
- enabling working environment
- encouragement to innovations
- development
- While the outcomes were studied under:
- Work Appreciation
- Satisfaction

The respondents were asked to give scores on the above mentioned individual factors. Then aggregate mean score was derived for factors as well as the outcomes. An aggregate score of similar statements was calculated under the above-mentioned 7 prerequisites. These aggregate scores were handled as means. The aggregate scores were then analyzed on a scale of 1-5. A smaller value pointed out a divergent opinion from the statement, and a greater value was considered to be an opinion concurrent with the statement. The critical value of the scale was defined as 3. Values below 3 indicated a need for development in the respective areas of entrepreneurship. Likewise, values higher than 3 pointed to a positive dynamic from an entrepreneurial point of view. Combined mean of the individual prerequisites was also obtained. From the aggregate mean, a holistic understanding of the effects of the prerequisites was established.

These aggregate means were then used as scores to find the correlation between prerequisites and outcomes. Correlation between the two helped to gain valuable insights into the factors affecting entrepreneurship and their possible outcomes, in context of the sustainable development of organisations.

Results and Discussion

The study comprised of 70% lower-level managers and 30% middle-level managers. At such positions decision-making is common. Leadership is imperative for molding a group of people into a team, shaping them into a force that serves as a competitive business advantage. Study revealed that entrepreneurship was not specific to a particular work field, department or work profile, but is diverse in its interpretation. With this assumption, selected respondents worked in

73

various departments with diverse work profiles - Central Engineering, Contacts and Commercials, Content, HR department, Enterprise Business Unit, Training, Business Development, Technical Support Group, Finance, Services, International Marketing, International Business, etc. Thus, the pursuit of innovative solutions to challenges confronting the organizations, including the development/ reinvention of products and services, markets, management techniques, and technologies organizational operations (e.g., production, marketing, sales, and distribution), as well as changes in strategy, organizing, and dealing with competitors are innovations in the broadest sense.

Organizational Environment and Management Practices

Sustainable development of organisations can be ensured with a continuing stream of successfully implemented innovations. For this to happen, it is important for the organizations to be designed for innovation. Thus, the study attempts to gain an insight into the endeavors of the organization to encourage internal innovation. More than half (53.3%) of the respondents revealed that innovation is encouraged in their organization. Whereas, only a small percentage (13.3%) of respondents thought internal innovation is being encouraged rarely in their organization.

They clarified that in today's competitive market, corporate entrepreneurship is the surest way for the organisations to sustain and thrive. But the extent to which innovation is encouraged varies from organization to organization. Respondents expressed, it was not until recently that their organizations realized the worth of sustainable development through corporate entrepreneurship. They felt that over the past few years, their organizations had started appreciating the importance of entrepreneurship. They believed that the reason of limited encouragement of the same is its short duration of implementation. Contrary to the above experiences, few respondents also felt that the management was not encouraging enough innovation in their organization. They expressed that the reason for the same is situation based selective encouragement of entrepreneurship. In spite of this, respondents believe that organisations will soon fully integrate policies and practices which are sustainable, innovative and profitable, for a brighter future.

Respondents also shared varied experiences with these efforts. They largely believed that these efforts were of mutually beneficial to the employees and their organizations. As quoted by one of the respondents, "My organization is wonderful - our firm encourages innovation and this helps both the individual & the organization".

To achieve better understanding, the study attempts to explore the organizational culture and structure, communication problems, and administrative flexibility. Results revealed that a little less than half (46.7%) of the sample always considered the suggestion proposed by their team members, whereas others laid stress on considering under situation; indicating a positive approach towards innovative ideas. Respondents expressed that if entrepreneurs were given essential services and permissions to work on their innovative ideas, the chances were that a truly novel project would be successful.

Sustainable Development of Organisations: Corporate Entrepreneurship

Pre-requisites to Entrepreneurship

The present study attempts to understand the factors that promote sustainable development of organisations through corporate entrepreneurship. Literature suggests that entrepreneurship within a company is depends primarily on the employee. Emotional commitment [30] and the competence, beliefs and vision of senior managers [31] were identified as the factors essential to nurture entrepreneurial talent within the organisation. However, Zahra stated that not only the individual employee but also organisational values – individual and competition centered- have an impact on the outcomes of corporate entrepreneurship [32].

Table 1 analyzed to assess the perceived prerequisites. Results corroborated with the findings of the study, "How about measuring entrepreneurship?" [33]. every variable's value was over the critical value (3.0), wherein Enabling Work Environment scored the highest (mean 4.3). Respondents believed that the senior management encouraged development and provided them with sufficient authority to perform their job in the best possible way by allowing them to work independently.

Table 1 Showing Distribution of Sample based on the Prerequisites to Entrepreneurship

Prerequisites	Aggregate scores	Aggregate of all the Prerequisites
Encouragement by management & organization	3.7	
Individual motivation	4.3	
Transparency, openness, Communality	3.9	
Individual competence	4.0	4.0
Enabling work environment	4.3	
Encouragement to innovation	3.7	
Development	4.3	

Mean = 5- Strongly agree; 4 -Agree somewhat; 3-Neutral; 2-Disagree somewhat; 1-Disagree strongly
Aggregate score: < 3= positive towards corporate entrepreneurship; >3 = need for development in areas of corporate entrepreneurship

Individual Motivation and Development also scored the highest mean (4.3) and was perceived as a source of satisfaction by the sample. Respondents were not only confidant about their ability to perform but were motivated to work in an entrepreneurial way. They also stressed on professional development and teamwork.

Individual Competence with a mean of 4.0 was observed to be a desirable prerequisite for entrepreneurship. Respondents felt that they had the vision and were also eager to present new ideas to the management. These entrepreneurs actively developed themselves at the workplace.

Transparency, Openness and Communality (mean 3.9) is also identified as important prerequisite for encouraging corporate entrepreneurship nurturing sustainable organisations. Respondents perceived that information is useful to an organization only if it is available to the concerned person(s) performing the task. They stated that information flows freely, both horizontally and vertically, in innovative organizations.

Encouragement by Management and Organization & Encouragement to Innovate scored a mean of 3.7, which also settles well on the scale. Respondents stated that it was impossible to bring forth novel ideas in an environment where the management is not encouraging.

The combined mean of the prerequisites is 4.0. This ascertains that the respondents appreciate their organization's efforts towards corporate entrepreneurship vis-à-vis sustainable development.

Outcomes of Entrepreneurship

Results exemplify that, at individual level, appreciation of work & job satisfaction and external satisfaction in work are the outcomes of successful implementation of corporate entrepreneurship. It is interesting to note that during the interview the respondents reiterated the importance of work appreciation as motivator to perform better.

Table 2   Distribution of Sample based on the Outcomes of Entrepreneurship

Outcomes	Aggregate scores	Aggregate of the Outcomes
Appreciation of work and job satisfaction	4.1	4.0
External satisfaction in work	3.9	

Mean = 5- Strongly agree; 4 -Agree somewhat; 3-Neutral; 2-Disagree somewhat; 1-Disagree strongly
Aggregate score: < 3= positive towards corporate entrepreneurship; >3 = need for development in areas of corporate entrepreneurship

It is evident from table 2 that the aggregate mean of the outcomes of entrepreneurship is 4.0. This indicates that the respondents recognise work appreciation and external satisfaction as potential outcomes of entrepreneurship. The results of the present study validate the findings of the study by [34] on "How about measuring entrepreneurship?"

Correlation between Prerequisites to Entrepreneurship and Outcomes of Entrepreneurship

Findings confirm a high correlation ($r=0.797$ at $p \leq 0.01$) between the prerequisites to entrepreneurship and outcomes of entrepreneurship. This indicates that the more an organization will encourage the prerequisites the better will be the outcomes of entrepreneurship in terms of appreciation of work and job satisfaction & external satisfaction in work. This will allow a win-win situation for both the organization and the employee; encouraging greater individual enterprise and responsibility towards the organisation. Employees will be motivated to work towards the organization's growth – economically, socially and environmentally.

Table 3 Correlation of Outcomes of Entrepreneurship with Prerequisites to Entrepreneurship

Variable	Correlation Coefficient
Outcomes of Entrepreneurship	.797**

**. Correlation is significant at the 0.01 level (2-tailed).
*. Correlation is significant at the 0.05 level (2-tailed).

Therefore, as competition becomes more global and time-based, modern corporate organizations should not only improve their procedures for new product and new business development, but also improve their culture. A favorable work environment where the employee can work autonomously will ensure greater work satisfaction and commitment towards the organization. Thus, nurturing entrepreneurs is the surest way of lengthening the life-span of an organization and making it a sustainable organisation.

Conclusion

The present paper highlights the importance of implementing corporate entrepreneurship toward sustainable organisations. Findings validate the potential prerequisites to entrepreneurship and their outcomes. Prerequisites to entrepreneurship and outcomes of entrepreneurship are also found to be highly correlated. This indicates that the more an organization will encourage the prerequisites the more likely are the corporate entrepreneurs to appreciate their work and experience job satisfaction. Consequently, employees will work towards sustainable development and success of their organisation. These findings are relevant to both the academia as well as the industry. Above mentioned prerequisites can be used by organizations as potential factors nurturing corporate entrepreneurship. They can act as guidelines for the employee's or employer's performance, thereby striving towards organization's growth and sustainability. Academia can identify relevant and effective approaches for implementing the same.

References

[1] Wong, L. and Avery, G.C. Creating sustainability in organisations: Beyond being green. International Journal of Interdisciplinary Social Sciences, 3(2), 2008, 69-76.

[2] Sustainable Europe Research Institute (SERI) Overconsumption? Our use of the world's natural resources. Available from: http://www.foe.co.uk/ sites/default/files/ downloads/overconsumption. pdf. [Accessed 15/02/14].

[3] Stead, W.E. and Stead J.G. Can humankind change the economic myth?

[4] Wikipedia. Communitarianism. 2004. Available from:

[5] Wong, L. and Avery, G.C. Creating sustainability in organisations: Beyond being green. International Journal of Interdisciplinary Social Sciences, 3(2), 2008, 69-76.

[6] Daly, H.E. Steady state economics. (2nd Ed.) (Washington DC: Island Press, 1991).

[7] Kearins, K. Making sense out of mixed meanings: Is sustainability a responsibility of business? Chartered Accountants Journal, 83(1), 2004, 62-63.

[8] Eccles, R.G, Ioannou and Serafeim. Working Paper on The Impact of Corporate Sustainability on Organizational Processes and Performance, Harvard Business School, 2013 available at: http://www.hbs.edu/faculty/Publication%20Files /12-035_a3c1f5d8-452d-4b48-9a49-812424424cc2. pdf . (accessed February 2014).

[9] Wong, L. and Avery, G.C. Creating sustainability in organisations: Beyond being green. International Journal of Interdisciplinary Social Sciences, 3(2), 2008, 69-76.

[10] Avery, G.C. and Bergsteiner, H. Honeybees and locusts: the business case for sustainable leadership. (New York NY: Routlage, 2009).

[11] Placet, M., Anderson R., and Flower, K.M. Strategies for sustainability. Research- Technology management, 48(5), 2005, 32-41.

[12] Antoncic, B. and Hisrich, R.D. Clarifying the entrepreneurship concept. Journal of Small Business and Enterprise Development, 10(1), 2003, 7-24.

[13] Jennings, D. F., & Lumpkin, J. R. (1989) Functioning modeling corporate entrepreneurship: An empirical integrative analysis. Journal of Management, 15, 1989, 485-502.

[14] Pinchot, G. Intrapreneuring: Why do not have to leave the corporation to become an entrepreneur. (New York: Harper & Row, 1985).

[15] Schollhammer, Hans. Internal Corporate Entrepreneurship, In C. Kent, D. Sexton and K. Vesper (eds.), (Encyclopaedia of Entrepreneurship, Prentice Hall, Englewood Clipp, NJ, 1982).

[16] Stevenson, H.H. and Jarillo, J.C. A paradigm of entrepreneurship: Entrepreneurial management. Strategic Management Journal, 11, 1990, 17-27.

[17] Lumpkin, G. T., and Dess, G. G. Clarifying the entrepreneurial orientation construct and linking it to performance. Academy of Management Review, 21(1), 1996, 135-172.

[18] Antoncic, B. and Hisrich, R.D. Entrepreneurship: Construct refinement and

[19] Heinonen, J. and Korvela, K. How about measuring Entrepreneurship?. Paper presented at 33rd Entrepreneurship, Innovation and Small Business Conference, Milan, Italy, September, 2003.

[20] Tools for enhancing innovativeness in enterprises. Vikalpa. 31(1), 2006, 1-15.

[21] Schein, E.H. Organizational culture and leadership (3rd ed.). (San Francisco, CA: Jossey-Bass, 2004).

[22] Owen. A.L. "Risk, entrepreneurship and human capital accumulation," Finance and Economics Discussion Series 1997-37, Board of Governors of the Federal Reserve System (U.S.), 1997.

[23] Owen. A.L. "Risk, entrepreneurship and human capital accumulation," Finance and Economics Discussion Series 1997-37, Board of Governors of the Federal Reserve System (U.S.), 1997.

[24] Pinchot, G. Entrepreneuring: Why do not have to leave the corporation to become an entrepreneur. (New York: Harper & Row, 1985).

[25] Pinchot, G. Intrapreneuring: Why do not have to leave the corporation to become an entrepreneur. (New York: Harper & Row, 1985).

[26] Drucker, P. Innovation and Entrepreneurship. (London: Heinemann, 1985).

[27] Pinchot, G., and Pellman, R. Entrapreneuring in action: A handbook for business innovation. (San Francisco: Berrett-Koehler Publ, 1999).

[28] Heinonen, J. and Korvela, K. How about measuring Entrepreneurship?. Paper presented at 33rd Entrepreneurship, Innovation and Small Business Conference, Milan, Italy, September, 2003.

[29] Heinonen, J. and Korvela, K. How about measuring Entrepreneurship?. Paper presented at 33rd Entrepreneurship, Innovation and Small Business Conference, Milan, Italy, September, 2003.

[30] Kanter, R. M. The Change Masters. (London: Allen & Unwin, 1984).

[31] Guth, W.D. and Ginsberg, A. Guest editors' introduction: Corporate entrepreneurship. Strategic Management Journal, 11(Summer), 1990, 5-15.

[32] Zahara, S. A. Predictors and financial outcomes of corporate entrepreneurship: An exploratory study. Journal of Business Venturing, 6(4), 1991, 259-285.

[33] Heinonen, J. and Korvela, K. How about measuring Entrepreneurship? Paper presented at 33rd Entrepreneurship, Innovation and Small Business Conference, Milan, Italy, September, 2003.

Chapter-VI

Resource use Efficiency in Sericulture: A Case Study of Village Khanour in District Mandi of Himachal Pradesh

Sanjay Kumar et.al*

Abstract

Sericulture was one of the healthier options available to the farmers, because it was labour intensive at the village level, employing both men and women at all stages of production. Silk had importance in developing countries mainly because of its positive socio-economic consequences. In India silk was mainly produced in five states viz. Andhra Pradesh, Karnataka, West Bengal, Tamil Nadu and Jammu and Kashmir. Sericulture was also adopted in a few pockets of lower Himachal Pradesh by the farmers. To explore the causes of its limited adoption, Village Khanour was selected for this study because sericulture had been extensively practiced here. This study expresses the resource use efficiency in mulberry silk and constraints in its adoption. To examine the resource use efficiency of sericulture, the Cobb-Douglas production function was used on the primary research carried out in this village. The result of this study shows that this Mulberry Silk production was an eco-friendly, as no chemical fertilizers were used during any stage of silk production. Economically too, this project was income generating and framers could earn from Rs. 5000-40,000 per season. This type of alternate auxiliary practices has shown a considerable impact on the livelihood of the farmers of this small hilly village.

Keywords- Sericulture, Khanour, Eco-friendly, Mulberry, Resource use Efficiency

---

*Department of Geography and economics in different colleges of Himachal Pradesh

Introduction

Sericulture is both an art and science for raising silkworms [1]. India's traditional bound domestic market and an amazing diversity of silk attire that replicate 'geographic specificity' has helped the country to achieve a leading position in silk manufacturing. India is the second largest producer of raw silk subsequent to China and the biggest consumer of raw silk and silk fabrics. An analysis of trends in international silk production suggests that sericulture has better prospects for growth in the developing countries in comparison to developed countries. It is a farm-based, labour intensive and commercially attractive economic activity falling under the cottage and small-scale sector. It particularly suits rural-based farmers and entrepreneurs, as it requires low investment but, provides relatively higher returns [2]. It provides income and employment to the rural poor especially farmers with small land-holdings and weaker sections of the society.

India is a home to a vast variety of silk secreting fauna which also includes an amazing diversity of silk moths. This has enabled India to achieve the distinctive position in production of all the five commercial varieties of natural silks namely, Mulberry, Tropical Tasar, Oak Tasar, Eri and Muga. Silk obtained from sources other than mulberry are generally termed as non-mulberry or Vanya silks. The bulk of the commercial silk produced in the world is mulberry silk that comes from the domesticated silkworm, which feeds exclusively on the leaves of the mulberry plant. Rearing is done on naturally growing trees in the forests. The market contribution of Indian silk exports in the global silk trade is 4 – 5 % which is immaterial considering the fact that India is the second largest producer of raw silk [3]. This is because India has a huge domestic market for silk goods and about 85 % of silk goods produced are sold in the domestic market as well as India exports approximately 15 % of its output of all types of silk goods [4]. But the silk potential is yet to be fully tapped as against the potential yield in India [5].

As a cottage industry, sericulture provides abundant opportunities for women in the rural areas particularly in silkworm rearing and reeling. The men folk work largely in the field and do the weaving. Sericulture is a remunerative crop which suits almost all categories of farmers [6]. With short gestation periods, the returns are quick. The estimated return in case of mulberry sericulture during the study period is

84

approximately Rs. 5,000-40,000 per annum. The growing demand of silk in the domestic market can make the industry a valuable enterprise which in turn can provide employment for the rural masses ensuring assured economic returns at the individual family level.

Objectives of Study

To study the nature of resource use, their productivity and economic returns in sericulture in the study area

To examine the problems encountered by the farmers in sericulture enterprise in the study area

Methodology

The study was conducted during the month of April and May 2014 in Khanour Village of District Mandi. This village was specifically and purposively selected due to its extensive farming of sericulture. The information required in present study was collected using structured questionnaire from 35 households engaged in sericulture. Triangulation technique was adopted to verify the collected information. In order to meet the requirement of different objective of the study various analytical, mathematical, statistical and econometric tools have been employed for analysis.

The present study was undertaken in Khanour Village in Dharampur block of District Mandi of Himachal Pradesh. The area is located between 31o71'N latitude and 76o93'E longitude. Agriculture is the predominant occupation of the households, but around 30% of the household's rear cocoons during the month of March to May. The production span of cocoons is generally 45 days. In this village mulberry silk is only produced with single crop in a year.

Cobb-Douglas Production Function

To examine resource use efficiency for cocoons production, the Cobb-Douglas production function has been used. The Cobb-Douglas model which was chosen for estimating the resource use efficiency was of the following form:

$$Y = aX1b1 \ X2b2 \ eu \tag{1}$$

Where,

> Y = income from sale of cocoons (Rupees)
>
> X1 = Represents human labour (Rupees)
>
> X2 = Value of mulberry grass (Rupees)
>
> b1 and b2 are the elasticity coefficients of the respective variables.
>
> a = constant term
>
> u = Represents error term
>
> e = 2.7183 = the base of natural logarithms.

Although the Cobb-Douglas function is curvilinear, it can be changed into a linear function by taking the logarithms of both sides of the equation as follows:

$$\log y = \log a + b1 \log X1 + b2 \log X2 + u \qquad (2)$$

The natural logs were converted into common logarithms i.e. upto base 10.

The function has been estimated by least square regression technique by using the data for the individual variable with respect to the sample farms.

It is well known fact that R2 will increase as the number of variables considered in a regression equation increases. Therefore, to eliminate this effect in case of more than one variable in the function adjusted R2 ($\bar{R}2$) were calculated as under:

$$\bar{R}2 = 1 - \frac{(1-R^2)(n-1)}{n-k} \qquad (3)$$

The significance of $\bar{R}2$ was tested with the help of t-test as under:

$$F = \frac{R^2(n-k)}{(1-R^2)(k-1)} \qquad (4)$$

Where,

$\bar{R}2$= Adjusted coefficient of multiple determination.

N = Number of sample observation.

K = Number of estimated parameters estimated from the sample.

Returns to Scale

Returns to scale were estimated by the sum of the elasticities (Σbi) of the various inputs used in the production process. The established rule for the returns to scale is that if:

Σbi = 1, implies constant returns to scale.

Σbi < 1, implies decreasing returns to scale.

Σbi >1, implies increasing returns to scale.

Resource use efficiency

In order to find out how much of a particular input could be used profitably by the farmers and to determine input output ratio, the marginal productivity of each input for different crops as well as for whole farm production function was compared with its factor cost. The ratio of MVP to MFC [7] was used to determine the resource efficiency ® with the help of following formula:

$$r = \frac{MVP}{MFC} \qquad (5)$$

where,

MVP = Marginal value product

MFC = marginal factor cost of input (price per unit input)

The equation for getting MVP value is as given below

$$MVPxi = bi \frac{\bar{Y}}{\bar{X}i}$$

MVPxi = Marginal value product of input Xi

$\overline{Y}$ = Arithmetic mean value of output.

$\overline{Xi}$ = arithmetic mean value of the input being considered

Economic theory states that whenever;

MVPxi > MFCxi, there is under utilization of resource Xi

MVPxi < MFCxi, there is over utilization of resource Xi

MVPxi = MFCxi, there is optimum utilization of resource Xi

Results and Discussion

Estimates of Production Function for Sericulture

In the present paper, the value of output per ounce is the dependent variable. The independent variables selected for the study are human labour (Rs. /ounce) and value of mulberry grass (Rs. /ounce). Cobb-Douglas production function was studied for cocoons production in the study area. For the entire regression coefficient, the value of standard errors, t values and adjusted coefficient of multiple determination ($\overline{R}2$) have been worked out .The statistical significance of the regression coefficients was evaluated at 1% level of significance, which were considered an optimum probability standard for agriculture production functions. The total output is calculated in money terms alongwith all the independent variables which were also calculated in money terms. The market prices of 2014 prevailing in the local markets were considered for the calculation of value of all the dependent and independent variables. The results are presented in the Table 1. The log linear production function for cocoons production is given in the Table 1 a total of two variable X1 (human labour) and X2 (mulberry grass) were found statistically significant at 1% level of significance for the study area. The results indicate that these factors were the determinant factors influencing the cocoons production.

Table 1 Cobb-Douglas (Log Linear) Production Function for Sericulture

Particular	Sericulture
$\sum bi$	1.04
Deviation from unity	0.04
Returns to scale	Increasing

Note: (***) indicates significance at 1% level.

Source: Field survey

The value of adjusted coefficient of multiple determination ($\bar{R}2$) was found to be 0.879. It suggested that two independent factors i.e. X1 and X2 were determining 87.9% of the total variation of cocoons production. The variables X1 and X2 were positively related to the total cereals output i.e. the rise in the value of these variables the total output was likely to increase on an average basis.

Returns to Scale of Sericulture

The production function for cocoons production shows increasing returns to scale as the total sum of regression coefficients was found 1.04. The returns to scale calculated from the production functions show that returns can be increased by more than 1% if the independent variables are simultaneously increased by 1% in the study area.

Table 2 Returns to Scale for Sericulture Production in Study Area

Variables	Sericulture Production		
	Regression coefficient	S.E.	t-value
Constant	0.154	0.268	0.577
X1	0.661	0.146***	4.516
X2	0.384	0.154***	2.490

Source: Field survey

Resource Use Efficiency for Sericulture

The addition of one unit (in Rs.) of X1 (human labour) and X2 (mulberry grass) on cocoons production would return upto Rs. 1.05 and Rs. 1.43 respectively when other inputs remain constant in the study area. For the variable X1 (human labour) the Allocative efficiency ratio (r) was 1.05. The ratio for this variable was greater than one which clearly indicated it's under utilization in the production of cocoons production in the village. The use of human labour should be increased.

Table 3 Resource Use Efficiency in the Study Area for Sericulture Production

Sericulture Production				
Resources	Elasticity	MVP	MFC	$r = \dfrac{MVP}{MFC}$
X1	0.66	1.05	1	1.05
X2	0.38	1.43	1	1.43

Source: Field survey

This ratio (r) was also greater than one for X2 variable which indicated that this input was used below optimum. This input should increase in order to get more output. Therefore, the use of both variables should increase to get optimum use of these variables in the production of cocoons.

Problems in Sericulture Production

Table 4 enlists the importance of different constraints in introducing sericulture in term of multiple per cent of sample households.

Table 4 Problems in the Adoption of Sericulture as Enterprise (Multiple per cent)

Sr. No.	Problems	(Per cent)
1	Lack of technical knowledge and training	17.14
2	Lack of marketing facilities	77.14
3	Price fluctuation/ low price	94.29
4	Lack of capital/ credit	34.28
5	Lack of labour availability	65.71
6	Shortage of feeds of silkworm	42.85
7	Others(diseases)	68.57

Source: Field survey

Table shows that 77% respondents reported that there is no organized market for the transaction of cocoon. The farmers are compelled to sell at low price as only one buyer visit the village, which is also due to low scale of production and remoteness of the area. 94% respondents were stated that price of cocoons fluctuate on seasonal basis, which restrict them to expansion of this enterprises. Lack of labour availability was the other major problem stated by 66% respondents. Shortage of feeds is another important problem faced by the 43% farmers. The main reason for shortage of feeds or lesser growth of area under plantation is due to the pressure of increasing population on wasteland for food crop production. Cocoon production is also affected by diseases, therefore, 68% farmers reported as an important problem in the study area. Lack of technical knowledge and training and lack of credit were also reported as problems by some of the respondents.

Conclusion

The present research shows that sericulture is one of the leading farming occupation and an alternate to the farmers from regular or traditional farming. The production techniques are eco-friendly, which makes this occupation a boon to the environment as well as to the climate. This type of alternate auxiliary practices has shown a considerable impact on the livelihood of the farmers of this small hilly village. The statistical results also highlighted the fact of lack of transportation and marketing availabilities for healthier advancements.

Improvement in transportation facilities and availability of suitable markets shall enhance sericulture. Economically too, this venture was profit generating and framers could earn upto 40,000 per season. In future, if the rationalized approach is being followed this project could prove ecologically as well as economically beneficial to the farmers of this small vicinity.

References

[1] http://agritech.tnau.ac.in/sericulture/seri_index.html

[2] R.Anitha, Indian Silk Industry in the Global Scenario, International Journal of Multidisciplinary Management Studies, 1(3), 2011, 100-110

[3] http://sgo.sagepub.com/content/3/3/21582440

[4] S.Lakshmanan , H. Jayram , Manpower utilization in mulberry sericulture: An empirical analysis, Manpower Journal, (33), 1998, 49-63.

[5] N.B. Vijay Prakash and S.B. Dandin, Yield Gaps and Constraints in Bivoltine cocoon production in Mandya District of Karnataka- An Economic Analysis, Indian Journal of Sericulture, 44 (1), 2005, 283-286.

[6] Chandrama Goswami and Manisha Bhattacharya, Contribution of Sericulture to Women's Income in Assam -A Case Study in Goalpara District of Assam, India, International Journal of Scientific and Research Publications, 3(3), 2013,1-6

[7] M. Goni, S. Mohmmed and B.A. Baba, Analysis of Resource-use Efficiency in Rice Production in the Lake Chad Area of Borno State, Nigeria, Journal of Sustainable Development in Agriculture & Environment, 3(2), 2007, 36-40.

Chapter-VII

Some Therapeutic Uses of Local Flora Among the Tribes of Patalkot in Chhindwara District of Madhya Pradesh, India

Sanjay Pawar, Nikhil Kanungo*

Abstract

Chhindwara district lies between latitude 21 to 22° North and longitude 78 and 79° East. It is located in south-west of Madhya Pradesh and is a well-known tribal district. Patalkot valley is spread over an area of 79 Sq. Km. at an average height of 2750-3250 feet above Mean Sea Level lies between 22.24 to 22.29° north, 78.43 to 78.50° east. The place is located at a distance of 62 Km from the district headquarter in the North-West direction, and 23 Km from Tamia in North-East direction. People living in interior and inaccessible remote rural areas of Patalkot have excellent knowledge about medicinal utility of local flora for curing their various health disorders, due to low cost and sometimes it is a part of their social life and culture. The main tribe found in the area belongs to Mavashi, Bhariya and Gond. Information was obtained through structured questionnaire administered to traditional healers and herbalists in the region.

The study revealed 22 species of plants belonging to 17 families were documented with their scientific name, family name, Hindi names, local names, active ingredients and medicinal uses. A few decades back these herbs was very common in this region but due to commercial exploitation, the natural population is decreasing at an upsetting rate, some herbs has become almost wiped out in these parts.

Keywords: Ethno-medicine, Patalkot, Traditional knowledge, Conservation, Tribes

*Department of Botany, Govt. Autonomous Post-graduate College, Chhindwara, Madhya Pradesh, India

Introduction

The tribal pockets or tracts are the store house of information and knowledge on the multiple uses of plants. Presently, ethno-botany has become increasingly valuable in the development of healthcare, source of new food products and conservation programs in different part of the world. Madhya Pradesh with its wide variety of plants and tribal population affords ample scope for studies concerning various aspects of socio-religious and cultural and folklore medicine. Extreme commercial collection of local medicinal plants from their natural habitat, due to the growing demand for herbal, cosmetic and pharmaceutical industries may be a result of failure of plant populations. Earlier the tribal's of the region were harvesting the medicinal plants at a particular time and date and time only and have belief that at this particular time it has more therapeutic value. It is evident from the modern science that at particular time the herb contains optimum active ingredients. These types of traditional harvesting practices will be helpful in providing quality raw material on sustainable basis and tool for conservation. Some ethno botanical studies were made by Acharya (2004) [1], Rai et al., (2000) [2], Upadhyay et al., (2011) [3], Kanungo et al., (2013) [4] and Pawar et al., (2013) [5] in Patalkot region.

Methodology

Authors have explored the area of Patalkot valley that includes - Gaildubbha, Rathed, Kareyam, Bharia Dhana, Bijauri, Pandu Piparia, Sajkui, Lahagadua, Karrapani, Sidhouli, Chhindi, Jaitpur and Chimtipur. The data including local name, mode of preparation, medicinal uses, parts used were collected using interview, questionnaire, collecting samples and discussions with the practitioners.

Frequent visit to the tribal villages in Patalkot region of the district were made during the years 2010-13. A close association was maintained with the people to understand their indigenous knowledge system. Herbarium specimens were prepared following standard method (Jain and Rao, 1977) [6] and deposited at the Govt. P. G. College, Chhindwara. M. P.

Result and Discussion

Alangium salvifolium (L.F.) Wong.

Family:	Alangiaceae
Hindi names:	Ankol
Local names:	Akol
Active ingredients:	Alangidiol, Stigmasterol, ankorine, marckidine, marckine, tubulosine, alangicine, cephaeline, psychotrine
Medicinal uses:	Dried powdered leaves were taken for liver cirrhosis, fatty liver and chronic hepatitis. Bark and seeds were used in skin disease. Ripe fruits (1-2) was used daily for seven days for psoriasis.

Semecarpus anacardium Linn.

Family:	Anacardiaceae
Hindi names:	Bhilava
Local names:	Bhilma
Active ingredients:	bhilwanols, phenolic compounds, biflavonoids, sterols and glycosides.
Medicinal uses:	Leaves in poultice form used for rheumatism. Bark paste with coconut oil externally applied on affected body parts in skin eruption. Seed oil with the help of a needle tips are applied on nose tip for allergic body itching. Seed oil is applied on the cracks heel once daily till cure.

Wrighitia tinctoria ssp. tinctoria R.Br.

Family:	Apocynaceae
Hindi names:	Kutaj
Local names:	Indrajau
Active ingredients:	beta-amyrin and glucoside
Medicinal Uses:	Leaves has anti-inflammatory and anti-dandruff properties. The milky latex is applied on cavities to cure toothache. Stem bark is crushed and taken orally in stamach ache.

Powdered leaves mixed with coconut oil are applied for psoriasis.

Glossocardia bosvallia (L.F.) DC.

Family:	Asteraceae
Hindi Name:	Pitta papda
Local names:	Pathar chur
Active ingredients:	5, 6, 7, 4', tetrahydroxy 3-methoxy flavone -7-O-β-D xylopyranosyl (1→4)-O-β-D-glucopyranoside which showed antiviral activity, along with two known compounds 6, 4'-dimethoxy-5, 7-dihydroxy-flavone and Isoorientin
Medicinal uses:	Plant extract was used in gastric trouble and fever. Paste of fresh pants applied on sore and wounds. Leaf decoction is given in hypertension and as heart tonic. A paste of the fresh plant is applied to promote healing of sores and wounds.

Tridax procambens Linn

Family:	Asteraceae
Hindi names:	Ekandi
Local names:	Ekandi
Active Ingredients:	It contains sterols, campesterol, stimasterol, β-sitosterol and saturated and unsaturated fatty acids.
Medicinal Uses:	A whole plant is squeezed between the palms of hands to obtain juice. Fresh plant juice was applied twice a day for 3-4 days to cure cuts and wounds. The crushed leaves are applied to arrest bleeding in bruises and cuts. Leaves extract has strong wound healing properties.

Vernonia cinerea (L.) Less

Family:	Asteraceae
Syn.:	Cyanthillium cinereus
Hindi Names:	Sahdevi

97

Local names: Sahdevi
Active ingredients: Quercetin, stigmasterols, sitosterol, vernolide.
Medicinal Uses: Whole plants were shade dried and used to make pillow for sleeplessness. Plant juice is used for indigestion, piles, cough, asthma, ringworms and malaria.

Stereospermum colais (Buch.- Ham. ex. Dillw.) Mabb.

Family: Bignoniaceae
Syn.   Stereospermum chelonoides (L.f.) DC.
Hindi names: Padher, Paroli
Local names: Padar
Active ingredients: 1(17)-methyl anthraquinones, sterequinone- A and -D, their biogenetic precursors sterequinone-B, -C, and a new naphthoquinone sterequinone-E along with a known naphthoquinone, sterekunthal-B, have been isolated from stem bark.
Medicinal uses: The decoction of root or stem barks is used in the treatment of asthma and cough. Fruits effective in migraine pain, headache, which inhibit pain response mediated via both central and peripherally mechanisms.

Bauhinia variegata Linn

Family: Caesalpiniaceae
Hindi names: Kachnar
Local names: Lalkachnar
Active ingredients: The stem bark has hentriacontane, octacosanol and stigmasterol, while stem contains beta- sitosterol, lupeol and a flavanone glycoside.
Medicinal uses: It can be used in cough conditions, asthma, abdominal distention also acts as a gargle for sore throats, prevent from skin diseases, or internally as a remedy for diarrhea, cough, bleeding piles,

menorrhagia, scrofulous enlargement of neck glands, ulcers, skin diseases. A decoction of the bark is taken for dysentery.

Olea dioica Roxb

Family:	Oleaceae
Hindi names:	Ban Jamun
Local names:	Jangal jamun
Active ingredients:	Fatty acids in seeds (palmitic, oleic, linoleic and bhenica)
Medicinal uses:	Bark and fruit paste is applied in rheumatism. Root extract (10 ml) is used externally in chest pain.

Celastrus paniculatus Wild

Family:	Celastraceae
Hindi names:	Malkangni
Local names:	Malkangni
Active ingredients:	Celatrine and paniculatin, fatty acids, viz., oleic, linoleic, linolenic, palmitic, stearic, crude lignoceric acid, benzoic and acetic acid as volatile acids. Sesquiterpene polyalcohols
Medicinal uses:	Seeds are use in gastric troubles and sharpening of memory, also used to cure sores and ulcer. Oil being a powerful stimulant for neuromuscular system is also used for the treatment of rheumatism, gout and paralysis.

Terminalia cuneata Roth

Family:	Combretaceae Terminalia arjuana
Hindi names:	Arjun
Local names:	Kahua
Active ingredients :	β-sitosterol, chebulin, anthraquinone glycoside, terchebin, tetrachebulin, vitamin C, chebulinic & tannic acid,

	arachidic, palmitic, stearic, oleic, linoleic
	& behenic acids, 2-a-hydroxymicromeric
	acid, maslinic acid, 2-α -hydroxyursolic acid
Medicinal uses:	Used in heart diseases, bilious affections,

arachidic, palmitic, stearic, oleic, linoleic & behenic acids, 2-a-hydroxymicromeric acid, maslinic acid, 2-α -hydroxyursolic acid

Medicinal uses: Used in heart diseases, bilious affections, blood dysentery, inflammatory conditions and in the fracture of bone. The bark is useful as an antiischaemic and cardio protective agent in hypertension and heart diseases, especially in disturbed cardiac rhythm, angina or myocardial infarction.

Diplocyclos palmatus (Linn.) Jaffrey

Family: Cucurbitaceae
Hindi names: Shivlingi
Local names: Mahadevi
Active ingredients: Alkaloids, flavonoids, triterpinoids saponins, steroids and proteins, resins with, Sugars, starch. The seeds have been reported to contain 12% oil, protein also contains goniothalamin, bryonin, punicic acid and lipid.
Medicinal uses: Seeds are use in sterility due to blocked tubes in women. Seeds in combination with other plant drugs are use for helping conception and prevent miscarriage.

Citrullus colocynthis (L.) Schrad

Family: Cucurbitaceae
Hindi names: Indrayan
Local names: Kadu kachari
Active ingredients: cucurbitacin, Seeds contain the phyto sterolin (ipurand), 2 phytosterols, 2 hydrocarbons, a saponin, an alkaloid, a polysaccharide or glycoside, and tannin
Medicinal uses: 3-5 seeds were fried in ghee and used in jaundice for 5- 7 days. The pulp or leaves is a remedy for cancerous tumors. Whole

plant powder is use in diabetes. Pulp is also used in constipation.

Sida cordata Linn

Family:	Malvaceae
Hindi names:	Bala
Local names:	Kahrenti
Active ingredients:	Ephedrine, vasicine and pseudoephedrine constitute the major alkaloids from the aerial parts of the plant, which also show traces of sitosterol and palmitic, stearic and hexacosanoic acids. Sterculic, malvalic and coronaric acids have been isolated from the seed oil, along with other fatty acids [7]
Medicinal uses:	The rejuvenating action of this herb extends to the nervous, circulatory, and urinary systems. It has a diuretic effect and is useful in urinary problems, including cystitis. Being cooling and astringent, it is used in inflammations and bleeding disorders. It is used in asthma and liver problems, due to its ephedrine content. It possesses psycho-stimulant properties, affecting the central nervous system.

Martynia annua Linn

Family:	Martyniaceae
Hindi names:	Bagnakhi
Local names:	Ulatakanta
Active ingredients:	Glycosides, tannins, carbohydrates, phenols, flavonoids and anthocyanin, glycosides, tannins, carbohydrates, phenols, flavonoids and anthocyanin
Medicinal uses:	Seeds used for arresting of graying of hairs. The fruits used as local sedative and used as antidote to scorpion stings to venomous bites and stings.

Soymida febrifuge (Roxb.) A. Juss.

Family:	Meliaceae
Hindi names:	Rohan
Local names:	Raktarohan
Active ingredients:	Plant contains lupeol, sitosterol, methyl angolenate. Bark contains tetranortriterpenoids, yields gum. Heart-wood contains febrifugin, naringenin, myricetin, dihydromyricetin. Wood and bark contains deoxyandirobin. Leaves contain quercetin, nitinoside
Medicinal uses:	Bark used in the treatment of diarrhoea, dysentery and fever. It also used as a gargle in stomatitis and applied to rheumatic swellings.

Cissampelos pareira Linn

Family:	Menispermaceae
Hindi names:	Patha
Local names:	Kadupan
Active ingredients:	Cissampareine, arachidic acid, berberine, linoleic acid, stearic acid and tetrandrine.
Medicinal uses:	Root extract prepared in local liquor is used to reduce fever. It relieves heavy menstrual bleeding and help to prevent abortion. A rhizome decoction or pounded leaves are also use in jaundice, rheumatism and heart trouble.

Tinospora cordifolia (Willd.) Miers ex Hook. f. & Thoms.

Family:	Menispermaceae
Hindi name:	Amrita, Giloe, Jiwantika,
Local names:	Guduchi
Active ingredients:	The glycoside-giloin, and a non-glucoside-gilenin and gilosterol have been found. The bitter principles has been identified as columbin, chasmanthin and palmarin. The alkaloid tinosporin, protoberberine, tinosporic acid, and tinosporol have been identified in

	leaves, which are rich in proteins, calcium and phosphorus.
Medicinal uses:	The stem is one of the constituents of several Ayurvedic preparations used in general debility, dyspepsia, fever and urinary diseases. The stem is bitter, stomachic, diuretic, stimulates bile secretion, causes constipation, allays thirst, burning sensation, vomiting, enriches the blood and cures jaundice. It benefits the immune system in a variety of ways.

Butea monosperma (Lamk.)Taub.

Family:	Papilionaceae
Hindi names:	Palas
Local names:	Palsa
Active ingredients:	The root contain glycine, glycosides and aromatic compounds. Flowers contain butrin, butein and butin.
Medicinal uses:	The petiole is chewed and the juice is sucked to cure cough, cold and specially in the case of painful urination. A small piece of root from young plant, usually less than 2 years is use for 15 days as a remedy against impotency. Seeds are chewed and taken with milk to treat anemia and urinal complaint.

Pueraria tuberosa (Roxb. ex.willd.) DC.

Family:	Papilionaceae
Hindi names:	Vidhari kand
Local names:	Vidari kand
Active ingredients:	Quercetin, Puerarostan, Puerarone, Tuberosin
Medicinal uses:	Tuber (10 g) paste is mixed with milk twice daily for rejuvenate and to have good strength and stamina. It is also given to the lactating women to increase breast milk and in general debility, nervous breakdown and spermatorrhoea.

Clematis gouriana Roxb. ex. DC.

Family:	Ranunculaceae
Hindi names:	Churanhar
Local names:	Badarshinthi
Active ingredients:	quaternary aporphine alkaloid, magnoflu-orine.
Medicinal uses:	Leaves juice applied on hair to kill the lice. Stem & leaves extrect were externally applided on affected body parts to cure itching. Paste of leaves is applied on wound. Root paste is mixed with boiled rice water and decoction obtained is given thrice a day in dysentery. Root are applied externally in leucoderma. Whole plant powder is given with curd two times in a day for piles.

Cardiospermum halicacabum Linn.

Family:	Sapindaceae
Hindi names:	Kapal podi
Local names:	Safed gumchi
Active ingredients:	Glycosidic triterpenes, tannins, quebrachitol, beta sitosterols, campesterol and stigmasterol.
Medicinal uses:	Leaf extract is used in acute and chronic inflammatory rheumatism. Plant extract is used in dermatitis and keratosis. The leaf juice has been used as a treatment for earache. 2 to 3 drops of juice of the leaves can be used as ear drops for earache, purulent discharge from ears.

Conclusion

The study concludes that the role of herbal medicine for the treatment of various diseases and disorders among tribes is crucial. They use different plant parts of local weeds and trees. Majority of the preparations are taken orally and applied on the skin. Local healers play an important role in the life of these communities. A society can be made in the villages that will look after the conservation of important medicinal and economical plants. Universities, Colleges, NGOs and other agencies should come ahead and take up a village of their own region. These organizations can play essential role in conservation of significant medicinal plant.

A medicinal plant garden/ herbal garden and green house can be prepared in the village itself. At one side there is need of Ex-situ and in-situ conservation, on the other hand, preservation by documentation of traditional Ethno-medicinal-botanical knowledge is highly desirable. Local healers of targeted region should be given support time to time.

References

[1] Acharya, Deepak Medicinal plants for curing common ailments in India. Positive health: 102. 2004.

[2] Rai, M.K.; Pandey, A.K. and Acharya, D. Ethnomedicinal plants used by Gond tribe of Bhanadehi, distt. Chhindwara, M.P. Journal of non-timber forest; 7 (3/4): 2000, 237-241.

[3] Upadhyay, R. Trivedi, S. and Mehrotra, N. N., Phytochemical studies and Antimicrobial Activity of traditional medicinal plant Alangium salvifolium (L.f.) Wang. Search & Research Vol-II No. 2, 2011 (183-184).

[4] Kanungo, N. Pawar, S. and Barmaiya, K. K.. Ethnomedicinal plants used in kidney stones by Traditional healers in Patalkot velley of Chhindwara district of Madhya Pradesh. Indian Stream Research Journal ISSN: 2230-7850; 2013 32-36.

[5] Pawar, S. Barmaiya, K. K. and Kanungo, N, Ethno – medicinal plants used by tribes of Patalkot (District Chhindwara) M. P; Pro. Nat. Conf. on Ethnobotany (NCEB-2013). Jagat arts, commerce & L.H.P. Science college, Goregaon, Gondia (M.S.), 2013, 36-40.

[6] Jain, S. K. and Rao R. R. A hand book of field and Herbarium methods (Today and tomorrow Publishers, New Delhi. 1977).

[7] Indian Herbal Pharmacopoeia vol. II (Indian Drug Manufacturers Association, Mumbai. 1999).

Chapter-VIII

Preserving Traditional Medical System- A Case Study of Amchis in Dharamshala, Himachal Pradesh

Natasha Sharma and Chandra Prakash Kala*

Abstract

The variations in the traditional knowledge on medicinal plants among different groups of user are experienced over the years. The variations may depend on the geographical conditions, people perceptions, availability of resource and policy interventions. The decline in traditional knowledge through generations is reported worldwide. The study was undertaken in Dharamshala block of district Kangra, Himachal Pradesh with respect to the importance of Tibetan medicinal system in preserving the traditional knowledge. The sampling unit comprised of Tibetan doctors and the young people residing in this area. The semi structured questionnaires were used to gather information. Tibetan doctors were personally interviewed and were questioned about the practices and development of Tibetan medicinal system in past few years. The Tibetan doctors acquire knowledge from their ancestors as reported by them during the study. They collect the medicinal plants on the basis of the nature of diseases, recipes of codified Tibetan medicines and periodic harvesting calendar. They have developed many medicinal formulations for curing chronic and acute diseases. In general, the traditional knowledge is declining with time, but as observed in the study, within the Tibetan community the traditional knowledge is being passed on from one generation to the other. About 68% of young people in the community are pursuing their career in the Tibetan medicines. The findings are discussed in view of the preservation of Tibetan medicine system and sustainability of the system by adopting innovative interventions.

Keywords- Preservation, traditional knowledge, medicinal plants, sustainable harvesting, Tibetan medicinal system.

---

* Indian Institute of Forest Management, Nehru Nagar, Bhopal - 462 003, Madhya Pradesh, India

Introduction

Traditional knowledge has been defined as a cumulative body of knowledge, know-how, practices and representations maintained and developed by people with extended histories of interaction with the natural environment. These sophisticated sets of understandings, interpretations and meanings are part and parcel of a cultural complex that encompasses language, naming and classification systems, resource practices, rituals, spirituality and world-views'[1]. Since ages humans have indispensably associated with the nature and its resources. The knowledge and practices derived by the use of the natural resources, mainly the wild medicinal plants, has been passed to different generations. The knowledge and traditional medicinal systems have not been well documented except the few making it on the verge to disappear [2]. Community based traditional medicinal systems are helpful for the sustainability and management of the natural resources.

Himalayan communities in themselves are well accustomed with the traditional medicinal system comprising of Ayurveda, Chinese and Tibetan therapeutic system. They altogether rely on the traditional medicines as well as the allopathic or the modern medicinal system. With the strengthening of the modern allopathic system, the traditional systems have lost the uniqueness [3]. Although, with time the traditional knowledge is on the verge to diminish but there are traditional healers still practicing in various parts of the world [4]. According to the Department of Ayurveda, Yoga & Naturopathy, Unani, Siddha and Homoeopathy [5], total number of registered practioners till date are 686319 out of which 56% are Ayurvedic practitioners comprising of traditional vaidya and professional ayurvedic doctors. Recently, Department of AYUSH under Ministry of Health &Welfare, Government of India has included Sowa-Rigpa (Tibetan medicinal system (TMS) along with the other traditional medicinal system.

Sowa Rigpa also called as 'amchi system of medicines' is one of the oldest medicinal systems in the world. History stretches to 3rd century AD when TMS originated. But it came into force in the 7th century AD [6]. It is a holistic medicinal system which uses medicinal plants and minerals. TMS comprises of peculiar methods to diagnose, describe and treat the particular disease [7]. Over a period of time, TMS have gained significance due to its quick results. Till date, the total number of registered Tibetan dispensaries in India is about 22, yet no practitioner is registered under AYUSH [5]. These dispensaries exist in 6 Indian states with the maximum of 28.6% in Arunachal Pradesh. Among many literatures on Tibetan Medicines, the most authentic and authoritative text is the Four Great Tantras or the Four treatises which forms the main source book of TMS till today. It is basically the summary of the Tibetan peoples fight against the diseases by making healthy use of the natural resources. The Four Great Tantra is said to be compiled by the Father of Tibetan Medicine, the Yuthog Yonten Gonpo.

Dharamshala, a block of district Kangra in Himachal Pradesh of India is a home to the Tibetans in exile. During the "Tibetan uprising" in the year 1959, the 14th Dalai Lama escaped from Lhasa (capital of Tibet) and settled up at Dharamshala along with 80,000 Tibetan people. As per Demographic Survey of Tibetans in Exile 2009, by Planning Commission of Central Tibetan Administration [8], about 1, 28, 014 Tibetans are living in this exile community (India 94,203; Nepal 13,514; Bhutan 1,298; and rest of the world 18,999). Tibetan community is in itself incredibly diverse and with the establishment of Central Tibetan Administration the people are supported through social and educational services. Men-Tsee-Khang [The Traditional Tibetan Medicine Institute (TMAI)] was re-established in 1961 in Dharamshala, to promote and practise Sowa- Rigpa. They now provide health services to the people worldwide and produce medicine in environmentally sensitive manner.

With the course of time, TMS has frequently attained a significant level. People from different parts of the world depend on this traditional healing system. Thus, variations in traditional knowledge are experienced with advent of TMS. These variations depend on the geographical conditions, people perceptions, availability of resource and policy interventions. There is a need to document the traditional practices towards the modern disease cure. Also, with the abrupt dependence on Tibetan medicines and its subtle demand in the international market, the influential and sustainable approaches need to be measured and further to suggest possible strategy for the preservation of the traditional TMS. With this background a study was undertaken in the Himalayan state of India in order to document and analyse the TMS for the welfare of human beings.

Materials and Methods

Study area

Dharamshala, one of the administrative blocks of district Kangra, Himachal Pradesh is known as "Little Lhasa". It is a quasi-capital for the Tibetan population residing in the place. Dharamshala located on the southern aspect of the Dhauladhar mountain range in the Western Himalayas. The place is surrounded by the dense coniferous forest. Dharamshala lies between 32° 13'30.52"N and 76° 18'37.66"E with the altitude varying from 1500 m to 2000 m above sea level. As per the Census 2011, the total population of Dharamshala block is 1, 36, 536 out of which rural population is 93,744 and urban is 42,792. Dharamshala is divided into two regions, one the lower Dharamshala and the upper Dharamshala. The lower Dharamshala inhabit the local 'pahari' community and the upper Dharamshala is composed of both local as well as majority of Tibetan community.

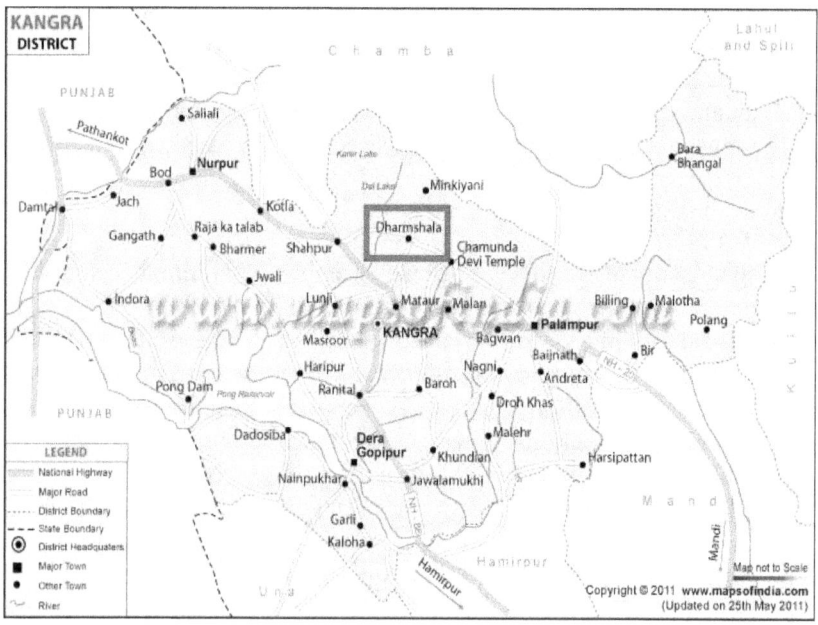

Map of District Kangra, Himachal Pradesh. (Source: Maps of India)

Tibet in Exile

In the year 1959, the escape of the 14th Dalai Lama to the state of Himachal Pradesh with to the establishment of the Tibet in exile remunerated Dharamshala. In the year 1960, they formed Central Tibetan Administration (CTA) which worked as the government-in-exile for the Tibetan people. It has become the government headquarters and several thousands of Tibetans are settled here. It is considered as a home of His Holiness 14th Dalai Lama and many Tibetans, a tourist place and an administrative capital. In the recent year, the people who have resided in the place in the way back 1960 have been also listed in the electoral list. Tibetan people in the region have established market which is internationally famous. Many of them have been a part of CTA and work for the development of the community in different departments. The old people, who were well known traditional healers in Lhasa, have been practicing the profession and are transferring traditional knowledge to the next generation. The young generation is highly influenced by the education and many of them have been in world's renowned universities.

Climate

The climate of Dharamshala is humid subtropical with maximum summer temperature of 36°C. From July to mid-September is the monsoon season with maximum rainfall up to 304.8 cm. The autumn temperature on an average is between 16-17 °C. Winters are cold and snow, sleet and hailstorms are common during this season. The spring season is short and depends on the departure of the winter season. The region experiences some common natural events like earthquake and landslides.

Sampling and Collection of data

For the purpose of study, the sampling unit was defined as the Tibetan community. Among the community semi-structured questionnaires were designed for different groups, including traditional healers commonly known as amchis, Tibetan doctors, interns and young people. The questionnaire included the demographic profile, profession, experience, utilisation and conservation of traditional knowledge. About 15 amchis and Tibetan doctors were interviewed. Besides, 30 interns were also consulted. The selection of amchis was based on snowball sampling. The interns and young people were

111

randomly selected from the region. Further, due to unavailability of some Tibetan doctors during the field surveys, the information was collected through online questionnaire survey. Besides, extensive literature [9]-[16] was surveyed which comprised of important publications.

Data analysis

Data were analyzed at species level. The number of medicinal plant species used for the treatment of various diseases was calculated and informant consent factor (ICF) was calculated following Trotter and Logan [17] method. For measuring some important variables and their significance descriptive and analysis of variance was used in the SPSS 20.0 software [18].

Results and Discussion

Traditional knowledge

Traditional knowledge on use of Ethno medical plants

According to the TMS, disease is an imbalance of three major principles called as 'Nyes- pa' i.e. 'rLung' (wind), 'mKhris-pa' (fire) and 'Badkann' (earth and water) [19]. The traditional Tibetan doctors diagnose and treat the ailments on the basis of these principles. The present study documents 31 plant species commonly used for the treatment of various diseases. For each species informant consensus factor was calculated. Out of 31 medicinal plants, about 74% of the species had informant consent factor between 0.9 – 0.96 (Table 1). The highest consensus factor species were Aconitum heterophyllum, Acorus calamus, Bambusa sp, Berberis lyceum, Carum carvi, Dracocephalum heterophyllum, Emblica officinalis, Ephedra sp., Gentiana sp., Hippophae sp., Juniperus communis, Myristica fragrans, Melia sp., Nardostachys jatamansi, Picrorhiza kurrooa, Rheum sp., Rosa sp., Saussurea lappa and Terminalia chebula.

Terminalia chebula is called as 'the king herb' in Tibetan medicines which is a good astringent (Zhang, 1997). Emblica officinalis is a very common plant species which is said to balance all the three principles ('Nyes-pa') [16]. According to them Emblica officinalis (Kyu ru ra) along with Terminalia chebula (Arura) and Terminalia bellerica (Baru ra) are the major constituents in the Tibetan medicine for cleaning of body as the 'Triphala churna' in Ayurveda. Based on the extensive

112

literature survey these species were listed as major constituents in the Tibetan formulations. Among the pure formulations documented in the traditional literature, the species with highest ICF were constituents of Agar-8, Agar-12, Agar-15, Nutmeg 20, Thapring, Brag-Khung-Ril-Bu, Padma28, Aru 7, Aru 35 and Bhim Mitra formulations. The main constituents of Agar-8 and Aru-7 have been found in the Trans Himalayan region of India [15]. Nutmeg 20 called as Zati helps in promoting mental wellness and disorders related to one of the three principles i.e. rLung (wind) [16]. Thapring which is very common Tibetan medicine nowadays has anti cancerous and hepatoprotective properties [20] [21].

According to the Tibetan traditional healers or doctors the traditional system uses natural herbs, some precious stones, salts, mineral and some animal extract. Among the common minerals gold, silver, copper, iron, calcite and mercury are used in traditional medicinal systems [22]. Gold promotes longevity whereas Iron helps in curing liver poisoning and anaemia [15]. Mercury has also been detected in some precious pills in TMS [23]. The study undertaken in the Dharamshala region revealed that Tibetan precious pills constitute of mercury and the prolonged effects were detected among the population having those pills [24].

Method of Examination

The process starts from the examination, collection, preparation and treatment are spiritually interlinked [25]. The examination of the patient is revealed by the combination of pulse rate, urine analysis, touch, narration of diseases, tongue, previous reports or test as well physical examination (Fig 1). The pulse and tongue analysis have been derived from the Chinese medicinal system and the urine analysis is owned by Tibetans themselves [26]. The preparation of the medicine is entirely based on the detected measure of disease and on the potency to cure the disease without any side effects.

Diseases Diagnosed among the different population

The diseases treated by the Tibetan medicines were listed based on the records collected by different Tibetan clinics in the past five years. Maximum percentage of digestive disorders, diabetes, arthritis, cancer and asthma are treated among the population (Fig.2). The population treated generally comprise of patients from Punjab, Delhi, Karnataka,

113

Tamil Nadu, West Bengal, Gujarat, Jammu and Kashmir, Haryana, Uttaranchal and Himachal Pradesh. Internationally, patients from Russia, USA and other parts of World have also resorted to these Tibetan medicines. According to the Men- Tsee- Khang's annual report, 2008 [27] about 92% of its patients are from Indian subcontinent.

Source of Traditional knowledge

About 27% of the informants have acquired knowledge from their ancestors (grandparents/parents) while 62% have a professional degree or are learning from the professional Tibetan medical colleges (TMC). A total 11% of the informants have acquired knowledge through self-practice and literature. The informants have been studying the Tibetan medicine literature since 10 years and practicing side by side (Fig. 3). The professional college comprise of doctors or traditional healers who have gained traditional knowledge from all the three sources. Many studies have revealed the loss of traditional medicinal knowledge among the lineages due to the advent of other employment opportunities and lack of the interest by the younger generation [28]-[31]. But with the high demand of the Tibetan traditional medicines much of the younger generation is keen to learn about their traditional medicine system.

The data was segregated based on the formal and informal learners. The formal learners comprised of informants who have attained knowledge through professional course/degree. The informal population comprised of informants who are either self learnt or have acquired knowledge from parents and grandparents. Out of the total number of informants about 22% of females and 40% males have or are gaining knowledge formally and 7% of females and 31% males have learned informally as per the survey. Maximum formal learners belong to 21-40 age groups comprising both male and female. The informal learners in the survey belong to 41-60 and >61 age groups (X^2 = 38.67, df=2, p<0.05).

Collection of Medicinal Plants

Amchis or the Tibetan doctors collect the plants on the basis of the nature of diseases, recipes as codified in Tibetan literature and periodic harvesting calendar. Among the informants 24% of them buy the medicinal plants from the herbal mandis located at Amritsar and Delhi.

About 43% of them collect from the wild (Figure 4). Out of these 43%, many of them (25%) purchase from the local people who are collectors by profession. Very few bring the medicines from the amchis resided in Spiti or Leh region of India. About 33% collect raw material from the cultivated fields all around the country i.e. herbal gardens and home gardens. The collection is purely based from the wild in the Trans Himalayan region where only the amchis or Tibetan healers utilize the raw material [14].

Conservation Methods

According to the traditional Tibetan healers, the indigenous methods for the collection and utilisation of various plants parts as used in the Tibetan medicines are based on three factors i.e. periodic harvesting calendar, nature of disease and recipes of codified Tibetan medicines. The practice of plant collection is deeply linked with spiritual prayers. Before collection, spiritual ritual is carried out in view of getting fruitful and good outcomes. The culture and religious calendar known as tahangsung rikhi is considered for the collection of medicinal herbs. This is a period when most of the medicinal plants used in the preparation of medicine complete their life cycle. The dhuchi man char i.e. medicine rain period is significant in this calendar as it is believed that after the first winter shower the herbs attain maximum medicinal potential. Undergrounds parts are collected during this period. During the spring season bark and leaves are collected. The traditional healers who collect from the wild consider availability to be an important indicator [32]. Also, if the collection is from wild they collect medicinal plants based on the requirement. They believe that to store medicinal herbs is difficult as it can lose its medicinal value with time [25]. Therefore, the indigenous methods used are regarded to be sustainable, when the surrounding environment is under peer pressure with the demand.

Cultivation of the important medicinal herbs used in the TMS is a way forward for the conservation of the species and its knowledge as the conservation challenges have been complex due to changing climate. The adoption of cultivation practices for the medicinal plants can often best be achieved by different institutions developing the traditional Tibetan medicine. The sharing of the knowledge has always supported the conservation of the traditional practices [33]. According to them, the knowledge transferred to the global community has not posed any ethical problems and is an asset to be used for the wellness of human beings.

Figures and Tables

Table 1: Medicinal plants used in Tibetan medicines and different formulations

Botanical Name	Tibetan Name	Family	Diseases	Informant Consensus Factor (ICF)	Formulations
Acacia catechu Willd.	Seh ldeh	Legumi nosae	Insomnia, mental illness, nose bleeding, body pain and skin disorders	0.54	Thapring, Nutmeg 20, Medicinal'ba m7
Aconitum heterophyllum Wall.	Pogma r	Ranunc ulaceae	Stomach disorders, gall bladder diseases, brain disorders, cancer	0.94	Brag-Khung-Ril-Bu, Padma28, Thapring
Acorus calamus L.	Su dag	Araceae	Arthritis, inflammation of kidney channel, ear nose, eyes and lungs, cold, fever, stomach and intestinal parasite pain	0.94	Thapring, Aru 35, A-Ru-Sman-Nag, Brag-Khung-Ril-Bu, Garuda 5
Bambusa sp.	Chu gang	Poaceae	Asthma, cough, diarrhea,infecti ons,fever, pulmonary disorders	0.95	Agar8, Agar 12, Agar15, Gyu-Thog's Bamboo Pith 25, Nutmeg 20, Zangs-Thal 25, Blue Poppy 8

Berberis lyceum Royle.	Kerba Nakpo	Berberi daceae	Diabetes, gall bladder And eye Problems, inflammation of lungs, nausea and high fever	0.93	Aconite 13, Skyer-Shun 8, Spang-Rgyan 10, Tik-Ta 8
Betula utilis D. Don.	Takpa	Betulac eae	Antiseptic, jaundice, asthma, irregular menstruation	0.73	-
Cartham us tinctorius L.		Asterac eae	Lung diseases, indigestion,arth ritis,gout.	0.50	Tik-Ta25, Sorig, Nutmeg 20, Brag-Zhun 9
Carum carvi L.	Goh– nyod	Umbelli ferae	Loss of appetite, muscles contractions, cold, cough, Fever, food poisoning, eyeInfection, gastric dysfunction	0.92	A-Wa 15, Bhim Mitra, Cinnamon 6
Chenopo dium album L.	Niew	Chenop odiacea e	Stomach disorders, piles, anemia	0.53	-
Commip hora mukul Hook.	Gu gul	Bursera ceae	Blood dysfunction, body pain, influenza	0.62	Gser-Thang 18, Thapring,
Delphini um sps.	Jakang	Ranunc ulaceae	Diarrhoea, Intestinal Disorders, Wounds	0.59	Devil Dung Pill, Thapring

Dracocep halum heteroph yllum L.	Jibkar	Lamiac eae	Liver disorders, heal wounds, oral diseases, toothache ,blood pressure	0.94	Sandalwood18 , Gyu-Dril 13
Emblica officinali s Gaertn.	Kyu ru ra	Phyllant haceae	Hair loss, balance all three principles and is an diuretic	0.96	Agar 15, Agar 17,Agar 19, Aru18,Aru23, Carex15, Gyu-Dril 13, Gyu-Thog's Bamboo Pith 25,
Ephedra sp.	Chhe Dum	Ephedra ceae	Liver disorders, hemostatic effects, bronchial disorders, hypertension	0.92	Safflower 7
Gentiana sp.	Khyi Chye Karpo	Gentian aceae	Nerve and liver disorders, fever, lung dysfunction, tuberculosis.	0.94	Aconite 13, Da-Li 18, Gentiana 10
Heracleu m lallii Wall.	Tukar	Umbelli ferae	Stomach disorders, earache, leprosy, joint pain and blood pressure	0.65	Devil's Dung Pill
Hippoph ae sp.	Tora	Elaeagn aceae	Lung diseases, stomach-intestinal disorders, amenorrhea,	0.94	Bse-Ru 25, Buckthorn 5, Gyu-Thog's Bamboo Pith 25, Blue Poppy 8
Juniperus communi s L.	-	Cupress aceae	Diabetes, blood pressure	0.92	Aru 18
Juniperus macropo da Boiss.	Shugp a	Cupress aceae	Kidney disorders	0.50	-

Myristica fragrans Houtt.	Za–ti	Myristi caceae	Heat imbalance in liver and stomach, indigestion	0.94	Agar8, Agar 12, Agar15,Bamb oo Pith 25, Sorig, Rhubarb 15, Da-Li 16,Nutmeg 20, Ga-Bur 25
Melia sp.	-	Meliace ae	Indigestion, inflammation of lungs, fungal infections	0.92	Agar8, Agar 12, Agar15, Nutmeg 20
Nardosta chys jatamansi (Don.) DC	Pangp yo	Valeria naceae	Lung, heart and liver disorders,woun ds, cough, cold, Fever, hypertension, tumours, epilepsy, skin diseases, rheumatism, Paralysis	0.94	Aru 7, Brag-Khung-Ril-Bu, Brag-Zhun 9, Camphor 25
Oxytropi s microphy lla D.C.	Senak	Legumi nosae	Dysentery, inflammation of lungs, dog bite	0.62	Bya-Kyung Sngon-Po, Medicinal 'Bam 9
Picrorhiz a kurroa Royle Ex. Benth	Hon len	Plantagi naceae	Fever, cold, blood pressure, inflammation of lungs, cardiac disorders.	0.94	Tik-Ta 8, Gyu-Thog's Bamboo Pith 25,Agar 31, Aconite 13, Medicinal 'Bam 7, Bamboo Pith 9, Bamboo Pith 25,
Rheum sp.	Chutra	Polygon aceae	Bone fractures, sprain, indigestion, sores, menstrual and blood Disorders	0.94	Rhubarb 25, Calcite 35, Rhubarb 15

Rhodiola sp.	-	Crassul aceae	Dysentery, inflammation of lungs, irregular menstruation, leukorrhea.	0.75	Bya-Kyung Sngon-Po, Rhubarb 25, Bamboo Pith 25, Gentiana 15, Sandalwood 8,
Rosa sp.	Segoe Fo	Rosacea e	Fever, Diarrhoea and Bile disorders	0.9	Eight Lotuses
Saussure a lappa DC.	Sch. Bip	Asterac eae	Astringents, lung infections, cancer	0.93	Devil's Dung 25, Agar8, Agar 12, Agar15,Aru 25,Carex 15, Brag-Khung-Ril-Bu, Da-Li 16
Taxus wallichia na Zucc.	Thingr e salla	Taxacea e	Cancer	0.80	-
Syzygiu m cumini L.		Myrtace ae	Diabetes	0.80	-
Terminal ia chebula Retz.	Arura	Combre taceae	Astringents, inhibit growth of malignant tumors	0.96	Agar8, Agar 12, Agar15,Aru7, Aru23,Aru25, Bhim Mitra, Brag-Khung-Ril-Bu, Shilajit 9, Bamboo Pith 25, Rhubarb 15, Da-Li 18,Nutmeg 20

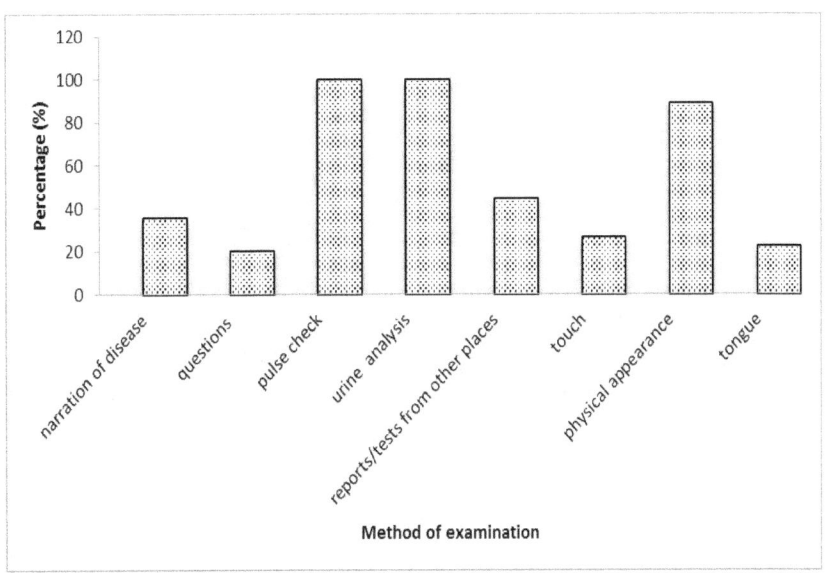

Figure 1 Methods of examination by the Tibetan doctors or amchis as per the survey

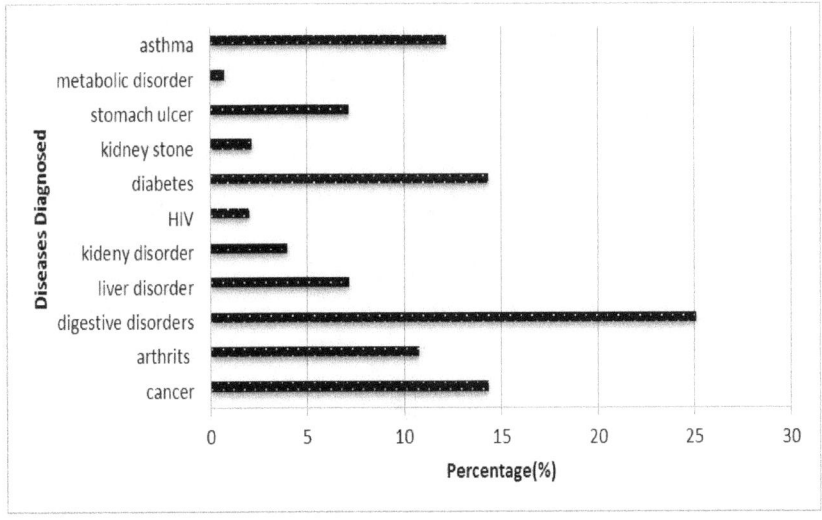

Figure 2 Percentage of diseases diagnosed and treated by Tibetan doctors as per the survey

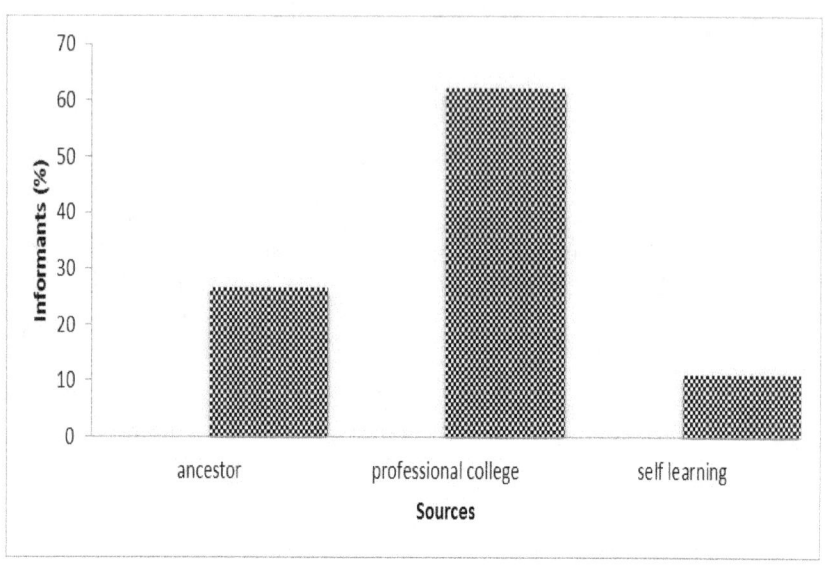

Figure 3 Sources of traditional knowledge as per the survey

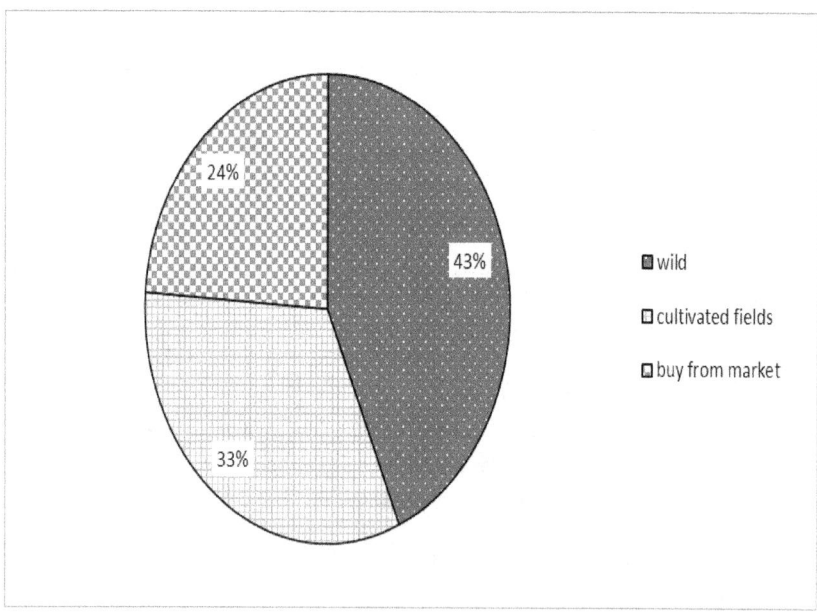

Figure 4 Collection of raw material as per the informant requirement

Conclusion

For the recognition and continuation of traditional TMS, establishing a synergistic approach between different associated knowledge holders, practices and institution is of great concern. These interactions may help to boost the learning, development of traditional practices and sharing of benefits among the population. It is extremely useful to interconnect with the institutions and develop policies to ensure the benefit of the traditional medicinal system. There is a need to ensure the involvement of different groups especially the young generation in the learning process. Therefore, establishment of legal system for the protection of traditional knowledge should be considered by the government.

Reference

[1] International Council For Science (ICSU), Report on Science, Traditional Knowledge and Sustainable Development, 2002, 24.

[2] S. Pei, G. Zhang, and H. Huai, Application of traditional knowledge in forest management: Ethnobotanical indicators of sustainable forest use, Forest Ecology and Management, 257, 2009, 2017-2021

[3] C.P. Kala, N.A. Farooquee, and U, Dhar, Prioritization of medicinal plants on the basis of available knowledge, existing practices and use value status in Uttaranchal, India, Biodiversity and Conservation, 13(2), 2004, 453-469.

[4] S. Nautiyal, R.K. Maikhuri, K.S. Rao, and K.G. Saxena, Medicinal Plant Resources in Nanda Devi Biosphere Reserve in the Central Himalaya, Journal of Herbs, Species and Medicinal Plants, 8, 2001, 47-64

[5] Anon., AYUSH in India 2013, Report (Department of Ayurveda, Yoga and Naturopathy, Unani, Siddha and Homeopathy (AYUSH), Ministry of Health and Family Welfare, Government of India, New Delhi, 2013).

[6] Dash, B., In Tibetan Medicine (Library of Tibetan Works and Archives, Dharamshala, 1976, 198-213).

[7] Tsarong, T. J., In Handbook of Traditional Tibetan Drugs (Tibetan Medical Publications, Dharamshala, 1986).

[8] Census, Demographic Survey of Tibetans in Exile 2009 (Planning Commission of Central Tibetan Administration, Dharamshala, 2009)

[9] L.D. Khangkar, In: An Introduction to Tibetan Medicine (Tibetan Medicine Series 9, Library of Tibetan Works and Archives, 9, 1985, 3–15.

[10] B. Dash, In Encyclopedia of Tibetan Medicine (Sri Satguru Publications, Delhi, I-III, 1994).

[11] T. Dommer, Tibetan Medicine and Other Holistic Health Care Systems (Routledge, Chapman and Hall, New York, 1988).

[12] T.J. Tsarong, Tibetan Medicinal Plants (Tibetan medical publications, West Bengal, India, 1994).

[13] N.A. Manjrekar, Study of the Local Health Traditions of Spiti (Foundation for Revitalization of Local Health Traditions, Bangalore, 1998).

[14] C.P. Kala, In Medicinal Plants of Indian Trans-Himalaya: Focus on Tibetan Use of Medicinal Resources, (Bishen Singh Mahendra Pal Singh, Dehradun, 2002).

[15] C.P. Kala, Health traditions of Buddhist community and role of amchis in Trans Himalayan region of India, Current Science, 89 (8), 2005, 1331-1338.

[16] T. Choedon, and V. Kumar, Medicinal Plants used in the Practice of Tibetan Medicine, RPMP Phytoconstituents and Physiological Processes, 34, 2012, 387-405.

[17] R.T. Trotter, and M.H. Logan. 1986. Informant consensus: a new approach for identifying potentially effective medicinal plants, In: Ektin N.L. (ed.): Plants in indigenous medicine and diet (Redgrave Pub. Co. Bedford Hill, New York, 1986, 91-112).

[18] IBM Corp. (Released), IBM SPSS Statistics for Windows (Version 20.0. Armonk, NY: IBM Corp., 2013)

[19] V. Dash, Tibetan Medicine: Theory and Practice (Sri Satguru Publications, Delhi, India, 1997, 92-113)

[20] Z. Weiyun, Recent development on application of Rhodiola spp. and its preparation, Journal of Gansu college of Traditional Chinese medicine, 14(4), 1997, 41-42.

[21] T. Choedon, D. Dolma, and V. Kumar, Proapoptotic and anticancer properties of Thapring– A Tibetan herbal formulation. Journal of Ethnopharmacology, 137, 2011, 320–326.

[22] R.B. Saper, S. Kales, Paquin J, Heavy Metal Content of Ayurvedic Herbal Medicine Products, Journal of American Medical Association, 292, 2004, 2868-28736.

[23] C. Moore, and R. Adler, Herbal vitamins; lead toxicity and developmental delay, Pediatrics, 106 (3), 2000, 600-602.

[24] S.Sallon, T. Namdul, S. Dolma, P. Dorjee, D. Dolma, T. Sudtshang, P. Ever Hadani, T. Bdolah–Abram, S. Apter, S. Almog, and Roberts. Mercury in

traditional Tibetan medicine– panacea or problem?, Human and Experimental Toxicology, 25, 2006, 405–412.

[25] T. Lobsang, and T. Dakpa, Fundamentals of Tibetan medicine (Mentsekhang Publication, Dharamshala, India. 4th ed, 2001).

[26] S. Dharmananda, Tibetan Herbal Medicine: With examples of treating lung diseases using rhodiola and hippophae, (Institute for traditional medicine, Portland, Oregon 2014,

[27] Bod gzhung sman rtsis khang, 2008. Annual Report (Mentsekhang Publication, Dharamshala, India, 2008)

[28] S. Ghimire, D. McKey, and Y. Aumeeruddy-Thomas, Heterogeneity in ethnoecological knowledge and management of medicinal plants in the Himalayas of Nepal: implications for conservation, Ecology and Society 9(3), 2004, 6.

[29] S.K. Uniyal, A. Awasthi, and G.S. Rawat, Current status and distribution of commercially exploited medicinal and aromatic plants in upper Gori valley, Kumaon Himalaya, Uttaranchal, Current Science, 82(10), 2002.

[30] S.K. Uniyal, A. Awasthi, and G.S. Rawat, Developmental process, changing lifestyle and traditional wisdom: Analysis from western Himalaya, The environmentalist, 23, 2003, 307-312.

[31] M.G. Stevenson, Indigenous knowledge in environmrntal assessment, Arctic,49(3), 1996, 278-291.

[32] S.K. Ghimire, D. McKey, and A.T. Yildiz, Conservation of Himalayan medicinal plants: Harvesting patterns and ecology of two threatened species, Nardostachys grandiflora DC.and Neopicrorhiza scrophulariiflora (Pennell) Hong . Biological Conservation, 124, 2005, 463-475.

[33] Y.C. Lama, S.K. Ghimire, and Y. Aumeeruddy-Thomas, Medicinal plants of Dolpo: amchi's knowledge and conservation. (WWF Nepal Program, Kathmandu, Nepal, 2001).

Chapter-IX

Plants used for Traditional Fishing Practices in *paniya* Tribes of Wayanad district, Kerala, India

Subin R & Kamarudeen V*

Abstract

Wayanad district is with a hilly terrain on the southern Western Ghats and located in the northeast part of Kerala state. Paniya tribe is very primitive tribal group of Wayanad region, with unique culture and tradition. Their arts, costume and practices closely related with the conservation of aquatic and natural resources. The study reveals that the Paniya community uses 12 different species of plants in the traditional fishing practices. Most of these plants have medicinal value as well as make use of low coast renewable inputs for the fishing practices. The plants are employed in making or acquire many different kinds of equipment or materials like Koortha, Chada, Kotta,etc...for harvesting the edible resources form the water bodies. Traditional method of fish practices decline due to the scarcity of species which is caused by human activity and over grazing by animals there for it has become essential and need of the hour to focus on conservation of these plant species. The results show that paniya community has indigenous knowledge on both plant conservation and sustainable fishing practices inherited from ancestors. This data regarding the plants may useful to developing eco-friendly methods of fish catching practices form the water bodies without using hazardous chemicals. This study is an attempt to document and enumerate the ethno botanical knowledge associated with the traditional uses and practices among paniya tribe.

Key words: Traditional Knowledge, Fishing Practices, ethno botanical plants

* *M S Swaminathan Research Foundation, Puthurvayal, Kalpetta, Kerala, India*

Introduction

Wayand is located in the south eastern part of Kerala, the region is home to the largest population of diverse indigenous tribes, the five primitive tribal group being the Adiya, Kattunaikka, Paniya, Kuruma and Kurichiya. The tribes of Wayand have a vast indigenous knowledge regarding ethno medicine and the traditional ecological practices. These primitive tribal groups developed large varieties of practice to survive and adopt for sustainable fishing practices through ancestors rich experience. These traditional knowledge developed over time in a community mainly through accumulation of experience and intimated understanding of the environment within the culture. These traditional knowledge needs to be recorded and can be of good use to devise innovative research articles for researchers, development practitioners, extension workers, environmentalists for sustainable development and management of aquatic resources. The traditional fishing practices ensure the sustainable way of fish harvesting from the water bodies without harm the local biodiversity. Paniya tribe is very primitive tribal group of Wayanad region, with unique culture and tradition. Paniya tribes are those who do the work; those who work for others (Shankar Rao 1990). Paniya tribes are those who do the work; those who work for others. The community having processes the wealth knowledge related to ethno medicine and other traditional livelihood practice. The community people gather a variety of edible resources from forest and water bodies includes fish, frog, crustaceous, mollusks, wild meat, tuber and wild vegetables. Their arts, costume and practices closely related with the conservation of aquatic and natural resources. The paniya tribe possesses t vast knowledge related to traditional fishing gears and practices.

Study Area

Wayand, the panoramic hills of Malabar in the south western ghat region, between Latitude: 11°39'34.45"N Longitude: 76°10'21.30"E, covering an area of about 2131 Sq km, the region receives a high rainfall. Meanwhile annual rainfall ranges from 3000 mm to 4000 mm, the attitude ranges between 700 to 2100 msl. The area is impregnated with rivers, reservoirs, ponds, estuaries, and paddy fields at rainy season, streams and their tributaries. The ethno ecological survey was conducted in nine villages in Wayand district viz Pandalam, Panamaram, Varadhoor, Vythri, Echome, Vellithodu, Kolambatta, kongiyambam.

Methodology

An ethno botanical survey was conducted during January 2014 to July 2014 for collect information from the paniya tribes inhabiting in 9 villages of Wayand region. During the survey, data acquired through participatory research tools such as group discussion, semi structured interviews, key informant survey and also on- site observation were taken to collect the data regarding the fishing practices followed by the tribes. The data collected were further verified and cross checked in different villages around the study area.

Result and Discussion

Paniya community possesses a wealth knowledge related to ethno fisheries techniques, these techniques are specialized according to season, geographical condition of water source and specious of fish. Five traditional fishing practices were documented in 9 villages of wayand region. The plants are used for making or constructing many different kinds of equipments and materials like Chada, koortha, Chonda, koodu, Nanju kuru, Urave ila. The list of plant species used for the traditional fishing among paniya community in the surveyed area is enumerated alphabetically with botanical name, family, local name, locality of collection, parts used and habitat (Table 1). A total of 12 plants were collected and identified during the field survey, which belongs to 7 families. The tree has highest diversity (8 species) followed by 2 shrubs and one climber.

The most dominated family is Arecaceae (4 species) followed by leguminosae, Menispermaceae, Poaceae, Myrteceae, Malvaceae, Urticaceae, Araliaceae, with single species. Stem of various plants (4 spp.) and leaves (2 spp.) are used for making fishing gears. Some plants like leaves of Hydrocotyle javanica Thunb and seeds of Anamirta cocculus (L.) Wight & Arn) some parts are mostly preferred for fish poison and frequently used by the Paniya community of Wayand region.

The data reveals that paniya community has indigenous knowledge on both plant conservation and sustainable fishing practices inherited from ancestors.The results shows that mainly six type of fishing methods

129

Table 1 - Plants related to traditional fishing practices

Botanical Name	Family	Local Name	Habit	Parts used
Ochlandra travancorica (Bedd.) Gamble	Poaceae	Mula/Eata	Herb	Steam
Calamus thwaitesii Becc	Arecaceae	Chooral	Climber	Stem
Anamirta cocculus (L.) Wight & Arn	Menispermaceae	Nanju	Tree	Seed
Syzygium cumini (L.) Skeels	Myrteceae	Njaval	Tree	Leaf
Grewia tiliifolia Vahl	Malvaceae	Chadachi	Tree	Leaf
Caryota urens L	Arecaceae	Pana	Tree	Fruit
Debregeasia longifolia (Burm.f.) Wedd	Urticaceae	Manili	Tree	Stem
Areca catechu L	Arecaceae	Kavungu	Tree	Stem
Gliricidia sepium (Jacq.) Walp	Leguminosae	Sheemakonna	Tree	Stem
Cocos nucifera L	Arecaceae	Thengu	Tree	Leaf
Hydrocotyle javanica Thunb	Araliaceae	Urave	Shrub	Leaf

Chada, Koortha,Koodu, Choonda, Nanju Kuru, and Uravila are practiced by the paniya communities in wayand region, for making the fishing gears they uses the different parts of various plant species. The study reveals that the community under study has thorough knowledge of life cycle, food preference, reproductive behavior, habitat and habit of the fishes found in the region.

The community also has a very good understanding of the plants that can be used as sedatives or as a raw material for making fishing gears for catching the fishes. During the recent years, the government of Kerala took several discussions about the management and conservation fresh water The discussion include ban on chemical, explosives and seductive plants for catching the fishes from the water bodies.

Hydrocotyle javanica Thunb (Bedd.) Gamble

Ochlandra travancorica

Debregeasia longifolia (Burm.f.)

Wedd Grewia tiliifolia Vahl

131

Syzygium cumini (L.) Skeels   Anamirta   cocculus   (L.)
                                 Wight & Arn

Conclusion

This study regarding the botanical plants may useful to developing
eco-friendly methods of fish catching practices form the water bodies
without using hazardous chemicals. The sustainability of traditional
fishing practices is very much important to protect the naturally
occurring aquatic diversity along with the surrounding environment.
This data may be useful in developing eco-friendly methods to ensure
the sustainability of fish harvesting for the community people.

References

1. Shankar Rao C N, Sociology Principles of Sociology with an Introduction to Social Thought, S Chand Publication, 1990

2. Tag H, Das AK & Katila P, Plants used by the Hills tribes of Arunachal Pradesh in ethno fisheries, Indian Journal Traditional knowledge, 4 (1) (2005) 57-64

3. Yumnam YJ & OP Tripathi 2013 Ethnobotony: Plants use in fishing and hunting by Adi tribe of Arunachal Pradesh, Indian journal of Traditional knowledge Vol. 12(1), January 2013, PP 157-161

4. Gurumayaum SD & MC Choudhary (2009) Fishing methods in river of Northeast India, Indian journal of Traditional knowledge Vol 8(2) April 2009, PP 237-241

5. Tysong H & Tiwari BK (2008) Traditional Knowledge associated with fish harvesting Practices of War khasi community of Meghalaya, , Indian journal of Traditional knowledge Vol 7 (4) 618-623

6. Sharma Rupan, (2001) Traditional Fishing Methods and Fishing Gears of Assam, Fishing Chimes 20 (12) 23

7. Nath P & Dey SC, fishes and fisheries of Northeaster India, Vol 1 Arunachal Pradesh (1989)194

Chapter-X

Climate Change and Farm Water Management: Problems & Solutions- A Case study of Pakpattan, Punjab
Aamer Hayat Bhandara*

Abstract

Agriculture is a major sector providing food and jobs to the global population. The sector accounts for 29% of the GDP in developing countries and provides jobs to 65% of the total population. Particularly in the situation of Pakistan, agriculture is the mainstay of the economy providing 44% of the jobs and contributing to nearly a quarter of the country's GDP on the other hand it is the major user of water in the country. Less knowledge about impact of the Climate Change, Agriculture farming and water in Pakistan is a major cause of absence of adaption practices in the irrigation sector. Pakistan is facing a huge water shortage for agriculture and the farmers do not completely know that why they are facing this. Some farmers have started adapting new technologies to use water efficiently but the majority is still outside the circle. The Project is to arrange training for farmers about the Climate Change, its impacts on Agriculture and Water and to find more efficient ways for Farm Water Management. Agriculture sector is the major user of water in Pakistan and most of the farmers use the traditional and conventional irrigation techniques. According to the current scenario in context of Climate Change it is very important to train the farmers in an efficient way to use the water in efficient and cheaper ways. This training will involve all the stakeholders of the Agriculture sector including all relevant officials of the Government, environmentalists, agro economists and business individuals who will discuss the problems of the Agriculture sector in context of Climate Change and on Farm Water Management. After this training farmer will be enable to utilize water in an efficient way and this will help them to understand the link between Climate Change and Water.

Key words: Climate Change, Agricultur, GDP, Pakpattan, Farm Management

---

Farmer, Hayat Farms, Pakpattan, Punjab, Pakistan

Introduction

Agriculture in Pakistan is responsible for 43% employment generation and supply vital input for agro-based industry. Agriculture sector has recorded modest growth of 1.2% in 2010-11 and has provided much needed support to boost exports, revival of manufacturing sector and responsible for upbeat in the consumption [1]. Agriculture income has created demand for industrial products. Pakistan is an agro based economic country but this is also a reality that after investing a huge amount of financial as well as natural resources its output is very low as compared to other developing countries like Nepal, India and Bangladesh. Water wastage is very high in our country. The old-fashioned method of flood irrigation is still in practice in country which wastes almost 50% to 60% of water. Ineffective communication system of rendering the information related to the new agricultural techniques and allied sciences in rural areas is also impediment in agriculture development in Pakistan.

This paper will provide a rigorous conceptual introduction, problems and a set of strategic interventions to achieve efficient and sustainable agricultural growth at the lower level in context of Climate Change and Water. Proposed solutions derive from a strategic analysis of the agricultural sector in Pakpattan and a prioritized set of highly-focused, integrated interventions. These interventions are designed to achieve sustainable growth in the agricultural sector; raise income for small farmers specially; and increase employment opportunities in rural areas.

For this paper it has been reviewed existing documents, and conducted extensive interviews and consultations with government officials at the provincial and districts levels, representatives of farmers, non-government organizations, and private sector concerns. (A list of people consulted is provided as an annexure.1). All the interviews were supplemented with a roundtable discussion with a distinguished group of prominent agricultural sector officials, scientists, economists, academics and parliamentarians. Most of the issues discussed in this paper are belonged to the professional experiences of small farmers of the rural setting of Punjab.

Pakpattan is a small district of Punjab and it is situated at the boundry of Southren and Central Punjab. The capital Pakpattan is located about 207 km from Lahore and 205 km from Multan- the district is bounded to the northwest by Sahiwal District, to the North by Okara District, to the South by the Sutlej River and Bahawalnagar District, and to the Southwest by Vehari District.

Pakpattan District is known for the fertility of its soil and most of the population of Pakpattan district makes a living on agriculture. The main crops are wheat, rice, cotton, maize (corn), sugar cane, etc. which are the major users of water.

If the agriculture sector of Pakpattan is strong it means the livelihood of the people is also good. A more vibrant rural economy will depend on Pakpattan's effort to stimulate the agricultural sector. Agricultural development will not only raise farm income and generate on-farm employment but, more importantly, it will promote expansion of the rural non-agricultural sector, which will have beneficial effects on rural poverty and social stability. So it is very imperative to discuss the significant problems and adoption of latest technologies at grass root level. Strengthening efficient and sustainable agricultural growth is a necessary condition for rural growth, employment generation, poverty reduction and social stability at national level. It is necessary to maintain a comprehensive approach to agricultural development and to ensure that sufficient resources are invested in the undertaking. For success, the agricultural development efforts should be more strategic, highly focused and integrated.

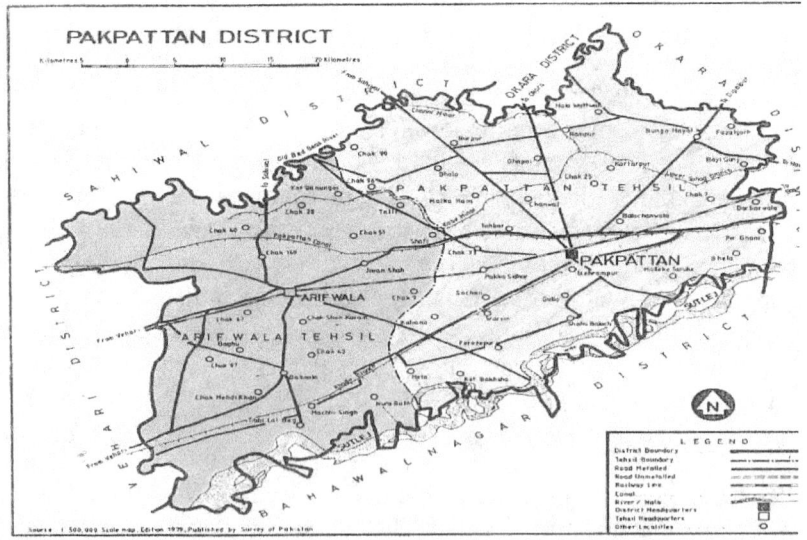

If we see the land utilization of Pakpattan then we will come to know that in this district the crop intensity is very high than other districts and more than 90% area is cultivated area which is best for all types of crops.

Particular	Area
Cultivated Area	609198
Area Under Forest	1541
Uncultivated Area	63473
Total	674212
Cropping Intensity	159.51%

Let us take the example of the vegetables sector of the district, after examine this sector we will come to know that this is the major hub of the production of vegetables in the country. Common vegetables grown grow are Cucumber, Potato, Carrots, coli flower and almost all the vegetables are growing I the district and being supplied in the whole country via major fruits and vegetables markets.

The agriculture of the district could be the water saver sector in the district by using the water conservation tools at the large level. For the enhancement of WCT it is very necessary to build the capacity of farmers through the training and the by realizing farmers about the water shortage due to Climate Change.

Objectives and Outcomes

a) Identify the Impacts of Climate Change on Agriculture
b) Become aware of important methods of risk factors
c) Recognize the importance of improving water conservation tools
d) Understand some practices can adopt towards adaptation
f) Learn methods of Community Based Adaptation

By the end of the training following outcomes regarding participants are expected:

- Able to understand the Climate, Climate Change and its impacts on agriculture and water.
- Awareness of water conservation tools.

- Recognition about the importance of the use of drought resistant varieties
- Awareness towards water course Lining

The objectives of this module, therefore, are that you will:

- Identify the Impact of Climate Change on Agriculture
- Become aware of important methods of risk factors
- Recognize the importance of improving water conservation tools
- Understand some practices you can adopt towards adaptation
- Learn methods of Community Based Adaptation

Methodology

The project would be in the form of training module for the farming community of Pakpattan.

The training will be undertaken by trained staff using audio visual, lectures and field demonstration of Climate Change adaptation technologies. EDO Agriculture will highlight the current position of agriculture of the district. DO Forrest will discuss the best plantation strategies in context of Climate Change? DO Water Management will tell the current water situation in the district and the methods of Water Conservation? Climate Change Expert will clarify the concept of Climate change, Impacts of Climate Change on Agriculture and its solutions. Environmentalist will discuss the connection between the environment, Climate Change and Agriculture. Agriculture Economist will discuss the overall link of the economy linked with Agriculture and Climate change.

At the end of the session there would be an optional visit to a farm for the practices of Water Efficiency, Organic Farming and Green Power Generation with introduction of solar water pumping technology and visit to Sir Ganga Ram's farm to see self-sufficient village power at Renalla Khurd.

Results and Discussions

Agriculture in Pakistan is responsible for 45% employment generation and supply vital input for agro-based industry. Agriculture sector has recorded modest growth of 1.2% in 2010-11 and has provided much needed support to boost exports, revival of manufacturing sector and responsible for upbeat in the consumption [2].

If we examine the agriculture sector in context of Climate Change then it is realized that Climate Change will affect the farming community globally. Due to climate change, we are already witnessing increase in the temperature, changing cropping and rain fall patterns, extreme droughts and floods, and shifting of pests and diseases. Moreover, the impact of Climate Change on agriculture has repercussions that extend far beyond the supply of food. Agriculture is not just the victim of Climate Change; it is also a significant cause of Climate change [3]. Agricultural activities are directly responsible for 20-22% of human generated greenhouse gas emissions. The emissions resulting from fuel and fertilizers are excluded. However agriculture is responsible for a much greater share of global emissions if removed forests for crops and live stocks are included.

However, a range of practices which come under heading of 'climate-smart agriculture' can increase food production, help farmers become more resilient to Climate Change, reduce greenhouse gas emissions and water saving.

Climate change has raised serious concerns for developing countries and Pakistan is not alone to face tremendous social, environmental and economic impacts [4]. The major problem small as well as large farmers are going to face in the upcoming era due to Climate Change is the water crises. The present and projected water need for different sectors in Pakistan is showing a rapidly increasing competition for water from other sectors. Now, agriculture sector of the country uses more than 93% of the fresh water resources of the country [5].

Table 1. Present and Projected Water Requirements of Pakistan

Water Use	Year 2001 (MAF)	Year 2025 (MAF)
Agriculture	100	127.5
Drinking and Sanitation	4.5	10.5
Industry	2.2	3.5
Environment	1.3	3.5
Total	108	143.2

Source: (Khan at el., 1995)

The present average water availability is very close to average requirements in the agriculture sector, but the projected demand is expected to rise by more than 25% as shown in the Table 1. Therefore, an impression of a looming serious water scarcity in Pakistan cannot be ignored. This needs to be viewed in terms of what could be done through agro-economic approach for crop production that would seek to develop cropping systems, technologies and management approaches that are both consistent with emerging market demands for crops(e.g., oil seeds and horticulture crops) and at the same time offer considerable opportunities for more efficient use of water.

Table 2. Annual Indus river water distribution and losses

Sr. No.	Distribution of Water	Distribution of Water in MAF
1	Annual Flow Available	152 MAF
2	Diverted to canals	101 MAF
3	Diverted to watercourses	76 MAF
4	Addition of tube well water	33 MAF
5	Total Water Available	19 MAF
6	Diverted to Farmers Field	65 MAF
7	Effective Participation	13 MAF
8	Total water Available for Crops	78 MAF
9	Net Crop Water Usage	67 MAF
10	Overall Total Available Water	198 MAF
11	Total Water Wastage	131 MAF
12	Overall water wastage %age due to conveyance and application losses	66%

(EDO Agriculture Pakpattan)

The annual water flow in the Indus water system shows that some more than 60% water is being wasted due to the conveyance and application losses (Table 2). These losses not only enhance the production cost as well as low yields of crops. The overall performance of the water / irrigation is poor, particularly in the recent years. We need to focus on the new technologies available at the gross root level. There are lots of technologies for water conservation but some are very costly while other can be used in limited local resources. In the paddy fields direct seed technology can be used for not only to conserve water as well as boosting in the yield and for the high profits. Modern techniques of irrigation can solve the problems of irrigation in Pakistan. This includes drip irrigation and sprinkle irrigation methods. By using this technique the farmers can save a huge sum of money which he pays for irrigation through tube wells and tractors. Drip Irrigation is although an expensive technology for small and medium farmers of Pakistan but it is more beneficent as compare to the conventional irrigation systems. There is no water saving in conventional method of irrigation on the other hand in Drip Irrigation a farmer can save more than 60% water (Table 3). Production quality is excellent in this technology and it is a good way to reduce labor costs.

Table 3. Drip versus Conventional Irrigation System

Parameters	Conventional Methods	Drip Irrigation
Water Savings	-	40-75%
Conveyance Losses	High	Negligible
Irrigation Efficiency	30-50%	80-95%
Weed Problems	High	Negligible
Water Quality Suitability	Only Fit	Saline to Fit
Disease and Pests	High	Relatively Less
Fertilizer Use Efficiency	Low	Very High
Water Logging Risk	High	Nil
Labor Costs	High	Less
Yield Increase	-	20-100%
Production Quality	Normal	Excellent

Data received from EDO agriculture Pakpattan

Conclusion

Based on the analysis, data and discussion presented above, it is suggested that the following key points need to be taken into account for developing the agriculture sector of Pakpattan in the face of Climate Change and farm Water Management.

- The overall performance of agriculture sector is insufficient.
- The productivity of irrigated agriculture is very low; it is suggested to provide training on Climate Change and Farm Water Management and latest water conservation tools to farmers.
- Alarming situation of power deficit in Pakistan can be rectified by improving the supply of electricity through on farm power generation with solar panels or biogas plants at subsidized prices.

Bibliography

1. Economic Survey of Pakistan, 2010-2011, Ministry of Food, Agriculture and Livestock, Finance Division, Economic Advisor's Wing, Islamabad (Pakistan) (2010).
2. Economic Survey of Pakistan, 2010-2011, Ministry of Food, Agriculture and Livestock, Finance Division, Economic Advisor's Wing, Islamabad (Pakistan) (2010).
3. Farming's Climate-smart Future by Charlie Pye-Smith
4. http://www.pide.org.pk/psde/25/pdf/agm26/day3/Uzma%20Hanif.pdf
5. Refrence of the Paper of Dr. Muhammad Irfan Khan

Chapter-XI

Morphometric Response and Germination Behavior in Some Arid Legumes to Salt Stress

Saroj Meena and Soumana Datta*

Abstract

Salinization of soil or water is one of the major environmental problems facing global agriculture leading to crop damage. Salinity problem is characterized by presence of excess of inorganic salts. In arid and semi-arid regions like Rajasthan in India, due to saline soil or water, many physiological and metabolic changes are induced in plant, affecting their growth, development and also quality and percentage of seed germination and early seedling growth. The stress induced by high concentration of Na+ and Cl ions causes inhibition of cell division and cell expansion through abscisic acid presence, closure of stomata, and decline in photosynthesis. The K+ ion in cells play a major role in maintaining cell turgor, enzyme activities and membrane potential. Similarly Na+ has strong inhibitory effect over K+ ion, and therefore disrupts its uptake by root leading to growth inhibition of growth. In the present study the response of legumes like Vigna mungo and Vigna aconitifolia, commonly grown in arid tracts of Rajasthan, was investigated under different level (0, 25, 50, 75, 100 mM) of NaCl. Germination percentage and seedling length was measured to understand the effect of Na+ ions. Salinity affected the germination percentage, germination kinetics, plumule, radical and fresh and dry weight of seedlings. Strategies to overcome such stress needs to be therefore elucidated further and shared with farmers to minimize crop losses.

Keywords: NaCl, Vigna aconitifolia, Vigna mungo, Seedling growth, Soil Salinity.

---

* Department of Botany, University of Rajasthan, Jaipur, Rajasthan, India

Introduction

In nature, plants are subjected to a multitude of stresses throughout their life cycle. Depending on the species of plant and the source of the stress, the plant will respond in different ways. When a certain tolerance level is reached, the plant will eventually die. A wide range of environmental stresses, (such as high and low temperature, drought, alkalinity, salinity, and UV stress and pathogen infection) are potentially harmful to the plants. In addition, the two major stresses in this that currently reduce plant productivity are drought and salinity (Serrano et al., 1999), and these stresses cause similar reactions in plants due to water stress. These environmental concerns affect plants more than is commonly thought.

Salinity is one of the most important abiotic stresses, limiting crop production in arid and semi-arid regions, where soil salt content is naturally high and precipitation can be insufficient for leaching (Zhao et al., 2007). According to the FAO Land and Nutrition Management Service (2008), over 6% of the world's land is affect by either salinity or sodicity, which accounts for more than 800 million ha of land.

Soil salinity in agriculture soils refers to the presence of high concentration of soluble salts in the soil moisture of the root zone. These concentrations of soluble salts through their high osmotic pressures affect plant growth by restricting the uptake of water by the roots. Salinity can also affect plant growth because the high concentration of salts in the soil solution interferes with balanced absorption of essential nutritional ions by plants (Tester and Davenport, 2003). It is also observed that existing salinity is a great challenge to food security. One-third of the land being irrigated worldwide is affected by salinity, but salinity also occurs in non-irrigated land (Allen et al., 1994).

Salinity Stress and Plant Response

At low salt concentrations, yields are mildly affected or not affected at all (Maggio et al., 2001). As the concentrations increase, the yields move towards zero, since most plants, glycophytes, including most crop plants, will not grow in high concentrations of salt and are severely inhibited or even killed by 100-200 mM NaCl. Both hyperionic and hyperosmotic stress caused by high salt concentration and because of this plant growth declines. Mostly the stress is caused by both Na+ and Cl- ion concentration in the medium of plant in which they are grown. This causes reduction in initial growth and inhibition in cell division. Some other catastrophic events i.e. disorganization of membrane, metabolic toxicity, photosynthesis inhibition occurs under high salt concentration condition.

Under higher salinity conditions, ion toxicity becomes a cause of death, so survival is measured (Niknam and McComb, 2000). Salt movement in plants into root and to shoot is due to transpiration flux which is required to maintain water status in plants. Toxic level of ion accumulation in plant is the result of unregulated transpiration. Due to salinity stomata close and as a result of stomata closure, photosynthesis declines and photoinhibition and oxidative stress occur. An immediate effect of osmotic stress on plant growth is its inhibition of cell expansion either directly or indirectly through abscisic acid. Plants regulate the ion movement in tissues to protect the actively growing and metabolizing cells.

Due to excessive Na+ ion accumulation in root surface, the K+ ion nutrition gets disrupted. During sodium stress, it is necessary for plants to operate the more selective high-affinity potassium uptake system in order to maintain adequate potassium nutrition. Potassium deficiency inevitably leads to growth inhibition because potassium, as the most abundant cellular cation, plays a critical role in maintaining cell turgor, membrane potential and enzyme activities.

An activity of many enzymes is inhibited due to entry of sodium ion in cytoplasm. It also depends on sodium/potassium ion ratio; if it is more it is harmful for plant growth. Even in the case of halophytes that accumulate large quantities of sodium inside the cell, their cytosolic enzymes are just as sensitive to sodium as enzymes of glycophytes. This implies that halophytes have to compartmentalize the sodium into the vacuole, away from cytosolic enzymes.

Materials and Methods

This study was carried out at the Department of Botany, University of Rajasthan, Jaipur. Seeds of Vigna mungo (Urad var. Uttara) and Vigna aconitifolia (Moth var. RMO-40) was obtained from Urad Breeder AGRI, Durgapura and Moth Breeder AGRI, Bikaner, Rajasthan. These seeds were superficially sterilized with 0.1% Mercuric Chloride solution for 3 min. and then thoroughly washed with distilled water 3 times each for 5 min, and then dried with paper towel. Dry seeds were placed in 90-mm-diameter Petri dishes on a layer of Watman No. 1 filter paper and then moistened with 4 different NaCl concentration (i.e. 25mM, 50mM, 75mM and 100mM), and seeds also grown in distilled water as control. Seeds were kept at room temperature ($25°C \pm 1°C$) under normal light for germination. Each treatment includes 3 Petri dishes as replicates which contains 120 healthy and homogenous seeds (8 Seeds/ Petri dish). All over 240 seeds (120 Urad + 120 Moth) were used. The number of germinated seeds was counted daily for 9 days after which no further seed germination occurred.

Germination percentage (%): Ni / N × 100 where Ni: number of germinated seed till that day and N: Total number of seeds.

Growth Measurement

Plant growth was estimated by measuring accumulation of root and shoot dry weight (after drying the plant material at 70°C for 48-72 h).

Statistical Analysis

In our experiment we used Two way ANOVA analysis by using GraphPad Prisim 5.01 software and considered P <0.05 as statistically significant value.

Results and Discussion

Total Germination

Seed germination percentage decreased with increase in NaCl concentration (M. Dash and S.K. Panda, 2001). Effect of salinity on total germination percentages of urad and moth is presented in Table 1. When salt was absent (0 mM), maximum seeds germinated. As a result, the percentage of germination was 98% in both urad and moth. But, increasing NaCl salinity decreased total germination of seeds. With the highest concentration (100mM), we have the lowest rate of germination i.e. 64 and 62% in urad and moth seeds respectively.

Kinetics of Plumule Emergence

According to Mohammad Housein et al., 2011, germination level, because of stress, delayed and reduced or prevented completely. We observed that the germination started the 2nd day of imbibition for

147

concentrations of 0 mM NaCl. But with the presence of higher concentrations of NaCl salt, the emergence of plumule was delayed and the period of the delay increased with the concentration. Due to the presence of high concentration of NaCl (100mM) the plumule emerged on the 5th day. In control seeds and seeds grown in 50mM NaCl, germination started one day after the imbibition. In higher NaCl concentration, the seeds germinated on the 4th or 5th day. Salinity not only decreased germination but also delayed it (Fig. 2).

Radicle and Plumule Length

According to A. Mahmood et al., 2008, plant growth in terms of height, root length, shoot length was maximum in the control plants and declined progressively with increased salinity levels as compared to control. The effects of salinity stress on radicle and plumule length have been shown in Table 2. Comparison of radicle and plumule length in different salinity concentration showed that with increase in salinity, seedlings radicle and plumule length decreased. When salt was absent (0 mM), radicle length was almost 9.40 and 7.52 cm in urad and moth respectively and plumule length was 7.66 and 7.49 in urad and moth respectively. With the presence of NaCl (25 to 100 mM), salt seems to have an inhibitor effect on the length of the radicle and plumule and it was seen to decreased depending on the concentration of NaCl. Reduction in radicle and plumule length in 100mM NaCl respectively was found to be 5.18, 3.75 and 5.14, 3.37 cm in urad and moth seed respectively.

Fresh and Dry Weight of Seedlings

According to Diego Ariel Meloni et al., (2004), Salinity caused a significant (p < 0.05) reduction on root and shoot dry biomass. The maximum fresh weight of seedling was observed for untreated plants i.e. 0.26 + 0.01 and 0.19 + 0.00 gm/plant, while on increasing NaCl concentration fresh weight of seedling decreased upto 0.16 + 0.02 and 0.14 + 0.01 gm/plant in urad and moth respectively. The dry weight of seedling was 0.04 + 0.00 and 0.02 + 0.00 gm/plant whereas in maximum NaCl concentration (100mM) dry weight was 0.03+0.00 and0.02 + 0.00 gm/plant in urad and moth respectively. This shows that on increase in the level of salinity the fresh weight decreased while minor changes were seen in dry weight (Table 2).

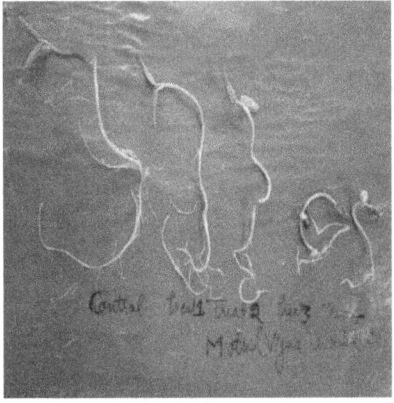 

Photograph showing the effect of different concentration of NaCl on seed germination and seedling growth of Vigna aconitifolia (Fig. 5) and Vigna mungo Table1. Effect of NaCl concentrations on germination rate of (A) Vigna mungo and (B) Vigna aconitifolia on 3d, 6d and 9d after treatment. *Values are germination percentage*

	Concentration of NaCl (mM)	3d		6d		9d	
		A	B	A	B	A	B
	0	96	90	98	98	98	98
Germination (In %)	25	78	80	94	92	94	94
	50	56	70	86	86	88	88
	75	48	64	74	74	74	76
	100	32	42	62	62	64	62

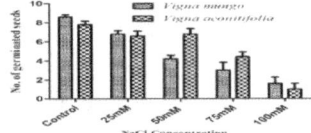

Fig: 1 Effect of different concentration of NaCl on no. of germinated seeds on 1ˢᵗ day in *Vigna mungo* and *Vigna aconotifolia*. Values are means ± SEM.

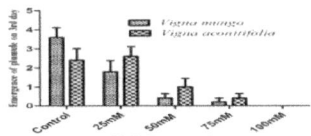

Fig: 2 Effect of different concentraton of NaCl on plumule emergence of *Vigna mungo* and *Vigna aconitifolia*. The data was recorded on 3ʳᵈ day. Values are means ± SEM.

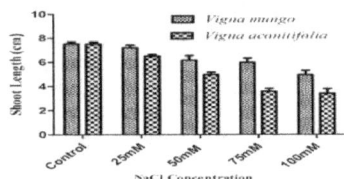

Fig: 3 Effect of different concentration of NaCl on shoot length of 9 day seedlings of *Vigna mungo* and *Vigna aconitifolia*. Values are means ± SEM.

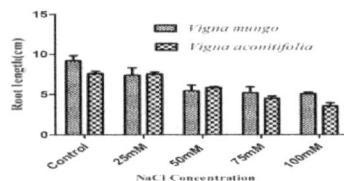

Fig: 4 Effect of different concentration of NaCl on rooth length of 9 day seedlings of *Vigna mungo* and *Vigna aconitifolia*. Values are means ±SEM.

149

Table 2: Effect of NaCl concentration on root length, shoot length, fresh weight and dry weight in germinating (A) Vigna mungo and (B) Vigna aconitifolia seedling on 9th day. Values are means + SEM

Concentration of 9th day NaCl (mM) A B		
Root length (cm)	0	9.40 + 0.86	7.52 + 0.35
	25	8.52 + 0.30	7.65 + 0.20
	50	6.10 + 0.85	5.96 + 0.10
	75	5.41 + 1.02	4.25 + 0.33
	100	5.18 + 0.16	3.75 + 0.31
Shoot length (cm)	0	7.66 + 0.16	7.49 + 0.13
	25	7.24 + 0.16	6.38 + 0.15
	50	6.46 + 0.25	4.94 + 0.28
	75	6.39 + 0.13	3.53 + 0.20
	100	5.14 + 0.44	3.37 + 0.15
Fresh weight (gm/plant)	0	0.26 + 0.01	0.19 + 0.00
	25	0.22 + 0.01	0.18 + 0.00
	50	0.19 + 0.01	0.16 + 0.00
	75	0.17 + 0.01	0.16 + 0.00
	100	0.16 + 0.02	0.14 + 0.01
Dry weight (gm/plant)	0	0.04 + 0.00	0.02 + 0.00
	25	0.03 + 0.00	0.02 + 0.00
	50	0.02 + 0.00	0.02 + 0.00
	75	0.02 + 0.00	0.02 + 0.00
	100	0.02 + 0.00	0.02 + 0.00

Conclusion

The reduction in final germination percentage can be explained by the increase of external osmotic pressure which affects the absorption of water by the seed and can be also due to the accumulation of Na+ and Cl- in the embryo which may lead to an alteration in the metabolic processes of germination. In acute cases cells death occurs in the embryo. We concluded that salinity levels used in present investigation affected all parameters of growth such as seedling vigor, dry and fresh weight of seedling, plumule, radicle and seedling length in comparison to the control seedlings. Vigna aconitifolia (moth) seeds showed less germination as compared to Vigna mungo (urad) when treated with

NaCl, thereby suggesting that urad is able to make more ionic adjustment compared to moth. Similar findings have been reported in Vicia sativa by Akhtar and Hussain (2009) and Medicago sativa by Wong et al., 2009. Phenotypic changes under environmental stress can be an indicator of the health of plants as suggested in our studies. Strategies to overcome such soil stress levels are therefore needed to minimize crop losses in the field as well as to restore soil health.

Reference

1. R. Serrano, F. Macia Culianz, and V. Moreno, 1999. Genetic engineering of salt and drought tolerance with yeast regulatory genes. Scientia Horticulturae, 78: 261-269

2. J. Zhao, D. Ren, D. Zhi, L. Wang and G. Xia, 2007. Arabidopsis DREB1A/CBF3 bestowed transgenic tall rescue increased tolerance to drought stress. Plant Cell Rep., 26: 1521-1528

3. M. Tester, R. Davenport, 2003. Na+ tolerant and Na+ transport in higher plants. Annals of Botany, 91: 503-527

4. J.A. Allen, J.L. Chambers, and M. Stine, 1994. Prospects for increasing salt tolerance of forest trees: a review. Tree Physiology, 14: 843-853

5. Maggio, A., P.M. Hasegawa, R.A. Bressan, M.F. Consiglio, and R.J. Joly, 2001. Unraveling the functional relationship between root anatomy and stress tolerance. Aust. J. Plant Physiol, 28: 999-1004

6. S.R. Niknam, and J. McComb, 2000. Salt tolerance screening of selected Australian woody species-a review. Forest Ecology and Management 139: 1-19

7. M. Dash, and S.K. Panda, 2001. Salt stress induced change in growth and enzyme activities in germinating phaseolus mungo seeds. Biologia plantarum, 44 (4): 587-589

8. Mohammad Hosein Bijeh, S. Rafsanjani Mehrnaz, Mohsen Ohadi Moussavinik, and Lak Amir Parviz, 2011. Effect of salt (NaCl) stress on germination and early seedling growth of Spinach (Spinacia oleracea L.). Annals of Biological Research, 2 (4): 490-497

9. Athar Mahmood, A. Mohammad, Raiha Qadri, Mahmood, Nadeem, 2008. Eff ect of NaCl Salinity on Growth, Nodulation and Total Nitrogen Content in Sesbania sesban. Agriculturae Conspectus Scientifi cus., 73 (3): 137-141

10. Ariel Meloni, Marta Rosalía Gulotta, Carlos Alberto Martínez, Marco Antonio Oliva, 2004. The effects of salt stress on growth, nitrate reduction and

proline and glycinebetaine accumulation in Prosopis alba. Braz. J. Plant Physiol., 16 (1)

11. P. Akhtar and F. Hussain, 2009. Growth performance of Vicia sativa L. under Saline condition. Pak.J.Bot., 41 (6) :3075-3080

12. X. Wong, G. Zahao and G.U. Hongru, 2009. Physiological and antioxidant responses of three leguminous speciesto salin environment during seed germination stag. African journal of Biotechnology, 8 (21): 5773-5779

Chapter-XII

Integrating First Nation Traditional Ecological Values (TEV) into Science-Policy Platforms for Sustainable Forest Management in Canada

Rosanne Van Schie*

Abstract

This paper is about re-imagining sustainable forest management (SFM) both internationally and specifically within Canada. It supports the need to integrate First Nation traditional ecological knowledge (TEK) into science based policy platforms for sustainable forest management in Canada. This need is based both on the Canadian legal situation with regards to consultation with First Nations, as well as international Indigenous rights instruments and agreements for protecting the interests of Indigenous Peoples to which Canada is a signatory (Van Schie and Haider 2013). The work is guided ecologically by King's (1995) suggestion on how the theory and practice of SFM can benefit from the study and knowledge of communities that have successfully avoided ecological collapse over the long term. To date western science and scientists have experienced challenges documenting and presenting TEK in science based policy platforms (Peters 2002). This paper presents scientists, public forest management planners and Canadian First Nations with a TEK safeguarded traditional ecological value (TEV) system to express TEK inputs within modern day technical forestry planning models. This synthesis solution was developed in co-operation with the Algonquin community of Mahingan Sagaigan, Wolf Lake First Nation (WLFN) in Quebec, Canada. The project researched and documented Algonquin TEK related to trees and understory plants into an Algonquin plants compendium. A point system was developed to score the plants according to their medicinal, edible, technological and ecosystem functions.

Key words: Traditional ecological knowledge (TEK), Traditional ecological values (TEV), sustainable forest management

* *Wolf Lake First Nation, First Nation University, Canada*

Introduction

"In Anishinabe teachings there are four orders of creation. First thephysical world was created along with the sun, moon, and the stars. The plant world is the second order of creation; plants depend the earth for nutrients and growth. Animals that fly, swim, and walk on four legs were the third order of reation. Finally the two legged humans were created as the fourth order. Without the other orders of creation human beings could not live, thus the circle connects all of creation. If the plant or animals on Mother Earth were to disappear so would the human beings, because humans are dependent on all others for survival". Mamiwini Adisokan- *The Algonquin Story 2010.*

In Elinor Ostrum's (2008) Stockholm Whiteboard Seminar on "Sustainable Development and the Tragedy of the Commons" she explains that, "It is very important for all of us to recognize that we are in dire times and part of the dire times are that there are many more humans on earth and we are making a larger impact on earth than our predecessors." That:

"there is a presumption that it always has to be the state, the big guys with the guns that tell us what to do" however " historically there have been better systems developed by local users who had the knowledge and ability to develop and sustain their own systems over long periods of time. So if we want our grandchildren to have resources and survive we have to manage things differently today than the way things were done twenty, thirty, forty years ago"(http://www. youtube. com/watch?v=ByXM47Ri1Kc).

The work of Elinor Ostrom was, in part, oriented towards understanding and promoting institutional arrangements crafted by local appropriators of common pool resources (CPRs) (Van Schie 2013).

Peters (2008) notes that any group with knowledge about its environment derived from tradition and experience can be said to possess traditional ecological knowledge (TEK), however, this terminology is most commonly used to refer to the knowledge of Indigenous peoples. Elias (2002) states challenges in implementing TEK in mainstream resource planning as it is conveniently dismissed by legislators and resource land managers as a subject for anthropologists. This was substantiated in Whitman and Cooper's 2000 report findings that there had been no empirical research conducted on TEK by management scholars. However this is changing in Canada, with key Supreme Court decisions behind them, Aboriginal peoples can now insist the Crown and industry respect and utilize their traditional knowledge in lands and resources initiatives. Since the 2004 Haida Taku River decision, Canadian federal and provincial lands and resource ministries have implemented Aboriginal guidelines for consultation and, in some cases, mandates to undertake traditional knowledge research. As a result, there are formal community government arrangements that agree traditional knowledge will take a prominent part in resource development and management plans. Co-operative efforts that include TEK in resource and environmental assessments over international boundaries are growing. For example, the 2013 *Health of the Salish Sea Report*, a joint initiative between United States of America Environmental Protection Agency and Environment Canada, describes trends that help identify priorities for future management action across international boundaries of the Salish Sea. The report incorporates "sustainable perspectives" where Coast Salish Nation traditional ecological knowledge (TEK) extends the study timeline to historical indicators drawing current attention to the significance of historical conditions and connections among indicators. However to this day, "Despite increasing recognition of the potential contribution of Indigenous knowledge to questions of environmental and resource management, its incorporation into decision-making processes appears to remain problematic" (Peters 2002:49).

Saint- Arnaud et al 2009 notes while a number of Canadian First Nations have worked on adapting national scale forestry criteria and indicator (C&I) frameworks (e.g., Canadian Council of Forest Ministers 2003, 2006), to their specific situations by developing local indicators (e.g., Lévesque *et al.* 1997; Natural Resources Canada 2000; Gladu and Watkinson 2003) however, the complexity of these frameworks can be a barrier to their use. (Natural Resources Canada 2000; Collier *et al.* 2002). Saint Arnaud et al 2009 further explains Sustainable Forest Management (SFM) evaluation criteria is based on national and international C&I frameworks (e.g., Center for International Forestry Research [CIFOR] and CCFM), has limited relevance within the local aboriginal context because of the specific cultures and histories of the communities. These differences do restrain communities' willingness and capacity to participate in these types of evaluative processes. (Parotta and Agnoletti 2007; Wijewardana 2008), have identified that national and international frameworks do not address local social and economic goals in an appropriate manner. Saint- Arnaud et.al. 2009 further suggests the need to modify criteria and indicator frameworks for First Nation communities so that they themselves can better represent indigenous values and needs within forestry operations.

This suggestion forms the basis of my research. Presently in Canada computer-based mathematical forest simulation models turn First Nation forest lands and resources into efficient forest factories, guided from afar as part of Crown government centralized timber management systems (Humphreys 2006 as cited in McDermott 2012). This standard processing of large complex data sets required the development of expert systems reliant on advanced mathematical and engineering knowledge that was and continues to be beyond the capacity of most First Nation citizens. Given this complexity, First Nations have been unable to intervene at the strategic planning level and are often left trying to hold forest planning actors accountable for active on-the-ground impacts (Power 1997 as cited in McDermott 2012). As such, this study focused on developing a means of incorporating TEK into modern day strategic computer- based planning platforms for sustainable forest management. Offering a solution to what Johnson (1992: 7-8) described as a need to reconcile two different world views.

The study's objectives were three-fold:

(1) To develop a community based cultural classification system to express traditional Algonquin knowledge and eco-system values for integration into modern day scientific policy platforms;

(2) To reconnect WLFN youth to their traditional Anishnabe knowledge while exposing them to science based forest ecology data collection methods.

(3) To empower Canadian Indigenous peoples and their knowledge once again in their forests and forest use planning after many years of power and identity loss.

These effort is designed to build cultural resilience through TEK affective labour activities that enhance bio-cultural diversity, community education, development and well-being. Singh 2013 describes affective labour as "the power to affect and be affected; and a focus on affects in our laboring (and everyday practices) draws attention to the potential of these practices to produce new ways of being, new subjectivities, and new forms of human communication and cooperation." This paper attempts to quantify TEK knowledge in hopes that it can be utilized without misleading interpretations from one culture to another in a common language, which does not exploit TEK but rather transforms it with positive implications for future SFM. Thus, this paper explores how natural resource management agencies can overcome existing knowledge and data gaps and be meaningfully engaged with Aboriginal communities in the long term protection and preservation of forests and biodiversity on their territories.

Wolf Lake First Nation

This research and development project takes place with Wolf Lake First Nation (WLFN) an Anishnabe community within the Algonquin Nation of Canada. The community is made up of 205 people, living not on reserve lands but lands within the Provinces of Québec and Ontario, where they assert Aboriginal Rights and Title as recognized by the Canadian Constitution. WLFN has struggled with the issues of self-determination and economic development that all First Nations across Canada have experienced. They have experienced cultural and landscape changes from industrial logging since 1850. WLFN, with other First Nations in Canada, are advocating for the United Nation Declaration on the Rights of Indigenous Peoples (UNDRIP) as a framework for advancing First Nations rights, dignity, survival, security and well-being (Van Schie 2013). In keeping with the key articles of UNDRIP, WLFN is motivated to create opportunities that protect and promote their TEK within modern sustainable forest management frameworks. For a decade now, the community has been "rethinking economy," focusing on research and development of Indigenous socio-economic alternatives to logging that protect and build on their rights, values and interests in a forest landscape that has some very dominant management actors.

As a result they are focused on creating economic and employment opportunities which are compatible with the cultural and environmental values and aspirations of the members (for example eco-tourism); and building on environmental education and stewardship opportunities that reflect and strengthen cultural values, with climate change mitigation and adaptation co-benefits, and possible eco-system service opportunities (Van Schie 2011). This is about re-thinking how forests can be managed more ecologically beyond current governments and forest company policies and how to meaningfully engage First Nations as witnesses to the past; our baseline on a once ecologically intact forest landscape.

The Québec Sustainable Forest Development Act (SFDA)

On March 23, 2010, the members of the National Assembly of the Province of Québec gave unanimous assent to the Sustainable Forest Development Act (SFDA) that as of April 01, 2013 changes the way public forests are managed throughout the province. Now comes the challenging task of managing public forests for values other than wood volume, pulp production and jobs (Van Schie 2013). The government proposes to implement sustainable forest management through eco-system based management. The new regime is intending to ensure protection of sensitive wildlife or flora species affected by forest management operations that slip through the coarse filter of forest modelling or are of social importance that is not taken into consideration by regulation. However, WLFN's ability to use TEK as an argument in harmonization of non-commercial timber values is undermined by current Quebec empirical data requirements. As such, WLFN currently faces institutional barriers in incorporating TEK in future forest management planning efforts on WLFN territory.

Methods and Materials
The Algonquin Plant Use Study

The community's starting point in this endeavour is that TEK knowledge of Algonquin plants and their uses persists only amongst a few members. In the spring of 2013, WLFN assembled and reviewed background reports and mapping on traditional Algonquin plant use with the objective of gathering sources on both the historic and contemporary role of plants in their culture. A compendium of research resources in excel format was developed to be used as the community study plant list and restoration reference tool. This is a dynamic compendium in that information can still be entered through future activities involving oral history, ethnographies, harvesting and management practices and future plant use activities. Sources for the Algonquin Plants Compendium to date include but are not limited to:

- Canadian Journal of Botany Use of plants for food and medicine by Native Peoples of eastern Canada by Thor Arnason, Richard J. Hebda, and Timothy Johns;
- Algonquins of Barriere Lake Traditional Ecological Knowledge of Plants Study;
- Traditional use of medicinal plants in the boreal forest of Canada: review and perspectives. Journal of Ethnobiology and Ethnomedicine 8: 7.
- Existing Land Use and Occupancy Study (LUOS) report and transcripts
- Existing 2012 WLFN -Nipissing University Community Plant Study
- 2013 Gracey and Pauline Ratt Workshop

The compendium sourced and recorded 144 plant species related to Algonquin traditional use and taxonomy. Plant types were then organized in terms of their use as medicine, food, technology, for animals or ecosystem indicators. They were then assigned a point value for each separate function. For example, plant species *Clintonia borealis* commonly known as blue bead lily or Moostoga (Moose Ears) for its appearance in Algonquin language. The plant has 5 separate medicinal uses, 1 technological use and 1 use as an indicator giving the plant a traditional ecological value (TEV) of 7.

A study site was then selected to set up 37 forest ecology research plots in a choice area of old growth pine and hardwood forest in the Maganasipi watershed both within and outside of the current Quebec protected area boundary. The area was chosen for its likelihood for rarer types of potential vegetation, as the area hosts sugar maple-northern red oak stands, balsam fir-cedar stands and balsam fir- spruce stands. WLFN has been aware long before Quebec's protected area strategy that Maganasipi watershed had a higher proportion of old growth forest than anywhere else on their territory. Since 2003, WLFN has focused forestry harmonization on measures that support the persistence of old growth forests and biodiversity within the Maganasipi to safeguard the long-term provision of ecosystem goods and services on which we all depend. Algonquins know this river as Maganasibi or Wolf River because of the valley's resident wolf population. One of the community's main objectives in this project is to prevent future logging activities that could potentially have a detrimental impact on this resident wolf population – a population that has lived relatively undisturbed in this watershed for thousands of years. By expanding the protected area they hope to insure the critical range and habitat of this vulnerable group as well as other threatened species. The Maganasipi River Protected area boundary is located between 46° 15' and 46° 27' north latitude and 78° 15' and 78° 28' west longitude in the Southern Laurentians natural province, more precisely in the Dumoine Plateau natural region and in the Lac Esber low hills physiographic unit. It is roughly 35 km west of the municipality of Mattawa Ontario and approximately 55 km southeast of Témiscaming Québec. It covers an area of 89.6 km^2.

The 2013 forest ecology sampling survey was intended to meet the following TEK and scientific study objectives concurrently:

1) Detect trends in relative understory plant abundance; and

2) Link species trends to forest eco-types, community priority uses and future forest harmonization and conservation efforts; and

3) Train WLFN youth at landscape level on local ecosystem knowledge, plant harvesting methods and environmental stewardship through monitoring trends in forest ecology and TEK ecosystem components and how they relate to human activities, with the goal of conducting data entry, data management to determine uses of data for future forest and animal habitat conservation efforts.

Elders Gracey and Pauline Ratt, known for their Algonquin knowledge of local plants, were asked to spend three days with community youth in selected forest types. During the day, the Algonquin ladies and the youth members would walk into natural old growth forest settings and the ladies would share their knowledge of specific plants and plant groups. Youth were taught the traditional names and Algonquin uses of the plants as well as the relationship of the plants to humans and non-humans. Fresh specimens were gathered and pressed by the youth and included Algonquin name, common name, cultural use, forest location and when and how it is harvested.

There was a consistency in Gracey and Pauline Ratt's knowledge shared in the field with published information on sources on Algonquin plant taxonomy and traditional uses. In the daily outings and evening gatherings the Algonquin women displayed a distinct

161

personal connection with the land, adherence to Algonquin ecological beliefs, and ease in relaying traditional ecological information in their language and translation of information about the plants they were so familiar with to Wolf Lake First Nation youth. The group learned that in Algonquin the plant names are generally descriptive and a reminder of their appearance, location or human and non-human uses. This was intriguing because WLFN's initial data sources had provided only Algonquin names and uses without translations or information related to Algonquin taxonomy. I discovered Algonquin language plant taxonomy requires further study as a repository of information on ecological interdependencies most often unknown and unexpressed to modern day SFM planners. While this work with WLFN is only preliminary and does not cover all of the vascular plant species found in the region, the results indicate complex language use that reflects the historical diversity of plant interactions within their eco-system.

Results

As is standard in forest management, simple ordination (detrended correspondence analysis) of the understory plant data, and how it relates to forest types was undertaken. Figure 2 shows forests that had a pine component in the overstory (either white or red pine) in red, forests that were dominated by eastern white cedar in green, and the other plots, which had a larger hardwood component in blue. Notice that this first axis (x axis) relates to how much pine there is, with red sites to the left and blue sites to the right. The second axis (y axis) is related to cedar, with cedar sites low on the axis, and the other sites high on the axis. The crosses show the various understory species and the dots are the 37 plots. Ok, but how does this relate to abundance and distribution of their Traditional Ecological Values (TEV)?

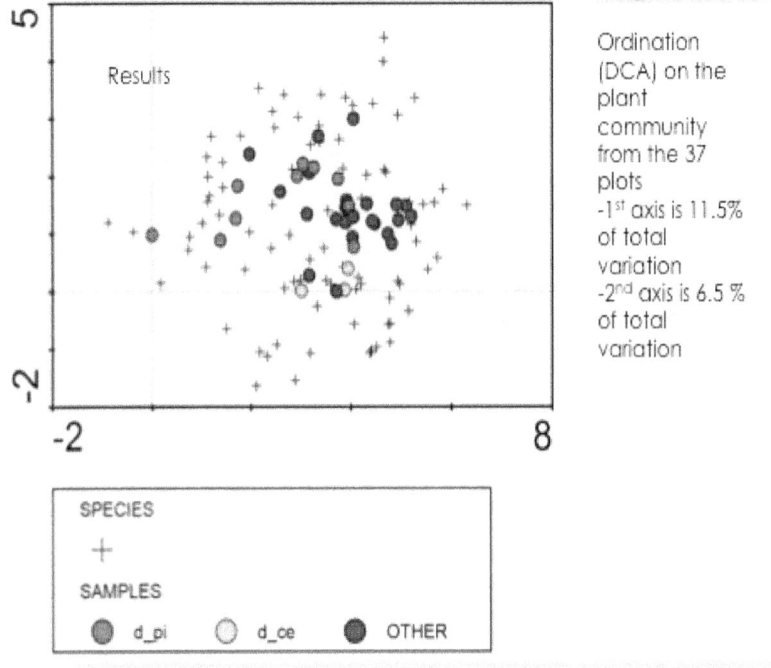

Ordination (DCA) on the plant community from the 37 plots
-1st axis is 11.5% of total variation
-2nd axis is 6.5 % of total variation

SPECIES
+
SAMPLES
● d_pi   ○ d_ce   ● OTHER

Figure 2

The next figure, Figure 3, shows the TEV of the 37 plots. Plots to the right have high TEV with respect to medicinal and "animal" values. You can see now why I focused on pine forests in Figure 2: these are the forests that tended to have lots of understory plants with medicinal and animal values, as did cedar plots. This is very preliminary of course, but we have developed a method to relate science-based understory plant data with TEVs. Although the plant data set is small here, if we use the much-larger provincial data sets, this method will allow us to classify all stands according to their TEV, and assess the extent to which current forest management practices actually protect TEVs.

163

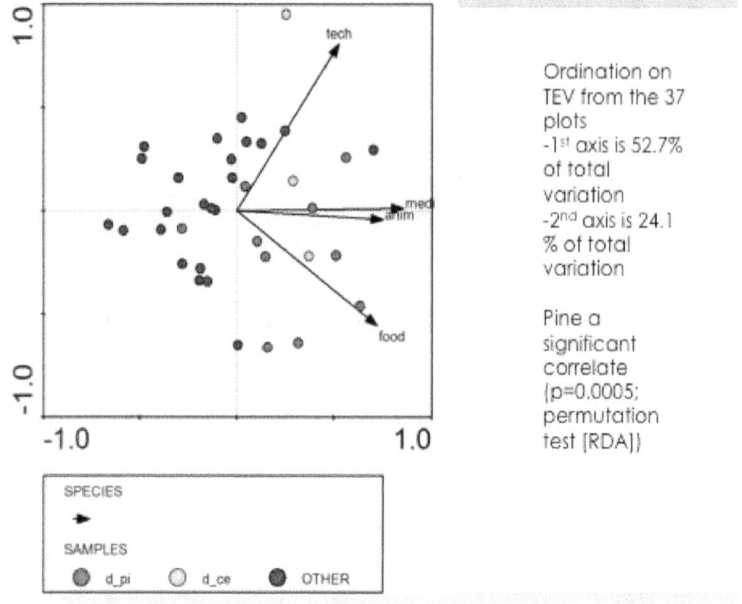

Ordination on TEV from the 37 plots
-1st axis is 52.7% of total variation
-2nd axis is 24.1 % of total variation

Pine a significant correlate (p=0.0005; permutation test [RDA])

Figure 3

Conclusion

The objectives of this preliminary project will be directed over time, learning more about integrating the different strata of Algonquin taxonomy and related TEVs in concert with Québec's sustainable forest development management plans. The synthesis of Aboriginal community TEV findings as a new constant in Québec strategic forest model management is an ongoing political effort by Wolf Lake First Nation and the author. Current work is focused on providing TEV synthesis into the Annual Allowable Cut (AAC) forestry calculations on WLFN territory that is useful to both the First Nation community and Crown forest planners. Maintaining the long- term needs of Algonquin communities will require a set of modeled TEV conservation strategies aimed at advance planning rather than operational planning, otherwise the most vulnerable components of the landscape are constantly under threat by industrial logging. Development of predictive modeling that includes TEV and understory plant forest cover relationships will assist both the Québec government and the Algonquin Lands and Resource Office in improving sustainable eco-system forest management practices throughout WLFN territory. This research and development is intended to awaken us to the pivotal role First Nations can play in conservation. Entering the confines of modern forest planning TEV value inclusion can bridge the gap between our growing needs on the planet and survival of all species.

References

1. Abrell, E., K. Bavikatte, H. Jonas. 2009. Bio-cultural jurisprudence. Chapter 7 in: Bio-Cultural Community Protocols, A Community Approach to Ensuring Integrity of Environmental Law and Policy, Natural Justice. (eds. K. Bavikatte, H. Jonas) UNEP. Available at: http://portaldoprofessor.mec.gov.br/storage/materiais/0000011925.pdf

2. Algonquin Nation Secretariat. 2011. Comments regarding the Government of Quebec's interim guide for consulting First Nations (Updated Version 2008). April 5, 2011. Available at: http://www.defendersoftheland.org/story/235 Anderson, M. K. 1996. "Tending the Wilderness." Restoration & Management Notes 14 (2): 154–66. 2001.

3. Anderson, M.K. 2006. Tending the Wild: Native American Knowledge and the Management of California's Natural Resources. Berkeley: University of California Press.

4. Anderson, M. K., and D. L. Rowney. 1999. "The Edible Plant Dichelostemma capitata: Its Vegetative Reproduction in Response to Different Indigenous Harvesting Regimes in California." Restoration Ecology 7 (3): 231–40.

5. Arnason, T., Hebda, R. J., & Johns, T. (1981). Use of plants for food and medicine by Native Peoples of eastern Canada. Canadian Journal of Botany, 59(11), 2189-2325.

6. Ausubel, K. 2008. "Remembering the Original Instructions." In Original Instructions: Indige- nous Teachings for a Sustainable Future, edited by M. K. Nelson, xxi–xxv. Rochester, VT: Bear and Company.

7. Bavikatte K, H Jonas. 2009. A biocultural critique of the CBD and ABS. Chapter 2 in: Bio-Cultural Community Protocols, A Community Approach to Ensuring Integrity of Environmental Law and Policy, Natural Justice. (eds. K. Bavikatte, H. Jonas)UNEP.Availableat:http://portaldoprofessor.

mec.gov.br/storage/materiais/0000011925.pdf
Bill 57- Sustainable Forest Development Act,
Chapter II- Provisions Specific to Native
Communities, Québec Official Publisher 2009.

8. Berkes, F. 1993. "Traditional Ecological Knowledge in
   Perspective." In Traditional Ecological
   Knowledge: Concepts and Cases, edited by J. T.
   Inglis, 1–9. Ottawa: International Program on
   Traditional Ecological Knowledge and
   International Development Research Centre.

9. Berkes, F. 1995. Indigenous knowledge and resource
   management systems: A Native Canadian case
   study from James Bay. In S. Hanna & M.
   Munasinghe (Eds.), Property rights in a social
   and ecological context, case studies and design
   applications: 9 9 - 109. Washington, DC:
   Beijer International Institute of Ecological
   Economics and the World Bank.

10. Belleau, A. 2012. MRN-DEX-08- presentation to Wolf Lake
    First Nation, Octobre 9, 2012. Ville-Marie
    Québec.

11. Collier, R., G. Parfitt, and D. Woollard (2002) *A Voice on the
    Land: An Aboriginal Peoples' Guide to Forest
    Certification in Canada*. Ottawa: National
    Aboriginal Forestry Association and Ecotrust.

12. CCFM—Canadian Council of Forest Ministers (2003).
    *Defining Sustainable Forest Management in
    Canada: Criteria and Indicators*. Ottawa: Natural
    Resources Canada.

13. CCFM—Canadian Council of Forest Ministers (2006).
    *Criteria and Indicators of Sustainable Forest
    Management: National Status 2005*. Ottawa:
    Natural Resources Canada, Canadian Forest
    Service.

14. Chief Forester's Office .2008. Assessment of the State of
    Forests and Québec's Performance in Sustainable
    Forest Management 2000-2008. Available at
    http://forestierenchef.gouv.qc.ca/images/stories/B
    AFD/

15. accueil/en/Assessment_of_the_State_of_Forests.pdf

16. Clayoquot Sound Scientific Panel 1995. Sustainable Ecosystem Management in Clayoquot Sound: Planning and Practices. Available at www.for.gov.bc.ca/hfd/library/documents/bib125 71.pdf

17. Colchester, M. (1994). Salvaging nature: indigenous peoples, protected areas and biodiversity conservation (Vol. 55). Diane Publishing.6:51

18. Collier, R., G. Parfitt, and D. Woollard (2002) *A Voice on the Land: An Aboriginal Peoples' Guide to Forest Certification in Canada*. Ottawa: National Aboriginal Forestry Association and Ecotrust.

19. DeLoria, V. 1992. "Spiritual Management: Prospects for Restoration on Tribal Lands." Restoration & Management Notes 10 (1): 48–50.

20. DeLoria, V. 1995. Red Earth, White Lies. New York: Harper and Row.

21. Egan, D. 1988. "Our Heritage of Landscaping with Native Plants: A Hermeneutical Study of Texts from 1919–1929." Master's thesis, Landscape Architecture Department, University of Wisconsin–Madison.

22. Elias, P. 2002. Notes on Traditional Knowledge to Algonquin Nation Secretariat Gibson-Graham, J.K. (2009). An Economic Ethics for the Anthropocene. Antipode, Vol. 41, 320-346.

23. Government of Québec. 2012. MDDEP-Réserve de biodiversité projetée de la Vallée-de-la-Rivière-Maganasipi Information document for public consultations Maganasipi Protected Area Document for Public Consultation. Available at http://www.mddep.gouv.qc.ca/biodiversite/reserv es-bio/reservebio_tableau.pdf

24. Henderson, S. 2011. "Pursuing Self Determination" Presentation to Assembly of First Nations Special Chiefs Assembly, December 2011.

25. Interministerial Support Group on Aboriginal Consultation. 2008. Québec Amerindians and Inuit of Québec. Interim guide for consulting the Aboriginal communities. Updated in 2008. Gouvernement du Québec. Available at:

www.autochtones.gouv.qc.ca, under the "Publications and documentation" Kenny, M.B., Parker W.H. (2004) Ojibway Plant Taxonomy at Lac Seul First Nation, Ontario, Canada, Journal of Ethnobiology, 24(1): 75-91.

26. Kimmerer, R.W. 2000. "Native Knowledge for Native Ecosystems." Journal of Forestry 98 (8): 4–9.

27. Kimmerer, R. W. 2011 "Restoration and Reciprocity: The Contributions of   Traditional Ecological Knowledge to the Philosophy and Practice of Ecological Restoration." in "Human Dimensions of Ecological Restoration" edited by David Egan. Island Press.

28. King, A. 1995. Avoiding ecological surprise: Lessons from long-standing communities. Academy of Management Review, 20: 961-985.

29. Lévesque, C., C. Montpetit, and S. Vincent (1997). *Vers une gestion intégrée et durable des activités forestières en Eeyou Astchee: L'élaboration d'un corpus de critères et d'indicateurs d'ordre culturel, social et économique.* Montréal: INRS.

30. Mamiwinni Adisokan. 2010. The Algonquin Story. Historical and Cultural Interpretive Kiosk, Wolf Lake First Nation.

31. Martinez, D., E. Salmon, and M. K. Nelson. 2008. "Restoring Indigenous History and Culture to Nature." In Original Instructions: Indigenous Teachings for a Sustainable Future, edited by M. K. Nelson. 88–105. Rochester, VT: Bear and Company. 88–105

32. McDermott, C.L. 2012. REDDuced: From sustainability to legality to units of carbon - The search for common interests in international forest governance. *Environmental Science and Policy.* In press. http://dx.doi.org/10.1016/j.envsci.2012.08.012

33. Morrison, J. 2005. Algonquin history in the Ottawa River watershed. Cultural Heritage pp. 17-32. Available at http://www.thealgonquinway.ca/pdf/algonquin-history.pdf.

34. Morse, S. J. (2012) Folk Taxonomy in Anishinaabemowin: A Linguistic Approach; a thesis for the degree Master of Arts in Linguistics. University of California Santa Barbara

35. Oeschlager, M. 1996. Caring for Creation: An Ecumenical Approach to the Environmental Cri- sis. New Haven, CT: Yale University Press.

36. Ostrom, E. 2008. Sustainable development and the tragedy of commons. Stockholm Whiteboard Seminar. Stockholm Resilience Centre YouTube video. http://www. youtube. com/watch?v=ByXM47Ri1Kc

37. Parrotta, J.A. and M. Agnoletti (2007).Traditional Forest Knowledge: Challenges and opportunities. *Forest Ecology and Management* 249:1-4.

38. Peters, Evelyn J. 2003. "Views of traditional ecological knowledge in co-management bodies in Nunavik, Quebec" Polar Record 39 (208): 49–60. United Kingdom Reid, L. 2005. "The Effects of Traditional Harvesting Practices on Restored Sweetgrass Populations." MS thesis, State University of New York College of Environmental Science and Forestry, Syracuse, New York.

39. Roark-Calnek, Sue. 2013. "Cultural Impacts Assessment Document" (Prepared for Wolf Lake First Nation and Eagle Village First Nation-Kipawa QC, 2013.)

40. Saint- Arnaud, Marie and H. Asselin, C. Dubé, Y. Croteau and C. Papatie. "Developing *Criteria and Indicators for Aboriginal Forestry: Mutual Learning through Collaborative Research"In* Stevenson, M.G. and D.C. Natcher (Eds.). (2009). *Changing the Culture of Forestry in Canada: Building Effective Institutions for Aboriginal Engagement in Sustainable Forest Management.* Edmonton: CCI Press and Sustainable Forest Management Network.

41. Schlosberg, D. (2004). Reconceiving environmental justice: global movements and political theories. Environmental politics, 13(3), 517-540.

42. SFU Center for Education, Law and Society (CELS) 2011, The Royal Proclamation of 1763 and how it affects Aboriginal Issues in Canada today, page 9. Available at: http://cels.sfu.ca/teachingApproaches/royal-proclamation.pdf

43. Shebitz, D., and R. Kimmerer. 2005. "Re-establishing Roots of a Mohawk Community and a Culturally Significant Plant: Sweetgrass." Restoration Ecology 13(2): 257–64.

44. Singh, N. M. (2013) The affective labor of growing forests and the becoming of environmental subjects: Rethinking environmentality in Odisha, India.

45. Sobrevila, C. 2008. The role of Indigenous peoples in biodiversity conservation- the natural but often unforgotten partners. The International Bank for Reconstruction and Development, The World Bank.Availableat:http://siteresources.worldbank. org/INTBIODIVERSITY/Resources/RoleofIndig enousPeoplesinBiodiversityConservation.pdf

46. Speck, Frank G. 1915. The Family Hunting Band as the Basis of Algonkian Social 1915 American Anthropological Association Issue American Anthropologist Volume 17, Issue 2, pages 289–305, April-June 1915.

47. St. Denis, Chief Harry. 2009. Fish Out of Water APTN Series. InterINDigital Entertainment (Ottawa Ontario) Joe Media Group (Calgary Alberta)

48. Thomas, C. W. (2003). Habitat conservation planning. Deepening democracy: Institutional innovations in empowered participatory governance, 4, 144.

49. Tobias TN. 2010. Living Proof-The Essential Data-Collection Guide for Indigenous Use and Occupancy Map Survey. Union of BC Indian Chiefs and Ecotrust Canada.

50. Tobin B. 2009. Setting protection of TK to rights – placing human rights and customary law at the heart of TK governance. In: Genetic Resources, Traditional Knowledge, and the Law (eds. EC Kamau and G. Winter). Earthscan: London. Pp. 109-118.

51. United States of America Environmental Protection Agency and Environment Canada 2013 Health of the Salish Sea Report available at http://www2.epa.gov/salish-sea/executive-summary

52. Van Schie, R. 2011. Forests and the Wolf Lake First Nation: more than economic value. In: National Round Table on the Environment and the Economy (Canada) Paying the Price: The Economic Impacts of Climate Change for Canada (Climate Prosperity; Report 04; page 112).

53. Westley, F., Carpenter, S. R., Brock, W. A., Holling, C. S., & Gunderson, L. H. (2002). Why systems of people and nature are not just social and ecological systems. Panarchy: Understanding transformations in human and natural systems, 103-119.

54. Whiteman, G. and Cooper W. 2000. Ecological Embeddedness Academy of Management Journal 2000, Vol. 43. No. 6, 1265-1282.

Chapter-XIII

Impacts of Temperature Variability on Rural Livelihoods and Adaptive Capacities in Kangra, Himachal Pradesh

Chintansinh Suratia, Harpalsinh Chudasama & Pramod K. Singh*

Abstract

Climatic variability and changes are exacerbating the ecological and human systems. The Himalayan ecosystem is considered to be a major climate sensitive hotspot as 1.3 billion people are directly or indirectly dependent on it. The study was carried out in Kangra district of Himachal Pradesh to assess sensitivity of livelihood assets to temperature variability. It also aims at assessing assets that serve as adaptive capacities to such perturbations. Sensitivity and adaptive capacities are documented based on peoples' perception using a fuzzy cognitive mapping approach, a semi-quantitative tool. Fuzzy cognitive mapping is a useful tool for climate change impacts and adaptation assessments which showcase the interaction between climate-human-environment spaces. Temperature variability is adversely affecting the livelihoods of the people living in the western Himalayas due to their dependence on climate sensitive resources. Our assessment indicates that natural, human and financial assets are most susceptible to temperature variability while physical, organizational, natural and human assets provide resilience to the rural livelihood in Kangra.

Key words: adaptive capacity, assets, fuzzy cognitive mapping, Himalayas, livelihood, perception

---

*Professor and Research Fellow, Institute of Rural Management, Anand (IRMA), India

Introduction

The climate variability and change is emerging as one of the most severe global threats, impacting various livelihood assets in the world. It is manifesting in increasing global mean temperatures leading to precipitation variation, increasing sea-level rise and frequency of extreme events affecting environment, socio-economic conditions and development activities [1]. Livelihoods of major population in poor countries are being affected by climate variability and change which in turn adversely impact health, safety and food security [2].

South Asia is extremely vulnerable to climate variability and change, which witnessed 0.1–0.3°C increase in temperature between 1951 and 2000, which has resulted to precipitation variability, rising sea level at a rate of 1–3 mm per year, and higher occurrence of extreme events [3]. The Himalayan and the Hindu-Kush glaciers form an essential part of South Asian ecosystem in terms of the resources and services they provide. The Himalayan system is characterized by intense monsoon precipitation, and the seasonality of the accumulation and melting of snow and ice cover. Anthropogenic factors such as emissions of greenhouse gases also contribute to increasing temperature in the Himalayan regions. The Himalayas have shown consistent warming over the past 100 years [4]. Various studies suggest that warming in the Himalayas has been much higher than the global average of 0.74°C over the last 100 years [3-5]. The indigenous communities living in remote and ecologically fragile zones, relying directly or indirectly on their immediate environments for their livelihood security, are extremely vulnerable to the impacts of climate change [6].

The hydrological cycle of the Hindu-Kush Himalayan region is nourished by the Asian monsoon. Melting glaciers in the Himalayas provide a key source of water for the region during summer season. About 70% of the summer flow in the Ganges and 50–60% of the summer flow in other major river are contributed by glacial melts of the Himalayas [7]. About 130 Million people are depended upon the perennial rivers such as the Indus, Ganges, and Brahmaputra – all fed by the unique water reservoir formed by the 16,000 Himalayan glaciers. The current trends in glacial melt suggest that the low flow will substantially be reduced as a consequence of climate change [8]. Reduction in water availability could extensively reduce the amount of food that can be produced, thereby affecting livelihoods within the river basins [9]. The climate change impacts delicate mountain forest

174

ecosystems, which includes upward movement of tree lines and shifts in the latitude of forest boundaries; changes in vegetation types and species composition; and an increase in net primary productivity (NPP) [10]. Climate change impacts the distribution and composition of plant communities and productivity of grassland ecosystems. Few grasslands have already degraded by 40% on the Tibetan plateau [11].

It is essential to study people's perception of climate and environment in general, in order to understand how humans would respond to climate change [12]. Perception based research brings observations, experiences and mind-set of local people [13]. Various studies have been carried out with the intention of understanding the impacts of climate variability and change on rural livelihoods in Himalayan region. A study by Rana et al. [14] on peoples' perceptions of climate change in Himachal Pradesh spotlights impacts of climate change on mountain agricultural activities. They conducted their study in Fatehpur, Bajaura, Palam, Lahul valleys and Theog region in Himachal Pradesh at different elevations. Another study on local perceptions assessed the impacts of climate change on biodiversity and agriculture [15]. A study was done in order to assess the vulnerability of mountain communities to climate change, for understanding the adaptation strategies taken to alleviate climate induced change on agriculture in mountain region of Nepal [16]. A similar study drew attention not only towards people's perception on climate change and its impacts but also on adaptations as well [17]. Exploring local knowledge of climate change is very crucial in the Himalayan mountain region [13]. For primary data collection, these studies used field observations, semi-structured questionnaires, personal interviews with local people, consultation with various institutions and community based organizations. The above studies often used participatory rural appraisal (PRA) and focused group discussion (FGD) to understand information on perception and awareness of climate change vulnerability induced by climate change and adaptation measures of local mountain communities to minimize such impacts. However, micro level studies of the impact of climatic variability and change on livelihoods of people and their consequent responses are relatively few [18]. Most studies are weak on quantifying social impacts of climate change and adaptation measures. The indicator based approach which has been used in most of the studies involves selection of indicators that a researcher considers to largely account for vulnerability. The weakness of such studies is subjectivity in choosing various indicators

175

[19]. Recent studies on people's perceptions about climate change in the central and western Himalayas have scrutinized only qualitative and descriptive results. In order to understand impacts and adaptation, interactions between natural and human systems must be understood, which none of the above study is able to capture.

The major aim of this study is to understand the interconnectedness between climate-human-environment spaces, using fuzzy cognitive mapping (FCM) approach. The FCM approach captures the interaction between natural and human systems adequately. The approach enables the quantification of peoples' perceptions about climate sensitivity and adaptive capacities. It is important to understand the livelihood asset bases of the community and respective sensitivities to climate change on relative asset classes. To know these sensitivities on assets comprehensively, we have employed modified DFID Sustainable Livelihood Framework [20]. One of the major advantages of using FCM is that it is semi-quantitative approach which is rare and does not necessarily require expert knowledge and can be constructed on the simple observations by local community. This approach helps in understanding the factors that affect the people's livelihoods and factors which contributes to providing resilience including relationships between these factors.

Study Area

The study area, Palampur block of Kangra district, of Himachal Pradesh is situated in the Western Himalayas between 31°2' to 32°5' North latitudes and 75° to 77°45' East longitudes. About 45% of the total geographical area is covered by forest and nearly 20% under agriculture. Kangra has population of 1,510,075 with a population density of 263 person/ km^2 where 94.29% of the total population lives in rural areas [21]. The topography in the district is highly undulating, varies from 400–5500 m altitudes. The district falls under Western Himalayan Region Agro-Climatic Zone, with humid/sub-humid to wet temperate climate. The mean annual rainfall in the district ranges from 900–3000 mm. The winter lasts from mid-December to mid-February, the winds during winter causes winter rains. The temperature in winters ranges from 0–20°C. Summers are hot and dry and last from April until June. The temperature in summers ranges from 25–38°C [22]. Medium deep to deep loamy-skeletal soils, and rock outcrops with shallow, sandy-skeletal soils are prominent soil types found in the region. The chief crops cultivated in the region are wheat, maize, paddy, barley, gram and black gram. Major oil seeds grown are mustard, sesame and linseed. Mango, citrus, litchi, guava, peach and papaya are major horticulture crops grown in the region. Major vegetables grown in the region are tomato, okra, cauliflower, cabbage, brinjal, peas and capsicum. The prominent livestock in the region are small ruminants, followed by large ruminants [23].

The study was conducted in eight villages of Kangra district namely Baah, Bhodhi, Bol, Dhanai, Dheera, Ghuggar, Jalag and Jamula. The community groups in Kangra comprised marginal farmers. Out of the total 35 maps drawn by the community, two maps were discarded due to lack of clear representation and 33 maps were used for the analysis. We ensured almost equal representation of both male and female. Table 1 gives an overview of stakeholder groups facilitated to construct fuzzy cognitive maps.

Table 1: Number of valid maps drawn by community participants

District	Stakeholder Groups	No. of Male Groups	No. of Female Groups	Number of valid cognitive maps	
				Summer	Winter
Kangra	Marginal Farmers	17	16	33	33

Methodology

Impacts of temperature variability and adaptive capacities are being captured using a Fuzzy Cognitive Mapping approach. FCM is a semi-quantitative tool that allows documentation of cause-effect relations such as climate and weather events' influence on certain aspects of ecosystems and humans [24]. FCM helps in capturing the functioning of a complex system based on people's perception. FCM approach was combined with sustainable livelihood framework to understand sensitivities of various assets to temperature variability and assets that serve as adaptive capacities.

Obtaining and analyzing cognitive maps

We selected marginal farmers (land holding less than 0.3 hectare) having a few livestock as stakeholder groups. After obtaining consensus of the participants on changes in summer and winter

177

temperatures over the last six to ten years, we demonstrated the construction of a fuzzy cognitive map to the participants. Then, we divided all the participants into four to five individual's groups. Men and women groups were formed separately to understand gender-based perceptions of climate related perturbations and coping strategies. The questions asked to obtain cognitive maps are listed below:

1. What changes have you observed in summer and winter temperatures over past 6–10 years?
2. What are the direct and consequential indirect impacts of temperature variability on your livelihoods?
3. What are the coping mechanisms/adaptation practices taken up in order to reduce the direct and indirect impacts of temperature variability?

Community participants' prepared cognitive maps for two central variables; increase in summer and winter temperatures. They also established the direct and indirect linkages. Furthermore, the weights were given to each connection on the scale of 0–10, with 0 being minimum impact and 10 being maximum impact. Individual maps were coded into adjacency matrices using an aggregated list of variables listed from the cognitive maps drawn by the community participants. Cognitive maps were transformed in adjacency matrices where the variables were listed on the vertical and horizontal axes. Weights given by the stakeholders were coded into the adjacency matrix. Each coded map was clubbed to make social cognitive map using matrix addition technique. The obtained social cognitive map is the perceived representation of all the stakeholders interviewed. Variables with similar characteristics are clubbed into lager category in line with the modified Sustainable Livelihood Framework. Later, the social cognitive maps were analyzed using FCMapper software. Cognitive interpretive diagrams (CIDs) [24] were prepared using visualization software called Visone, which helps in depicting the connections between the factors and also reflects the importance of different variables within the different asset classes. Variables in CIDs are represented on the basis of centrality which is the sum of indeegrees and outdegrees that helps in understanding the contribution of a variable in cognitive map and connectedness of the variable to another variable. Where, indegree means number of incoming links per variable and outdegree means number of outgoing links per variable.

Sampling

Sample size was determined by the Monte Carlo simulations using STATA to check the adequacy of sample size. Monte Carlo simulation technique has been used to determine sample size through accumulation curves. Average accumulation curves of the total numbers of maps versus the number of new variables are added per map to determine how the variables accumulated. FCMs are created with different groups until the representative population was sampled sufficiently. In this case, accumulation curve saturated at 32 maps.

Calculating sensitivity and adaptive capacity using weighted balance average

Sensitivities and adaptive capacities are categorized according to different livelihood asset classes. Sensitivity and adaptive capacity of various asset classes are calculated using weighted balance average, where each sub-component contributes equally to the overall index although having a varied number of sub-components [25].

Results and Discussions

Increased winter and summer temperatures, shorter winter periods and decreasing snow fall are the most perceptible manifestation of temperature variability among the stakeholders in Kangra. Declining snow fall is major reference point of stakeholders' observations about increasing temperatures. The perception of temperature rise is in conformity with the scientific evidences.

Network Statistics of Cognitive Interpretive Diagrams (CIDs)

The network statistics shows variables, connections and density of the CIDs. Total numbers of variables are 57 and 49 for summer and winter season respectively, which are further condensed into 28 and 26 variables for social cognitive maps. Community participants revealed the higher number of factors for summer season as compared to winter season (Table 2). Also, new factors added per map set higher for summer season which showcase that community perceive more threats in summer season. With merely two extra factors in summer season, number of connections is relatively higher than that of winter season. It leads to high density of CIDs for summer season, which indicates more interconnectedness between the variables. In CIDs (Fig. 1 and 2), the size of the variable indicates centrality, which is addition of variable's indeegrees and outdegrees. With larger number of outcomes and cause-effect relationships, higher complexity of cognitive map of summer season can be seen.

Network Statistics of Cognitive Interpretive Diagrams (CIDs)

Network Statistics	Increased Summer Temperature	Increased Winter Temperature
Number of Variables in Adjacency Matrix	57	49
Size of Condensed Cognitive Map		
Number of Variables in CID	28	26
New Factor/map in average	0.848	0.788
Density of Cognitive Map		
Number of Connections in CID	62	50
New Connection/map in average	1.879	1.515
Density in CID	0.0791	0.0740
Complexity - Influence Diversity		
Number of Transmitters in CID	15	13
New Transmitter/map in average	0.455	0.394
Number of Receivers in CID	1	3
New Receiver/map in average	0.030	0.091
Receiver/Transmitter in CID	0.067	0.231

Sensitivity of assets to temperature variability

Table 3 gives an overview of those asset classes which are impacted by temperature variability. Natural, human and physical assets are susceptible to temperature variability. Among all, natural assets (water, forest, land, agriculture and fodder) are most susceptible to increase in summer temperature while financial assets are being impacted the most due to increase in winter temperature. Higher susceptibility of financial assets for winter can be attributed to major decline in agriculture and horticulture production. Human assets also have been impacted due to rise in temperatures.

Table 3: Sensitivity of assets to temperature variability

Livelihood Assets	Summer	Winter
Natural	0.661	0.645
Human	0.542	0.579
Financial	0.498	0.714

As described above the most impacted natural assets due to increase temperatures are forest, agriculture production, water and land resources. Increase in summer temperature has led to decline in the surface as well as ground water of the region as perceived by the community, which has further impacted the agriculture production to a large extent (fig.1 and 2). With increasing temperatures, water resources like natural streams, traditional water structures (*naula* and *bowdi*) are drying up, the phenomenon observed in the recent few years only. Increase in temperature has resulted in less soil moisture and decreasing soil fertility which has hampered the agriculture production as perceived by community participants. With increasing temperatures as well as declining water resources, forest degradation has been accelerated and episodes of forest fire have increased. Intensified forest fires in summer have deteriorated the quality of air. Decline in ground water can also be attributed to forest degradation due to rise in temperatures. Wild animals are expanding their niche as resource availability in their original niche is insufficient for the survival which has intensified the human-wildlife conflict. Intrusion of these animals in agriculture field is one of the major concerns among stakeholders as incidences of crop destruction by animals are on rise. People are also dependent on a few non-timber forest produces (NTFPs) for their sustenance of livelihoods which are also diminishing due to growing events of forest fires, eventually adversely affecting their livelihoods. Livestock rearing which is also an integral part of the livelihood of the community has been impacted severely due to declining water resources as well as forest which supplements the green fodder. The fodder scarcity has severely affected health of livestock in the region.

Villagers observed decline in snowfall during winter. Lesser snowfall as compared to earlier have affected the soil moisture which has further intensified the pest infestation. Increasing attacks of pest have impacted the agriculture produce. Wheat production has been declining as temperature during winter is rising. While other food crops such as; paddy, maize and pulses are being impacted due to increasing summer and winter temperature. In regard to horticulture crops, citrus fruits have faced the brunt of rising temperatures. Production of oranges and malta are declining consistently in recent years. Temperature rise has largely affected the flowering and growth of these plants. Diminishing agriculture production has resulted in lesser food availability for self-consumption which has further resulted in deterioration of human health. Climatic parameters like fog and hailstorm in winter has impacted agriculture produce. According to community participants, fog was not prevalent earlier. Extreme fog in recent few years has impacted the growth of rabi crops. Hailstorm in winter has become rampant which is again destructive for crops.

Increased temperatures have led to proliferation of weeds in the region. Invasion of weeds like *lantana* and *parthenium* have reduced the availability of fodder as the land for fodder cultivation has occupied by these species. Also, adverse implications of weeds on human as well as livestock health were highlighted by community participants (fig.1 and 2).

Direct linkage between increase in temperatures and human health has been established by the stakeholders. Declining water resources and water quality emerged out as major contributor to deteriorating human health. Food unavailability due to declining agriculture produce has reduced the nutrition, affecting health of people. Increasing temperatures are also impacting work efficiency of farmers and forcing them to limit their working hours in fields. Increasing drudgery is observed among women as a result of drinking water scarcity due to increased summer and winter temperatures.

Financial reserves are indirectly being impacted due to increasing temperatures as the community is largely dependent on climate sensitive sectors. Impacts on land and water resources, agriculture and horticulture, and livestock are the major contributors for declining financial reserves. Lower agriculture produce and fodder unavailability increases the dependence on market for food and fodder, which further add to their financial woes. Stakeholders established a linkage between deteriorating health and increasing expenditures as the expenditure goes up to undergo medical care facilities. These factors altogether are pushing the community in a vicious trap of poverty.

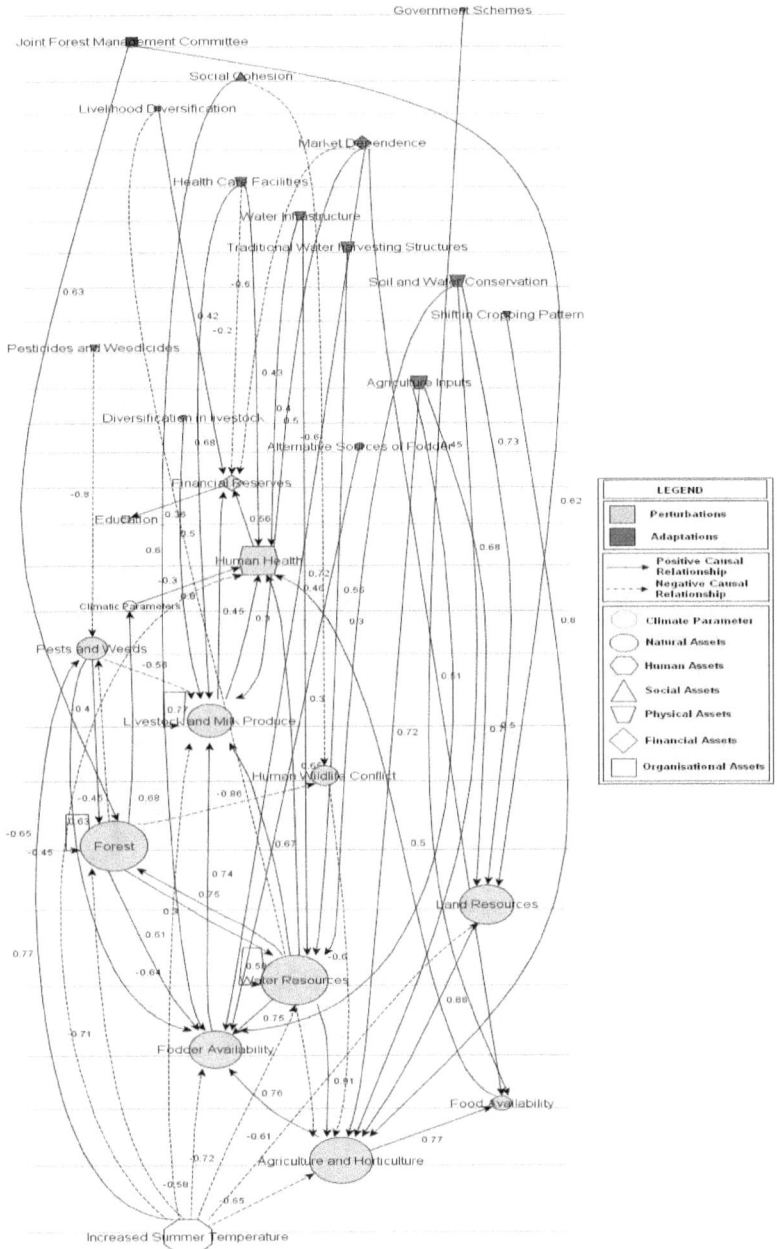

Fig. 1: Impacts of increased summer temperature on livelihood assets and adaptation options

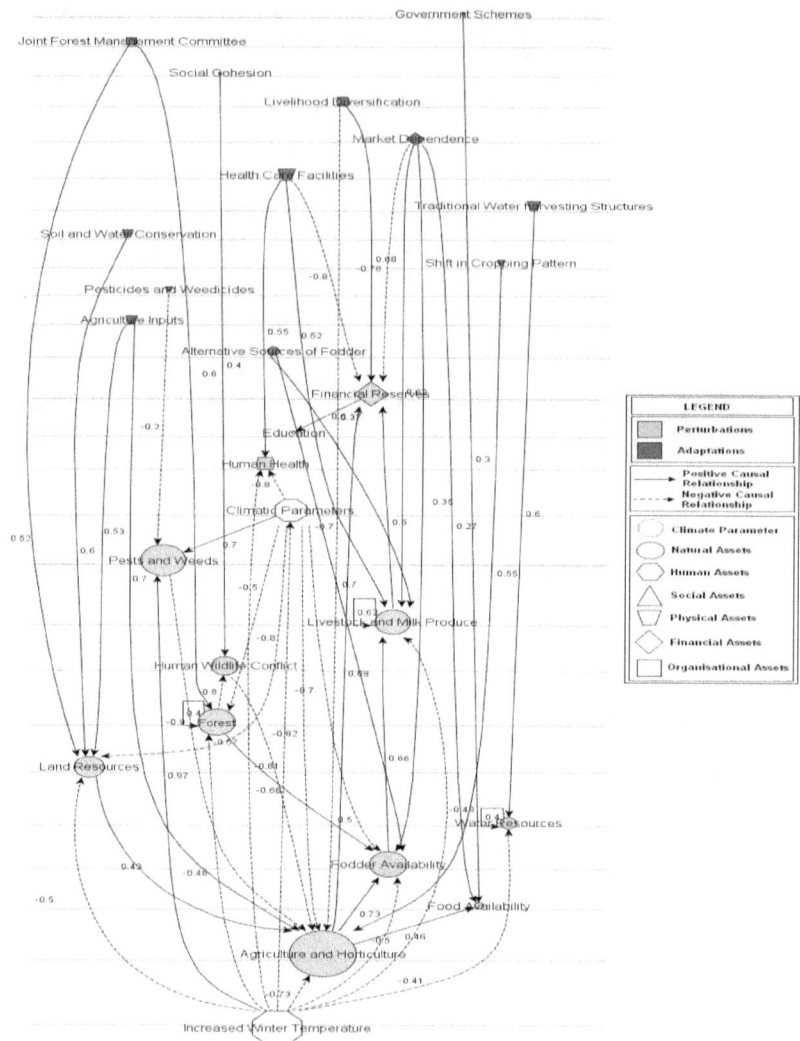

Fig. 2: Impacts of increased winter temperature on livelihood assets and adaptation Options

Assets Providing Adaptive Capacities

Physical and organizational assets are most effective in providing adaptive capacities to cope with temperature variability during summer while human and natural assets provide major adaptive capacities during winter. Increased role of human assets during winter can be attributed to farmer's inclination towards alternate livelihood strategies due to decline in agriculture production. Physical assets such as soil and water conservation structures like contour trenches, low cost check dams have brought positive impacts to land resources eventually benefitting agriculture. However, in past few years, a little amount of water retained in check dams due to lack of maintenance. Despite declining state of water in traditional water harvesting structures like *bowdi* or natural springs, it emerged out as the major adaptive capacity to cope with drinking water scarcity. Water infrastructure like tube wells, bore wells and hand pumps provide adaptive capacities to deal with scarcity of water. Agriculture inputs serve as major adaptive capacity to cope with increasing vagaries of temperature variability on agriculture production. Farm yard manure and compost have improved the quality of soil thereby increasing agriculture produce. Farmers are using high yielding varieties of seeds in order to maximize production. Pesticides and weedicides are being used largely to cope with pest and weed infestation. With increasing temperatures and declining agriculture productivity due to multiple factors, farmers have resorted to shift in cropping pattern. Farmers have replaced traditional crops with vegetables like cauliflower, tomato, potato and ginger. Diversification in livestock has also been observed due to erratic availability of fodder. Rearing of small ruminants has received more preference over large animals from past few years.

Table 4: Assets that serve as adaptation/adaptive capacity

Livelihood Assets	Summer	Winter
Natural	0.400	0.650
Physical	0.616	0.531
Human	0.416	0.675
Financial	0.488	0.410
Social	0.600	0.400
Organizational	0.566	0.473

Organizational assets have proven to improve land and forest resources. Joint forest management (JFM) has helped fairly in restoring the degraded land in the region. Plantation of broad leaves tree species have helped restoring the soil moisture which has also increased the fertility of soil to certain extent as perceived by the community participants. Plantation on degraded land has helped in reducing

185

surface runoff and soil erosion which has brought positive impacts on agriculture. JFM has increased the resilience of community to deal with the unavailability of fodder especially in hot summer months as it allows them to collect the green fodder from forest.

To avoid destruction of crops by wild animals such as wild boars and monkeys, villagers keep watch on their fields at night. Thus, social cohesion among people emerged as an adaptive capacity under social assets to reduce the crop destruction by wild animals. Dependency on market for fodder and food, public distribution system in order to avail food grains, medical care facilities to cure illness served as adaptive capacities. However, medical care facilities and dependency on market further exhausts the financial reserves. Due to declining agriculture produce, people tend to migrate in search of employment or engage themselves as daily wage laborers. Though, diversification of livelihoods helps villagers fulfilling their financial needs, it has major implications on land resources as most of the times land is lying barren

Conclusions

Fuzzy cognitive mapping based approach of impacts and adaptation assessments capture interconnectedness and dynamic relationship between climate-human-environment spaces. Fuzzy cognitive mapping approach does not only capture such interactions but also helps in quantifying the linkages established by stakeholders, and can be decisive in prioritizing the actions required to tackle the issues related to climate variability and change. The study captures the relationship between temperature variability and its direct manifestation on different assets which forms the base for sustainable livelihoods. It also seeks to understand the indirect manifestation of temperature variability on different assets and their consequential impacts of one asset on others. It can be discerned from the analysis that community participants perceive severe impacts of temperature variability on natural assets. Higher sensitivity of natural assets can be attributed to dependence of people on land, water and forest resources either directly or indirectly for sustenance of their livelihoods. Financial assets have high sensitivity due to increased susceptibility of natural assets. It can also be inferred that physical assets such as chemical fertilizers, pesticides, etc. are most effective according to community participants due to short term benefits they provide. However, they believe that excess usage of such agriculture inputs can bring undesirable results in long term. Soil and water conservation measures

186

under physical assets have proven to be advantageous for both land and water resources thereby improving agriculture. Organizational assets stand second in reducing the susceptibility of natural assets i.e. land and water resources. Hence, it can be inferred that natural assets seek attention for future actions and further enhancement of organizational and physical assets can bring positive impacts on rural livelihoods in Kangra.

Our study emphasizes on crucial role of community perception for generating knowledge about the impacts of climate variability and change, and planning adaptation strategies accordingly, as they have developed perceptions based on their own experiences. There is a lack of perception based impacts assessments that provides indicators to policy processes. Local assessments based on people's perception better represent the needs of adaptation, which can help in prioritizing actions to cope with climate variability and change as community perceive their risks better. Thus, it is imperative to involve stakeholders for impact analysis and planning of adaptations. Our assessment using fuzzy cognitive mapping approach goes beyond indicator based linear assessments and captures interconnected interactions and causal linkages between different variables. Such kind of assessments is important to harness local knowledge in complex systems, which can help policy makers in formulating better and apt adaptation strategies.

References

[1] RV Cruz, H. Harasawa, M. Lal, S. Wu, Y. Anokhin, B. Punsalmaa, Y. Honda, M. Jafari, C. Li, and N. Huu Ninh, Impacts, adaptation and vulnerability, *contribution of working group-ii to the fourth assessment report of the intergovernmental panel on climate change (IPCC)*(Cambridge University Press, London, 2007) 469–506.

[2] N Stern, *The Stern Review: Economics of Climate Change,* (Washington DC: Cabinet Office-HM Treasury, 2007).

[3] Intergovernmental Panel on Climate Change (IPCC), *Climate Change 2007: The Physical Science Basis,* Contribution of Working Group I to the Fourth Assessment Report of the Intergovernmental Panel on Climate Change, (Cambridge, UK: Cambridge University Press, 2007).

[4] TD Yao, XJ. Guo, T. Lonnie, KQ. Duan, NL. Wang, JC. Pu, BQ. Xu, XX. Yang, and WZ. Sun, δ^{18}ORecord and Temperature Change over the Past 100 years in Ice Cores on the Tibetan Plateau, *Science in China: Series D Earth Science, 49(1),* 2006, 1–9.

[5] SP Singh, I. Bassignana-Khadka, BS. Karky, and E. Sharma, *Climate change in the Hindu-Kush Himalayas: the state of current knowledge,* International Centre for Integrated Mountain Development (ICIMOD), (Kathmandu, Nepal: Hill Side Press Pvt. Ltd., 2011).

[6] United Nations Framework Convention on Climate Change (UNFCCC), *The First Ten Years,* (Bonn, Germany: UNFCCC, 2004).

[7] TP Barnett, JC. Adam, and DP. Lettenmaier, Potential Impacts of Warming Climate on Water Availability in Snow-dominated Regions, *Nature, 438,* 2005, 303–309.

[8] SR Bajracharya, M. Shrestha, and AB. Shrestha, Impact of Climate Change on Water Resources and Livelihoods in the Hindu-Kush Himalayan Region, *International Centre for Integrated Mountain Development (ICIMOD),* 2010, pdf

188

available at: http://globalstudies.doshisha.ac.jp/ english /i18n/images/theme2/Sagar_Bajracharya _Full_paper.pdf [Accessed on 16th June 2014]

[9] World Bank, *Turn Down the Heat: Climate Extremes, Regional Impacts, and the Case for Resilience.* A report for the World Bank by the Potsdam Institute for Climate Impact Research and Climate Analytics, (Washington, DC: World Bank, 2013).

[10] RR Nemani, CD. Keeling, H. Hashimoto, WM. Jolly, SC. Piper, CJ. Tucker, RB. Myneni, and SW. Running, Climate-Driven Increases in Global Terrestrial Net Primary Production from 1982 to 1999, *Science, 300,* 2003, 1560–1563.

[11] J Xu, RE. Grumbine, A. Shrestha, M. Eriksson, X. Yang, Y. Wang, and A. Wilkes, The Melting Himalayas: Cascading Effects of Climate Change on Water, Biodiversity, and Livelihoods, *Conservation Biology, 23(3),* 2009, 520–530.

[12] N Vedwan, and RE. Rhoades, Climate change in the western Himalayas of India: a study of local perception and response, *Climate Research, 19,* 2001, 109–117.

[13] BK Chapagain, R. Subedi, and NS. Paudel, Exploring Local Knowledge of Climate Change: Some Reflections, *Journal of Forest and Livelihood, 8(1),* 2009, 108–112.

[14] RS Rana, RM. Bhagat, V. Kalia, H. Lal, and V. Sen, Indigenous Perceptions of Climate Change vis-à-vis Mountain Agriculture Activities in Himachal Pradesh, India, *Indian Journal of Traditional Knowledge, 12(4),* 2013, 596–604.

[15] P Chaudhary, and KS. Bawa, Local Perceptions of Climate Change Validated by Scientific Evidence in the Himalayas, *The Royal Society,* 2011, published online,

[16] S Lama, and B. Devkota, Vulnerability of Mountain Communities to Climate Change and Adaptation Strategies, *The Journal of Agriculture and Environment,* 10, 2009, 65–71.

[17] KR Tiwari, KD. Awasthi, MK. Balla, and BK. Sitaula, Local People's Perception on Climate Change, its Impact

and Adaptation Practices in Himalaya to Terai Regions of Nepal, *Himalayan Research Papers Archive,* 2009.

[18] T Ingold, *The perception of the environment: essays on livelihood, dwelling and skill* (Routledge, London and New York, 2000).

[19] TR Deressa, M. Hassan, T. Alemu, M. Yesuf, and C. Ringler, Analyzing the Determinants of Farmers' Choice of Adaptation Methods and Perceptions of Climate Change in the Nile Basin of Ethiopia, *International Food Policy Research Institute,* 2008.

[20] PK Singh, and A. Nair, Climate Change Vulnerability Assessment for Sustainable Livelihoods Using Fuzzy Cognitive Mapping Approach. *Institute of Rural Management Anand (IRMA) Working Paper Series,* 248, 2013.

[21] Census of India, *Population of India,* Office of the Registrar General and Census Commissioner, (New Delhi, India, 2011).

[22] The Official Website of District Kangra, http://hpkangra.nic.in/index.html, 2014.

[23] Department of Agriculture and Cooperation, Agriculture Contingency Plan for District Kangra, Himachal Pradesh n.d.

[24] U Özesmi, and SL. Özesmi, Ecological Models Based on People's Knowledge: A Multi-Step Fuzzy Cognitive Mapping Approach, *Ecological Modelling, 176,* 2004, 43–64.

[25] C Sullivan, Calculating a Water Poverty Index, *World Development, 30(7),* 2002, 1195–1210.

Chapter-XIV

Cultural Imperatives and the Sustainability of Development

Neelam Grover*

Abstract

Development in all spheres is an essential prerogative of the world today but its sustainability vis-à-vis the environmental context is perhaps one of the most pertinent and universal concerns and challenges before humanity. Globalization, accessibility, connectivity and inroads of modernization, industrialization, and urbanization have left but few areas of the world untouched. As a consequence, indigenous identities face the risk of disappearance as external influences, especially the commercial perspectives gain significance and simple, evolved indigenous cultures and culture traits in their tangible and intangible expression are sidelined in the name of development. Perhaps the answer to sustainability of development lies in the indigenous cultures. This paper attempts to explore the possibility of adapting age old practices to modern day concerns. The idea is not to root out development but to recognize and strengthen the indigenous sustainable practices and adopt them to sustain development without either degrading the environment, stressing the natural resources, or altering the ecosystem by any imposition of exogenous alternatives unsuited to the existing cultural-ecological contexts. This alone will ensure that genre de vies, culture traits, cultural landscapes immortalizing the interaction between the habitat, habit, and inhabitant are not lost, nor fragile environments and ecosystems degraded. The focus will be on disappearing rural landscape identities.

Key Words: Development, Sustainability, Indigenous, Exogenous, Cultural Identities

* *Professor, Geography Department, University School of Open Learning, Panjab University, Chandigarh India*

Introduction

Development manifests itself through modification of the already existing cultural ecological context. With no alternative to development its sustainability is imperative both in respect of the environment and the culture of the inhabiting group. This is the challenge that grips the world today as environments, both physical and cultural are impaired. Elaborate scholarly works to understand, explain and suggest alternatives to attain sustainable development have been attempted and continue to do so at the international, national, and regional levels. But ecological settings and cultural imperatives are unique. As a result micro studies at the rural settlement landscape level become important and may perhaps provide an answer to attaining sustainability of development through indigenous wisdom and processes that have evolved over centuries to transform specific natural settings into cultural landscapes. This study is a case in point of a Gujar rural settlement landscape in a marginal setting which within a period of just about four decades is on the brink of losing its cultural identity following the development processes afoot.

Development and Sustainability

Development in all spheres is an essential prerogative of the world today and an integral part of our civilization and society. It distinctly involves the modification of the biosphere that results from the application of human, living and non-living, and financial resources to satisfy human needs and improve the quality of human life. It is definitely not an accidental one time effort but is rather a continuous process which must take into account the social, ecological, economic factors and the living and non-living resource base for the long term and short term advantages and disadvantages of alternative actions. As stated in the UNDP Human Resource Development Report it is "the process of enlarging peoples' choices". (1) However, the rich environment provided by nature to man replete with biotic and abiotic resources stands impaired today because of man's efforts to achieve infinite growth in a finite environment.

As a consequence of his developmental efforts, environmental concerns are the buzz word today as is 'sustainable development'. Central to this is human activities and the exploitative mode of development adopted by man. More crucial, however, is the fact that humanity is already caught in the vortex of the impact of environment

192

misuse and over-exploitation with ever increasing and more rapid development, industrialization, urbanization, consumption and consequent green house emissions, global warming and climate change. It is almost imperative, therefore, to examine and analyse the concept of sustainability of development for the future and its exclusiveness. In order to do this development has to be integrated into the physical and cultural milieu. An insight into the history of sustainable development will put this in perspective. Sustainable development, broadly defined as "meeting the needs of the present generation without compromising the ability of the future generations to meet their own needs" therefore, is the core issue. It was the Stockholm Conference on Environment and Development in 1972 that first addressed the need for environment protection along with socio-economic development and thus was born the notion of sustainable development which went onto become the focal point of the First Earth Summit held at Rio de Janeiro in 1992. The term itself was in fact, coined by the Brundtland Commission in its report entitled "Our Common Future" which set the agenda for the Rio conference. (2) In addition to raising public awareness to integrate environment and development it also brought in the recognition of the right of people to a healthy environment as also the right to development. As mankind began to experience the impact of environmental problems such as climate change, global warming, ozone depletion, desertification, loss of biodiversity, acid rain, depleting forest and water resources and sensed the endangering of human lives and the capacity of our planet to sustain an exploitative mode of development, the focus turned to the sustainability of developmental practices. Not only has this notion been widely accepted but has become the common agenda for all mankind reiterated as it was at the Earth Summit at Johannesburg held in 2002 wherein sustainable development was recognized as an "over reaching goal for institutions at the national, regional and international levels" and the need to incorporate the concept in the activities of all agencies. (3) Further at the Rio+20 conference in 2012 renewed political commitment for sustainable development, assessing the progress and implementation of the concept and devising and adopting new and emerging challenges were taken up as the main objectives. Emphasis was particularly placed on the development of green economies for sustainable development and reducing poverty, as also improving international co-operation for sustainable development so that developing countries can adopt better and more conducive practices. (4) Sustainability is based on a simple principle that everything that we need for our survival and wellbeing depends either directly or indirectly on our natural environment. It creates and maintains conditions under which humans and nature can exist in productive harmony and fulfill all of our social, economic and other requirements. Therefore a healthy environment is imperative but must include the physical as well as cultural imperatives.

Indian Rural Cultural Landscape

In order to understand this, a close examination of the Indian rural scenario is significant, where the relationship of the local inhabitants (culture groups) with the ecological context has evolved over a long period of time recognizing the symbiotic interaction between the physical and cultural imperatives as both sound and inevitable. The Indian rural landscape is an intricately woven mosaic anchored in rural settlements, big and small, hamlets, dispersed or agglomerations each being an expression of culture on the landscape, a rich micro-cosmos within the macro-cosmos of the Pan Indian tradition. With the myriad culture groups that comprise the Indian population, the Indian rural landscape, rather more specifically the Indian rural cultural landscape, therefore, is a vibrating and varying tapestry of many cultural hues but intimately linked by the thread of the Indian rural fabric. Each settlement therefore, while being unique is a part of the whole.

The rural cultural landscape emerges when a culture group at a certain stage of evolution decides to settle in an area perceived by it to fulfill the requirements of its mode of living. This eventually leads to the creation of a settlement whereby a group attaches itself to the land by establishing an abode as also demarcating a production territory. It is always coterminous with the adoption of a sedentary mode of living. It is through the rural settlement that a culture group makes its first impress on the landscape. Its three core elements, the settlement, the house type and the field pattern are molded from the materials provided by the site/territory into features characteristic of its culture. It was Meitzen who for the first time tried to establish the very close relationship between the ethnic (culture) groups and the type of settlement and the organization of space in the villages. (5) As such the rural settlement emerges on the landscape as an expression of the perennial interplay between the material foundation of the ecological context and the cultures whereby the terrestrial existence of man works itself out through two distinctive sets of features the secular and the religious; as a part of space contents, as the organizing element of the rural cultural landscape; and as the prism that reflects the culture of the people occupying that area, and as the symbol of the synthesis of the fundamental syndrome of habitat, habit, and inhabitant reaffirming that "any sign of human action in a landscape implies a culture, recalls a history and demands an ecological interpretation, the history of any people evokes its setting in a landscape, its ecological problems and its cultural concomitants and the recognition of a culture calls for the discovery of traces it has left on the earth". (6)

Through this interaction man creates imprints and landmarks that establish the identity and personality of an area. The rural settlements are therefore, not just local and regional indicators but also cultural artifacts. Culture, essentially being "learned behavior" (7) passed on down the line of generations, is the medium through which the natural landscape is evaluated and molded to create a cultural landscape, making the rural settlement the culmination of the adaptation of a culture group to an ecological setting. Thus settlements belonging to different culture groups become coterminous with the ecological settings, and each ecological zone becomes synonymous to a culture area. As the natural landscape is transformed into a cultural landscape, the mediator of this interaction being the culture group, through the concretization of culture nature interaction, the rural settlement emerges on the landscape as an expression of culture, with some attributes relating the settlement to an area and others helping its identification as an area.

Traditional Gujar Settlement Landscape

The focus of this study is a Gujar settlement, Tagra Kali Ram, within the Dun, occupying the upper part of the Kiratpur alluvial fan and the adjacent lower slopes of the southern flanks of the Lower Himalayas. A typical marginal land, it is one of the classic habitat areas of the Gujars in Northern Haryana, specifically the Kalka tehsil of Panchkula district. A recent visit (after a gap of nearly four decades) to Tagra Kali Ram brought home as never before that the typical Gujar rural settlement landscape had all but disappeared, a sheer testimony to the ravages that a rural cultural landscape experiences or is subject to as a consequence of development.

A brief insight into the cultural background of the Gujars and its translation onto the landscape shall perhaps put this study in better perspective. Traditionally, the Gujars form a prominent group among the pastoral castes.(8) Their culture history deeply rooted in pastoralism, reveals a gradual progress from pastoral nomadism to pastoralist farming and later to a farming pastoralist mode of living. Although widely acclaimed as one of the superior cattle-herding groups of the northern Indian sub-mountain tract (9) and regarded as among the best cattle-keepers, they as a group have been considered as inferior cultivators. (10). Presently, they are peasant farmers with a residual but strong pastoral element. They have several tribal elements in their culture and have been designated as one of the oldest tribal castes of India. (11) Their first impress on the landscape, their settlements, nowhere date back to more than 200 years, which only reflects their semi-permanent, dominantly pastoral, unsettled mode of living till as late as the seventeenth century. (12) Primarily concentrated in the marginally productive lands where they found much more conducive habitat for practicing their pastoral mode of living, their settlements provide a classic example of the relationship of the settlements with the evolution of their culture. Small, agglomerate, uni-caste, uni-religious and in several cases, uni-clan the Gujar settlements have agglomeration deeply rooted in the evolution of a minimal lineage into a maximal lineage, and finally into the uni-clan settlement. The morphological structure of the settlement comprising of gotra (clan) and lineage verahs (courtyards) evolving with the successive disintegration and elaboration of joint families into nuclear families has, therefore, been the main process involved in the agglomeration of the settlement and is a cultural phenomenon. Clan solidarity and strong familial ties have been complementary to agglomeration. Non-nucleated, the Gujar settlements have been loose agglomerate, only a heap of dwellings, revealing no preconceived ground plan or well defined street pattern.

A significant element of the traditional Gujar settlement landscape, is the Khera Baba of the founding clan, the material symbolization of ancestor worship, accepted and worshipped by all and an effective determinant of agglomeration, although not necessarily a point of nucleation. Further a diagnostic feature of the maximal and minimal lineage complexes was the verah, its significance all pervasive. Central to the organization of space within the complex, functionally, socially and culturally the verah provided the private and social space areas for inter-family as also intra-family interactions be it the performance of the rites de passage, seclusion and protection of women and children, and above all for tethering, stalling, and feeding the cattle which were inseparable and an integral part of the Gujar mode of living. The verah therefore fulfilled both religious and secular needs. (13)

Further the Gujar house, revealed the typical characteristics of a folk house, a structure built with locally available material, according to traditional design and building techniques. It is a part of the material culture of a people who have evolved ways of solving shelter problems using the available material, technology and values of their culture. The folk house is a visual representation of the attitudes, beliefs and aspirations of a specific culture group.(14) Traditionally it comprised five space units, the chabutra (a rectangular or square plinth), a quasi-private and social space; covered verandah, an exclusive domestic space including the kitchen hearth area, a store maybe and the locale of day to day household activities; the baharla moharla (outer room), essentially private space but often shared with the cattle; the andarla moharla (inner room), the exclusive domain for household storage of valuables and sleeping; and the cattle-room or shed an integral part of the house premises reiterating the strong pastoral element as a culture trait.. Moreover, the Gujar folk house was everywhere single storied (the world over associated with the gable and thatch dwellings of nomads which could not support another storey) and flat roofed, (adopted through contact with other farming groups) both culture traits imbibed perfectly as functional components of the house during the course of their evolution. The building materials used were essentially mud, wood, thatch, all locally available, while the construction of the house was essentially an activity involving both the family and community. Further each aspect of the house was endowed with cultural meaning, be it the direction and placing of the doors and windows or even the entrance to the verah complex itself.

The field landscape, characterized by small fields with no well marked field boundaries revealed joint and single ownership with each family having a fair share in terms of productivity of the different land types and the distance from the abadi controlled by the principle of compensation and mutual adjustment. Barani or rain-fed cultivation being the norm, the range of crops grown and the area under different crops in each season remained limited. A product of the land tenure system, technological know-how, the culture group and their genre de vie the field landscape and pattern is essentially an expression of the community decision through their culture and mode of living. Sir Malcolm Darling, a perceptive analyst of the Punjab rural scene, once wrote: 'only men with qualities of an ant could work so well under conditions so destructive of effort. Unfortunately, the Gujar......have little of the ant about them.......lazy pastoral habits still prevail.........They take not the slightest pride or interest in any agricultural pursuit, their fields are cultivated in the most slovenly manner; you see none of the neatly kept houses, well fenced fields, fat bullocks and wells kept in good repair which distinguish the industrious castes;......no fences protect their fields, their cattle are half starved, and their wells in the most dilapidated condition'. (15) This perfectly sums up their skills and their attachment to land.

Tagra Kaliram today is difficult to discern from the surrounding inroads of diversification and increasingly urban character. The evolved and a very evidently Gujar impress on the landscape stands today, torn as it were between the traditional heritage/genre de vie (16) and the modern. Transformation is inherent and concomitant with the evolution of a people, their mode of living, their value systems, their technologies and their adoption of ever changing and newly emerging traits and world view. The gradual change and progress affected by improved communication, education and provision of infrastructural facilities and subsequent widened vistas of interaction, external influences have had a distinctive bearing on the adoption of culture traits hitherto unknown. These over a period of time have got imbibed and become a part of the cultural baggage as an accretion or perhaps an induction into the value system. These inevitably have translated into concretized expressions on the landscape having great bearing on the rural cultural landscape, which stands visibly transformed. The level of transformation is very intimately linked to the traditional value system and culture traits. Thus in case of the Gujars, the traditional pastoralist group, whose attachment to land historically has been only somewhat superficial although the attachment to cattle rearing has been intrinsic, giving up the farming component of their genre de vie, is observed as fairly common. Adoption of newer, more lucrative occupations has been somewhat more easily accepted, especially in view of the fact that inhabiting the marginal lands, agriculture was for them never a lucrative option, due to the poor land productivity, barani or rain fed cultivation, and the fact that they were poor cultivators. The impact is visible on all the three core elements of the rural settlement landscape, the settlement, the house type and the field pattern.

The Changed Landscape

The small non-descript amorphous heap of dwellings comprising the loosely agglomerate settlement is gone. The settlement landscape stands quite changed today as continued evolution involving the disintegration of joint families into nuclear ones and further their evolution into maximal lineages have led to the expansion of the dwelling units either onto the verah or by constructing another storey. This undoubtedly reinforces their familial ties and clan solidarity, as the first choice remains to extend the house within the verah complex itself, but it also necessitates the moving of the cattle out of the verah complexes and into baras not necessarily adjacent to the houses. This tendency to isolate the cattle reflects their dwindling significance in their mode of living and a dilution of their symbiotic relationship as the Gujars move from the farming pastoral mode of living to the more modern tertiary and service sectors of the economy.

The settlement today is therefore, transforming into a compact agglomeration at the core with a tendency of the abadi deh spilling onto the adjacent farming lands. It is as if a forced dispersion is beginning to set in with the creation of a homestead on the owners' agricultural land. It is here that the maximal lineage verah complex is recreated indicative of the tremendous tenacity of the ground plan design. Also the availability of open land allows for the keeping of the cattle within the complex unlike in the core. It seems the changing genre de vie has led to first the ouster of cattle from the vassughar (residential area) to the verah, from the verah to a bara adjacent to the house and now to baras at the periphery, which have been perhaps instrumental in the creation of new minimal lineage units on the periphery. The settlement is now large having a population of 1957 according to the 2011 census, with several marked encroachments of the fields and production territory which is greatly reduced in extent. The initial abadi deh is completely overshadowed by the new extensions of the settlement, which are often related to the sale of the agricultural fields to outsiders, not necessarily Gujars or of the same caste and gotra and not also for purposes of farming but rather for house construction and some even for the use of the already poor soil for brick kilns. Thus the process of evolution of the settlement is no longer related to the evolution and extension of families belonging to the same clan. As such the minimal and maximal lineage verahs are conspicuously absent.

The most striking change and complete break from tradition, is the near universal proliferation of double storied houses hitherto unknown and clearly reflecting an adoption of a trait through contact with other groups which have come into the settlement mostly from the plains. This also reflects the paucity of land within the abadi deh and more lucrative income derived from the sale of their share in the production territory. The existing minimal lineage complex, therefore, of yester years stands transformed. Interestingly the once shared open space of the verah is broken into small diminutive verahs of the nuclear families, often quite well demarcated by boundary walls.

The expanding settlement, however, as before, does not reveal any preconceived ground plan and as such no well defined street pattern although at least three different orders of streets can be identified. The earlier access road, a wide pathway lined by boulders or thor (scrub) forming a low wall, linking the settlement to the fields and other settlements and channelizing the movement of the cattle and people has given way to a tarmac topped motor able road extensively used by the settlement dwellers as also others from the surrounding areas as an arterial link to other settlements and the tehsil headquarters and thereon to other towns and states. It is well demarcated but with shops on one side and also the pucca brick and cement walls of the transformed houses of the settlement. The off-shoots of this into the settlement form the axial street, onto which open all the village lanes. Providing for circulation within the settlement these are easily identifiable, being wider than the village lanes and commonly used for leading the cattle into the fields. Earlier this was just a plain mud and earth tract being demarcated by the backs or side walls of houses within the different verah complexes and rarely did a verah complex open onto this street. Today this is brick paved, lined with the high walls of the double-storied houses on either side with the verah complexes opening onto it directly. Also there are now more than one such arterial road.

The village lanes, narrow, rough pathways, providing circulation within the settlement, serving both to link as also separate the individual verah complexes, continue to serve the same purpose. It was onto these village lanes that the verah complex opened through just an ill defined gap in the low boundaries of mud, stone or thor that defined the verah complex as also the streets. The entrance was inevitably on the same level as the street since it was used for movement of cattle from the house to the fields and back. These village lanes also took on the role of an extended social space for inter family interaction as

200

anyone passing could interact with members of a household within the verah. In the present scenario as observed, the breaks and gaps as entrance to the verah complex is replaced by proper iron grill gates, sometimes very high and impressive. The purpose seems to be not just security but also a greater sense of privacy wherein no one can really see the activities being carried on in the verah complex which in many cases will be an individual small verah of the nucleated off-shoot of an evolving maximal lineage. The entrance remains level with the first order street but there is an increasing tendency to have the verah area of an individual house a notch or two higher, sometimes approached even by a step or two, especially where the cattle have been completely moved out of the verah complex and no longer share the intimate relationship with the owners. The narrow village lanes seem even more constricted, but continue to provide circulation among different maximal lineage units, not verah complexes, because those have almost disappeared.

The verah (open courtyard) in front of the vassughar (residential units), as mentioned earlier was the most diagnostic feature of the Gujar house. Insulated from the outside it served to organize the inter-family and social space and served as a cultural, functional and lineage spatial unit. In fact, no house was or is, even though in a diminutive form and in the absence of its cultural and social imperatives, independent of the verah. However, the settlement as an agglomeration of maximal lineage verah complexes is lost as is its importance to the present genre de vie of the Gujars.

Traditionally the five space units, the chabutra, covered verandah, baharla moharla (outer room), andarla moharla (innter room), and the cattle-room or shed have all but disappeared. . The verandah, the locale of the kitchen, store and several household chores and sometimes used as a place for stalling cattle, relating it almost exclusively to the members of the individual family, as it was here that all the intra-family interactions took place, has been the first to be encroached upon following the expansion of a minimal lineage and subsequent extension of the living quarters. Consequently, the functions of the verandah were transferred to the chabutra. Today they stand merged under a proper roof, the lean-to thatch structures and mud walls no longer exist. The kitchen is now well within the precincts of the house. There is no distinction between the inner and outer rooms, which allow access to any guest indicating the merging of the private and social spaces, and little or no segregation between the males and the females.

201

However, the most significant change is the increasingly frequent absence of the cattle-shed.

The cattle-shed has always reiterated the dominant pastoral element in the Gujar mode of living as it was everywhere an integral part of the Gujar house. In fact a hypothetical evolutionary sequence can be suggested whereby in the first stage, when pastoral element was all pervasive the humans and cattle shared the same room. In the next stage, the adoption of agriculture as a secondary occupation a slight degree of indifference to pastoralism comes to be reflected in the separation of human and cattle rooms, although close link is still maintained in retaining a connecting doorway between the two. Further still the two may have a common wall, though access to each is through individual entrances. Thus, although separation has set in, their traditional pastoral ties impel them to maintain close contact with their cattle, which are still an integral part of their mode of living. The increasing significance of agriculture and consequent declining dependence on cattle eventually leads to a severing of ties, whereby the cattle-shed is completely separated from the living quarters, although it is still retained within the premises in the verah. Eventually, when agriculture became the all dominant activity, the cattle-shed has been completely detached from the verah complex and now very often removed to the peripheries of the settlement or within the fields.

Even though agriculture has become gradually but increasingly important at no stage is the mode of living independent of cattle involvement, in that while milch cattle meet the daily household and very often economic requirements, it is the cattle again which form the major source of power behind all agricultural activities. However a new dimension is being added as the Gujars adopt other occupations i.e. the increasing total absence of cattle in their mode of living, which is clearly reflected in the house type, with the construction of double storey houses, the disappearing concept of the verah, the merger of the functional units of the house and the verah complex, the verandah emerging as the most diagnostic unit of the house and social space, the removal of cattle from the precincts of the house and therefore the disappearance of the khunta,(a peg dug into the ground to tether the cattle) khurli, (an elongated raised furrow to feed fodder to cattle) and fodder room from the house. At the same time, modern facilities such as modern, fully fitted kitchens with the latest gadgets, gas connections, refrigerators and other amenities, water and electricity supply are now incorporated into the houses.

The design of the houses stands changed as does the building material used, the mud and cow-dung mixture and wooden rafters replaced by the most modern, brick, mortar, cement, tiles and even marble and chips. This may also be related to the decline in the involvement of cattle in day to day living as there is a shift in the genre de vie to the tertiary service sector and therefore the impact of outside exposure which makes the house more a symbol of status than just a genre de vie related functional entity.

The Khera continues to evoke respect and reverence. However, while the original Khera remains intact and has come to be elaborately modified, it is now within the settlement and not at the periphery as before. Moreover, it is somewhat overwhelmed by the stature of other temples which have been established in the vicinity distinctly representing at least some gods of the Hindu pantheon. Impressive structures house the Lakhdata, for prosperity, Kali Mata, as representative of shakti worship of mother goddess for protection against evil, as also the Guga Marhi, for snake worship, a relict animistic typically tribal trait. It continues to exert a strong influence.

The field landscape has distinctly reduced in extent with some fields lost in the construction of the wide access road and others, especially in the direct vicinity of the abadi deh being overtaken for the purpose of development of modern commercial and residential areas by outsiders. All along the road, the string of modern houses of varied architectural design and shops have already lent a very urban character to the settlement. The intra clan cohesiveness is lost as the hitherto agglomeration stands transformed as a somewhat lineated settlement.

A Disappearing Cultural Impress

These observed changes bear testimony to the gradual dilution of a strong cultural impress evolved over centuries of adaptation of the culture group to the ecological setting. Change, progress, development are inevitable but not at the cost of disturbing fragile ecologies unable to sustain intensive use or the wiping out of cultures that are unable to withstand the onslaught of development. In fact in matters of sustainability the indigenous cultures have a lot to offer by ways of preservation, protection and optimum use of the limited available resources, modes of living that have sustained over centuries. Therefore, when the agenda is development it should not be exploitative of the physical, ecological setting or the cultural imperatives of a simple culture group.

In case of Tagra Kali Ram, a cultural landscape is being wiped out as is a culture of a simple pastoralist group and its secular and religious imprints on the landscape. If only the development process had been initiated to strengthen their livelihood through schemes of better facilities for cattle rearing, provision of suitable irrigation facilities so as to make the farming practices more productive and lucrative, if their education had helped them to better manage their cattle and enhance their incomes through improved milk production and supply, if the expansion of the settlement could have been better planned, perhaps many would not have chosen to sell their lands and adopt other occupations. But the increasing population, consistent division of the land, increasingly smaller houses and fields , unsustainable extensive farming practices have been unable to retain the interest of the younger generations in cattle rearing and the farming pastoralist mode of life offering at best meager earnings unsustainable of the increasing aspirations of a generation better connected, better educated and more aware. The minimal lineage or the maximal lineage at best, alone do not make up their world. Thus taking up more lucrative occupations outside the settlement itself and increasing awareness of their rights and greater exposure have all led to welcome development translated onto the landscape through the use of better building materials, better house designs, not necessarily suited to the traditional mode of living, better amenities....but these have also led to increased incursions and increased pressure of population and commercial activities. Will the marginal ecological setting be able to sustain these? The widespread use of concrete and bricks for house construction, the increasing intensity of pressure of population, the greater use of automobiles, the greater need for water, the diminishing cattle-heads and increasing land-use conversion from small agricultural field to luxurious bungalows and businesses have transformed a uni-clan rural settlement into an urban landscape. Thus a rural cultural landscape is almost obliterated.

Conclusion

The manner, in which the culture group comes to terms with the material foundation of the ecological zone, is ultimately controlled by the combination of its technologies and value systems and the historical circumstances in which the area is settled. In the process of settling, a culture group creates a cultural landscape, which is characterized not only by its culture but also by the material foundation of the ecological zone and which tends to attain the goal of maximization of functional efficiency and yet does not violate the integrity of its culture. At any point in time the rural settlements are not merely the landscape expressions of the interplay between culture and nature, between the value system and technology and the material foundation provided by the ecological context at that time, but also of the vestiges or relics of earlier occupancies characterized by their own processes, value systems and technology.

Development though necessary cannot be imposed. The people themselves must be involved in the process. They must contribute to and be party to the development and planning initiated involving any rural settlement. Their mode of living should be duly respected and recognized, strengthened and sustained so that the expression of their culture on the landscape, their settlement is not lost in the maze of development but rather maintains its own identity and the identity of the people who gave it that identity. Adopting sustainable practices and cultural imperatives is therefore of utmost significance. Thus sustainable development is not a fixed state but "a process of change in which the exploitation of resources, the direction of investments, the orientation of technological development, and institutional change are all in harmony and enhance both current and future potential to meet human needs and aspirations". (17)

References

[1] UNDP Report (1990). Human Resource Development Report, New York: Oxford University Press

[2] World Commission on Environment and Development, (1987) Our Common Future, New York: Oxford University Press

[3] United Nations Department of Public Information (2002); World Summit on Sustainable Development Johannesburg 2002

[4] United Nations (2012) Report of the United Nations Conference on Sustainable Development, Rio de Janeiro, Brazil 20-22 June 2012, New York: Oxford University Press

[5] A. Demangeon (1927) 'The Origins and Causes of Settlement Types's, in Readings in Cultural Geography, Philip L. Wagner and Marvin W. Mikesell (eds) Chicago: Chicago University Press, pp 506-576

[6] P.L. Wagner and Marvin W. Mikesell (1962) Readings in Cultural Geography, Chicago: University of Chicago Press p 23

[7] T.G. Jordan and Lester Rowntree (1976) The Human Mosaic: A Thematic Introduction to Cultural Geography, New York,: Harper and Row Publishers

[8] Crooke (1907) Natives of Northern India, London: Archibald Constable and Company Limited, pp.114-115; Denzil Ibbetson, (1981). Punjab Castes, New Delhi: Cosmo Publishers, p 184

[9] Sir D.C. Ibbetson (1885) Settlement Report of Karnal, Lahore: Government Press, p. 265

[10] Malcolm L. Darling (1925). The Punjab Peasant in Prosperity and Debt, Geoferry Camberlege: Oxford University Press pp 61-62

[11] Gerald D. Berreman (1963) Hindus of the Himalayas Berkely: University of California Press, pp.36-38

[12] Field inquiries and village records repeatedly bring forth the name of Mr. Kalerai, an Indian officer in the British employ, who made the Gujars aware of the value of land which was fast diminishing. He advised them to give up their nomadic habits in

the Siwalik Hills and Dun, to acquire land and settle down.

[13] Neelam Grover (1985) Rural Settlements: A Cultural-Geographical Analysis, A Case Study of Northern Haryana, New Delhi: Inter-India Publications and A.B. Mukerji (1976) "Rural Settlements of the Chandigarh Siwalik Hills (India): A Morphogenetic Analysis", Geografiska Annaler, Vol.58, Ser B, pp.95-115

[14] Fred B. Kniffen (1965) olk Housing: Key to Diffusion", Annals, Association of   American Geographers, Vol. 55, No. 4, Dec. pp. 549-577 See ref. 8

[16] Max Sorre (1962) "The Concept of Genre de vie", in Readings in Cultural Geography, P.L. Wagner and M.W. Mikesell, Chicago: University of Chicago Press, pp.399-401See ref. 2, p7

Chapter-XV

Conservation of Dal Lake, Kashmir-Missing Links or Gaps: A Case Study

Shabina Masoodi*

Abstract

Dal Lake, a tourist spot of international fame, is one of the prized lakes of world; it is part of India's beautiful national heritage and has been the centre of Kashmir's civilization. It has suffered a lot due to pollution and the present paper is an attempt to assess the missing links or gaps in its conservation plan on the basis of surveys, literature review, field studies and interaction with the lake experts and managers of the Dal Lake. The year 1971-1978 saw non-implementation of proposals because of lack of funds and limited State resource, the year 1985-1989 saw non-implementation of proposals because of geo-political reasons and uprisings in Punjab and in Kashmir. The J&K UEE Department who took charge of Dal Lake in early had main thrust on civil works, neglecting the scientific measures. The year 1996-1997 saw Dal Lake included under the National Lakes Conservation Program (NLCP), conservation plan with estimate was submitted but its approval delayed by the then Government. The Government of India suggested a new consultancy and again the modified plan which was submitted to the Central Government for funding. However the halfhearted approach impelled the state authorities to carry on with the project and now again it became a routine works program rather than a time bound project.

Most of the project proposals so far submitted and executed in the year 2010-11enabling to address the problem of lake and its dwellers and could not take care of important lake basin and exit channel flowing into river Jhelum.

Keywords: Non-implementation of proposals, neglecting the scientific measures, National Lakes Conservation Program (NLCP), halfhearted approach, Problem of lake and its dwellers

*Associate Professor, Department of Civil Engineering, SSM College of Engineering and Technology, Parihaspora, Pattan, Kashmir, J&K, India

Introduction

Dal Lake located at an altitude of 1587 msl (mean sea level), is situated in the Himalayan State, Jammu and Kashmir, in the extreme north of India and northeast of Srinagar, the summer capital of J&K. It has been the centre of Kashmir civilization, part of India's national heritage and is one of the most beautiful spots of tourist attraction. This shallow-post glacial freshwater body is bounded by Zabarvan Mountains in the east, overlooked by Shankaracharia Hill-lock in southeast and Kohi-Maran Hill-lock in southwest making its surroundings beautiful. The lake is multi-basined with (i) Hazratbal (ii) Bod dal (iii) Gagribal and (iv) Nagin are its four basins. It harbours a rich biodiversity of plants and rare and endangered animals which include several migratory bird species. Dal Lake is one of the few water bodies in the world having permanent human settlement within its confines. It is an important source of livelihood for above 60,000 people living in hamlets, houseboats and doongas (smaller boats for ferrying people and goods) through services like tourism, fishery, water sports, cultivation of vegetables in 'floating gardens'. Many aquatic plants are grown in the lake serving as food, fodder and compost for agricultural fields.

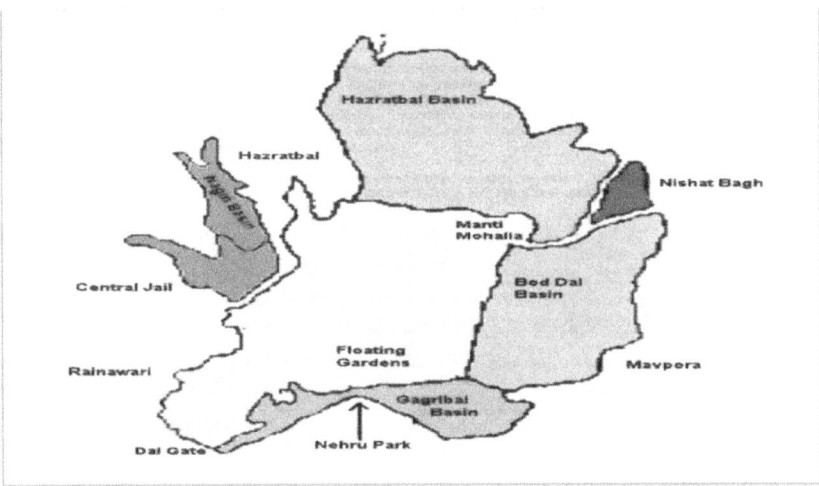

ecology and environment of Dal Lake due to which its area has got reduced. Dal Lake was spread over 75sqkms in 1200AD but at present it covers about 21.1 sqkms and has a depth of 5.4m and a shoreline of

15.4 km. Of the total area only about 11.4 sqkms is open water and the rest is under floating gardens most of which have now settled permanently. The major cause of this degradation has been unabated encroachments after converting floating gardens into permanent land masses, silting caused due to catchment area degradation, reduction and clogging of fresh water channels into the lake, nutrient enrichment of lake water resulting in excessive weed growth and changes in bio-diversity of lake and above all entry of untreated sewage and solid wastes from area in and around the Dal Lake which are a part of unplanned urbanization. A lake from which people drank water until 1980 is now so toxic that a gulp of it can send the person to the hospital. With rising temperature and presence of raw sewage it is rife with various water borne diseases.

MAJOR POLLUTANTS OF DAL LAKE PER YEAR

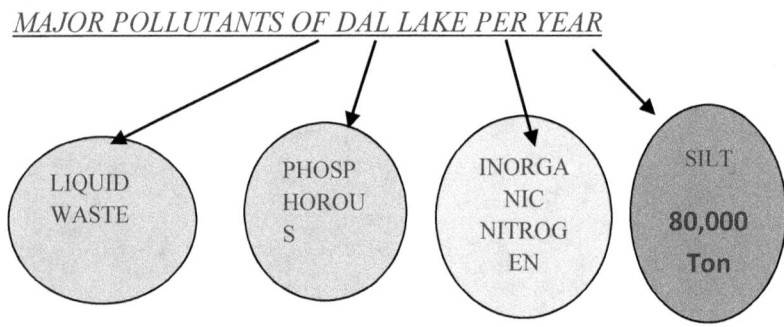

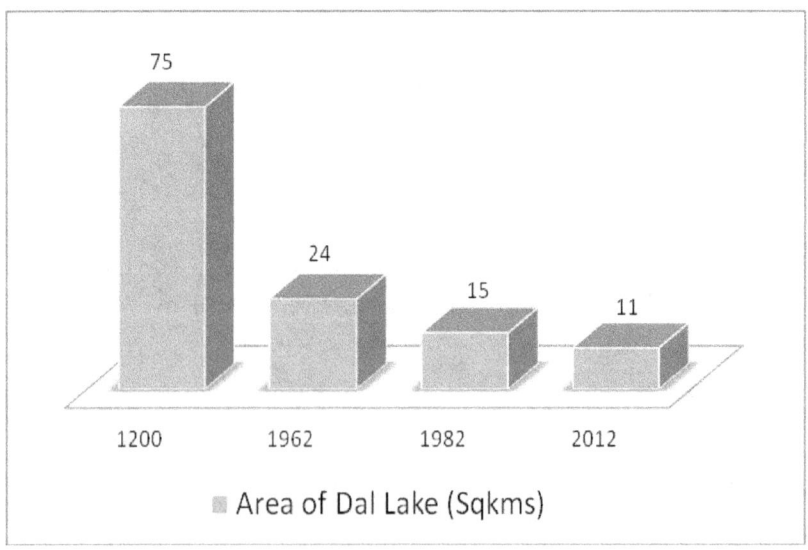

Acknowledging the ecological degradations of the lake and the concern of voices from all walks of life, the State Government engaged number of National and International Consultancies for preparation of conservation Plans of which the notable are Srinagar Master Plan of 1971, Lake Area Master Plan by Stein (1972), Enex Consortium Report (1978), Dal lake Development Report by Riddle (1985), ODA (1989), Project Report under National Lakes Conservation Plan (1997) and Project Report of University of Roorkee (2000). All the conservation plans have more are less arrived to the conclusion of following restoration measures for Dal Lake:

- Afforestation and soil conservation in catchment areas viz; Dachigam, Dara-Dhanihamma.
- Trapping of debris and sediment from the catchment area by way of construction of settling basin at Telbal.

- Marginal dredging of marshes, hamlets and landscaping the rest.
- Acquisition of land and structures within the lake body involving 6000 kanals of land and 3741 structures.
- Prevention and control of pollution by way of diversion of sewage and drainage from the peripheries including low cost options, house boat sanitation and Sewage Treatment Plants.
- Construction of green buffer areas/ Ecological barriers along Northern & Western foreshores.
- Delineation of the lake body by way of Northern and Western Foreshores.
- Improvement of Lake Hydrology and hydraulics by way of regulators. Modernization of Navigational lock at Dal gate, improvement of Nallah Amir Khan, construction of cut and conduit at Brari Nambal as outfall channel on river Jhelum and improvement of navigational routes.
- Establishment of Eco-Monitoring Laboratory.

Missing Links or Gaps

Although the basic limnological inputs were available during 1971-1978 from the local experts to the consultants yet in absence of complete and systematic data on Dal Lake the consultants had to rely on the available data and on their own resources and findings. On the basis of surveys, literature review, field studies and interaction with the lake experts and managers of the Dal Lake following gaps were noticed:

- The project proposals submitted for the Dal lake from 1971-1978 were not implemented because of lack of funds and limited State resources.
- The project proposals submitted between 1985-1989 could not be carried out because of geo-political reasons and uprisings in Punjab and in Kashmir which compelled the foreign agencies to stay back.
- The seriousness of the problem was felt by the Govt. in early eighties when a separate Department viz; Urban Environmental Engineering Department was established comprising of Civil and Mechanical Engineering wings to manage the Dal Lake affairs. The department followed the

proposals of Enex (1978) however the main thrust was being laid on civil works, neglecting the scientific measures. The lack of timely financial support resulted in slow pace of work, incomplete jobs and ultimately failure.

- The active restoration measures re-started by the involvement of Ministry of Environment & Forests, Govt. of India in 1996-1997 by inclusion of Dal Lake under the National Lakes Conservation Program (NLCP) and as such a fresh detailed project proposal was suggested.
- Accordingly a project proposal on Dal Lake conservation was submitted with an estimated cost of Rs.3971 Million in 1997 for approval and also with the suggestion that a separate autonomous Lake Authority comprising of all the wings viz; Engineering, Scientific, Forest, Revenue ,working under one umbrella and in tandem.

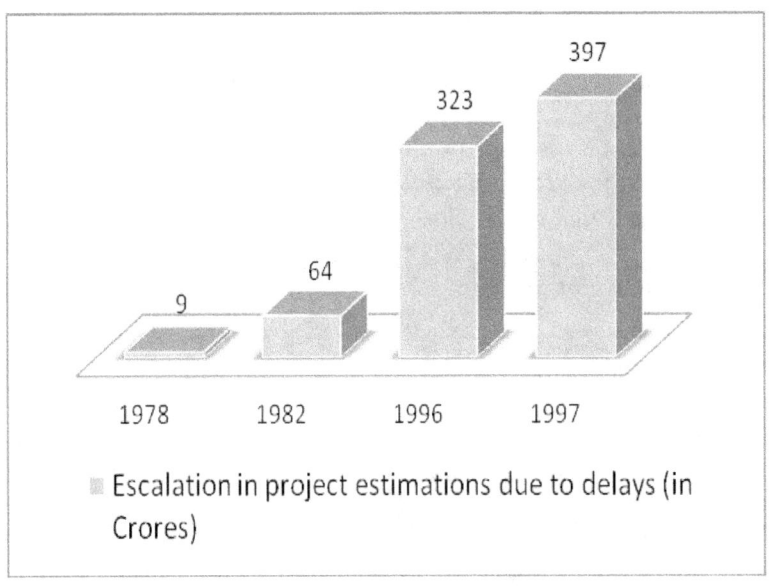

 Escalation in project estimations due to delays (in Crores)

- With the change in Govt. in the Centre the proposal of the lake got delayed and the ongoing works suffered again badly. The Govt. of India suggested a new consultancy and it was again the modified plan which was submitted to the Central Govt. for funding. Alternate Hydro Energy Centre (AHEC) of IIT, Roorkee was engaged as the consultant in October, 1999.

- However the halfhearted approach impelled the authorities to carry on with the project and changes in State administration further slowed down the project work and now again it became a routine works program rather than a time bound project.
- The state cabinet cleared the DPR in December, 2002 and submitted it to Government of India for funding.
- The Government of India sanctioned Rs 298.76 Crores in September, 2005 and the same was released in piece meals resulting in cost escalation and incompletion of various jobs. It was finally the year 2010-2011 the actual approval of funds took place for the Dal Lake although this project was supposed to be completed by 2010 which was subsequently extended up to 2012.
- Construction of northern foreshore road and western foreshore road taken up, against the advice of experts proved counterproductive as it encouraged encroachment on water body instead of containing it. Construction of these roads resulted in cutting off 206 hectares of lake body from it. Further construction of western foreshore road was stopped, the constructed portion of road closed and converted into a footpath resulting in wasteful expenditure.
- Encroachers gradually converted lake area near the areas identified for road into floating gardens by sowing weeds called plyach.

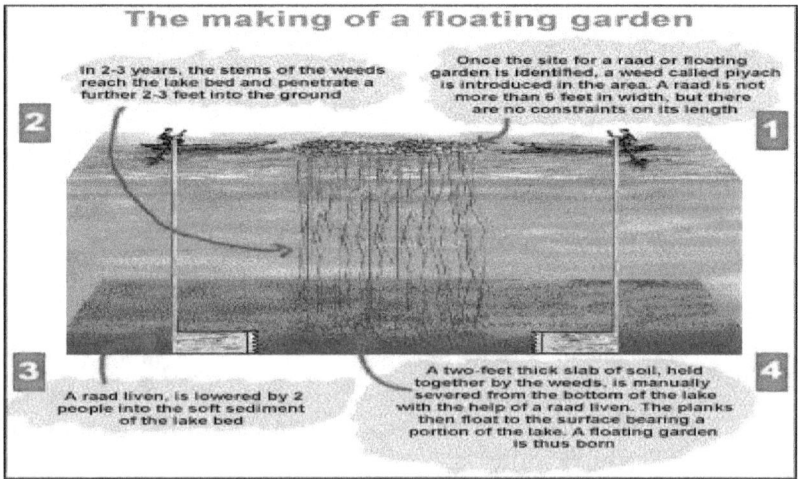

The making of a floating garden

2 — In 2-3 years, the stems of the weeds reach the lake bed and penetrate a further 2-3 feet into the ground

1 — Once the site for a raad or floating garden is identified, a weed called plyach is introduced in the area. A raad is not more than 6 feet in width, but there are no constraints on its length

3 — A raad liven, is lowered by 2 people into the soft sediment of the lake bed

4 — A two-feet thick slab of soil, held together by the weeds, is manually severed from the bottom of the lake with the help of a raad liven. The planks then float to the surface bearing a portion of the lake. A floating garden is thus born

- The ongoing conservation works are engineering dominated works and since 2002, the scientific wing was willfully derailed and onwards no scientific publication of any sort is on records which would have been a regular feature in the shape of annual reports depicting the water quality changes, environment impact assessment studies of dredging, de-weeding etc.
- Most of the project proposals so far submitted have not been able to address the problem of lake dwellers. One of the consultants had suggested the complete removal of the lake habitants which is neither possible nor practicable, as it involves huge sum for their relocation and rehabilitation. The lake experts too opposed the suggestion as they hold considered opinion that the lake dwellers form an important constituent of the lake ecosystem. The other consultant left the option of lake dwellers to the State Govt. and suggested that the number of souls in Dal Lake be adjusted as per the carrying capacity of the lake (without mentioning or studying the prevailing carrying capacity of the lake).
- For rehabilitation of Dal dwellers out of 1556 residential plots developed at a cost of Rs. 12crore, only 293 were allotted till 1996, 350 kanals of land were acquired for Rs. 3crore in 1988 for rehabilitation of families and Rs. 2crore spent on development of colony but due to improper co-ordination with Srinagar Development Authority, this work was stopped resulting in the entire expenditure proving unfruitful. Srinagar Development Authority pointed that the area was green belt in master plan and cannot be used for residential purposes.
- Achievement for acquisition of land and structures in the lake area was only 48% and 8 % respectively of the targets set. Land and areas were acquired sporadically and acquired area was not restored to lake and an expenditure of Rs. 7crore was incurred on acquisition till 1996 which did not serve any purpose. Acquired land continued to be used by people for cultivation.
- One of the important basins of the Dal lake viz. Brari Nambal lagoon as been totally neglected and no conservation measures what so ever have been mentioned in the DPR conservation. The lagoon continues to be a cesspool and is virtually ecologically a dead part of the lake with putrefied waters which can result in an epidemic calamity at any time.
- Another important component viz. "Chunti khul" an exit channel running from Dal lake to river Jhelum via Gawkadal is

also totally missing in the conservation plan, which needs maintenance and other engineering and hydraulic works for the normal flow of boat dwellers. Neglecting this outflow channel will also jeopardize the Dal lake conservation plan.

- Encroachment on lake body and unauthorized constructions in and around lake continued unabated during the implementation of the project. The number of encroachments and unauthorized constructions increased from 16 in 1978 to 1967 in 1996.

- The use of technology has not been with the time. The STPs which have been constructed till date have the technology which is not compatible with the weather conditions of Kashmir. These STPs do not perform up to their rated efficiency during winter especially in sub-zero temperature.

- Till 2008, Dal conservation program under NLCP was a cent percent funded by Government of India but after some objections were raised by the Government of India, operation and maintenance works and Dal dwellers rehabilitation works was entrusted to state government under State plan. State government projected the funds for maintenance of Dal Lake through Special Plan Assistance route. However, its Planning and Development department is objecting to this allocation. They want the nodal agency LAWDA to generate this revenue of their own which it is not able to do. Against the set target of 6crores/annum LAWDA has been able to generate revenue of few lakhs. This internal administrative tussle has affected Operation & Maintenance like functioning of STPs and dredging and de-weeding operations and created huge liabilities for LAWDA.

- The Government has not put much investment and time in social awareness programs related to Dal Lake conservation. There are many NGOs working in this field but their presence cannot be felt anywhere. There is no serious contact with the general society through media or even the latest buzz that is the internet or social media. Education and orientation programs regarding Dal lake conservation and for that matter conservation of all the water bodies are missing on the ground.

The CAG report of 2011 has highlighted the following points as part of Dal Lake mismanagement:

- The State Government had not conducted any survey for source water protection. A nodal agency for overall formulation, implementation and coordination of a comprehensive programme for pollution control in water bodies was not in place.

- There was considerable underutilization of funds ranging between 32 and 60 per cent during 2006-11 due to inaction of LAWDA to execute works like house boat sanitation, infrastructure development, etc

- The DPR for conservation of the lake had not been prepared on the basis of an exhaustive investigation and survey.

- The performance efficiency of STPs was not up to the mark as a result, 11.05 Crore spent on installation of these STPs had remained largely unfruitful. Also, non completion of IPS and works/trunk sewer/remodeling of drains had resulted into non-optimal use of installed STPs.

- Despite spending Rs. 70 Lakh on pilot studies for management of solid/liquid wastes of population residing in and around Dal Lake, no considerable headway had been made on the sanitation front.

- Improper land use planning by LAWDA prior to acquiring land and delayed decision of the State Government to change the originally envisaged land-use had rendered 8.32Crore unfruitful, besides adversely affecting the rehabilitation and resettlement programme of the lake-dwellers.

- The monitoring by scientific advisory committee and Board of Directors was poor. Also, the internal control mechanism was virtually non-existent.

Conclusion

The present studies and appraisal of the execution of Dal lake conservation plans reveals the following conclusions:

- Inability to take decisions regarding lake conservation at appropriate time has resulted in worsening of the health of the lake.
- Environmentalists believe that the JK government failed to implement its own comprehensive 256-page report that was submitted in the legislative assembly. The report was submitted by a 13 member house committee under the chairmanship of Sadiq Ali to the legislative Assembly in 2002. The report emphasized on the preservation of the water-bodies of Kashmir. It gave recommendations on how to save these reserves of water.
- The implementation of various restoration measures recommended by various agencies under NLCP could not be undertaken on time due to lack of infrastructural facilities.
- There was escalation in project cost due to failure in meeting the deadlines.
- There were administrative bottlenecks resulting in delay in release of funds.
- The main thrust of the conservation plan was being laid on civil works, neglecting the scientific measures.
- Most of the proposals are neglecting the basins and exit channels of the lake.
- There is no concrete proposal for people living with the lake.
- Above all the technology being used in various STPs in not compatible with the climate of Kashmir.
- The only ray of hope has been the honorable high court has been very instrumental in monitoring the lake conservation works. Public interest litigation was filed in 2003 in the state High Court. This ensured that many landmark decisions were passed by the Court for restoration of the lakes. The Court directions instructed the state to remove encroachments, illegal trees planted to reclaim lake, direct establishment of proper sewage treatment plants and cleaning of the lake. LAWDA cut almost 400,000 trees around the lake because environmentalists believed they were constricting its water.
- Since then the honorable courts have been continuously and keenly monitoring the lake conservation programmes.

References

1. 1978, Pollution of Dal Lake, Enex.
2. 1990. Impact of mechanical de-weeding on Dal lake eco system, Zutshi & Tickoo.
3. 1996, Impact of waste water on the vegetation pattern of Dal Lake, Kundangar.
4. 1996. Aeration of Dal lake (an interim report) HRL.
5. 1997, Dal Lake conservation & rehabilitation. (J&K LAWDA).
6. 1998, Technical report on Dal Lake (J&K LAWDA).
7. 1999, Technical report on Dal Lake (J&K LAWDA).
8. 2000, Technical report on Dal Lake (J&K LAWDA).
9. 2000. DPR conservation and management plan for Dal – Nigeen lake-AHEC Roorkee.
10. 2003, De-weeding practices in Dal Lake & impact assessment.Kundangar.
11. 2004, Thirty years of Ecological Research on Dal Lake, Kundangar.
12. 2009, Monitoring of Dal-Nigeen Lakes & other water bodies (J&K PCB).
13. 2009. Three decades of Dal Lake, Adnan & Kundangar.

Chapter-XVI

Traditional Use of Floral Bio-diversity in Context of Climate Change: Some Issues in Western Himalayan Region of India

Neeraj Kumar Sharma*

Abstract

Man has been living in the lap of nature since the dawn of evolutionary history and has been drawing most of his requirements from it, for that matter food, clothing or housing indeed everything. In fact jungle used to be his kitchen's market and he was having fairly very good knowledge about the useful plants. This local knowledge was embedded in their cultural tradition and was passed orally from one generation to next through songs, stories and drama etc. Also, earlier edible wild plants used to play an important role during tight times such as droughts and food shortages for rural population. As we have been advancing this traditional and very valuable knowledge about plants and their uses is very rapidly fading away from our minds. One of the reasons why we are losing interest in this could be agriculture intensification and our economic success ensuring our nutritional security. Moreover, such plants are innately resistant and adaptive to micro climatic changes such as low rainfall, high temperature etc., especially in comparison to exotic plant species. This has been proven in several ecology, conservation and restoration studies. However, since these wild plants fulfill a meager need and occupy barren lands both of which have been openly accessed and poorly managed and underestimated. Therefore, the decline of traditional ways of life and decreased use of wild edible plants are interlinked. In this research paper the author has tried to assess the traditional use of floral bio-diversity in context of climate change in western Himalayan region

Key Words: Evolutionary history, wild plants, traditional knowledge, ecology, microclimate

Associate Professor, Govt. Degree College Nagrota Bagwan, Himachal Pradesh

Introduction

Those were the lovely days! When, we were having lots of fun, no worries, after school hours outdoor games like hockey (both ball and stick made out of bamboo), gulli danda, kho-kho and stappu in open barren fields were a routine feature and home coming only after the sun set. Yes, I am talking about my childhood schooldays. Generally in the end of February or first week of March final examination used to be over and then use to start a long wait for final result to be declared on 31st March a normal schedule followed in all Government schools during those days. There was less flow of currency during those days and most of the villagers were living a life depended mostly upon mother-nature for health care to food and fuel requirements. The village children's during holidays or after school time used to try their hand in either digging out roots of Tarari plant or cutting Khajjor tree or watching fish catching activities by some elderly people in local Khad (Tributary) or bringing home some parts of wild plants as directed by their mother or grandmother while grazing cattle's in the jungle. This very valuable traditional knowledge is rapidly fading away from our minds not to talk about young generation, who have not been exposed and sensitized about it due to agriculture intensification and economic success, ensuring nutritional security. In this research paper an attempt has been made to assess the traditional use of floral bio-diversity in context of climate change in western Himalayan region.

Study Area

Himachal Pradesh, a prominent hill state of in western Himalayan region has an area of 55673 Sq Km and is located between 30022' - 33012' North Latitude and 75045' -79004' East Longitude. To East, it forms India's border with Tibet, to the North lies the state of Jammu and Kashmir, Uttarakhand in the Southeast, Haryana in South and Punjab in West. The entire territory of Himachal Pradesh is mountainous with altitude varying from 350m to 7000m asl. There is a general increase in elevation from West to East and from South to North. The study area is located in the lap of Dhauladhar range and included surrounding sites of village "Kohala" located approximately 5 km away from the major town Kangra of district Kangra of Himachal Pradesh (Fig.1).

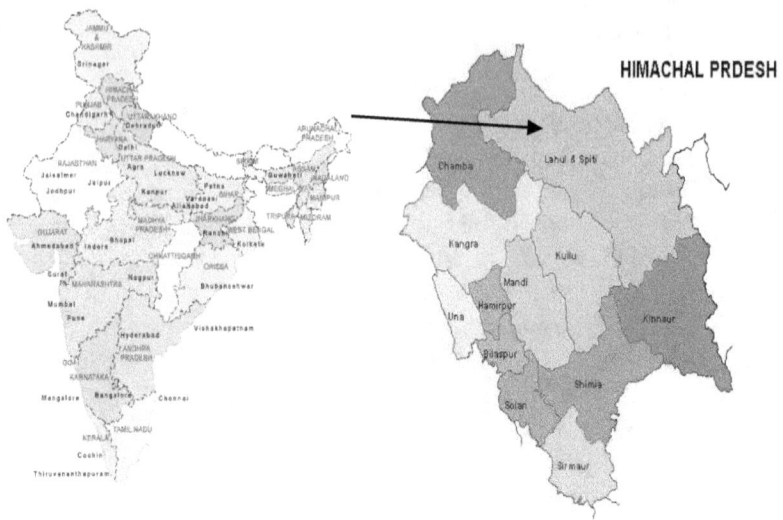

Methodology

The present study is based on the ethno-botanical surveys conducted with elderly persons about the traditional practices regarding uses of the wild plant species found in village "Kohala" and surrounding area along with recollecting author's personal childhood experience between November, 2013 and March, 2014. The plants have been identified with the available literature of Collett (1921), Chowdhery & Wadhwa (1984); Chauhan et al. (1999) and Chauhan et al. (1988), Singh (1996), Polunin and Stainton (1997), Gaur (1999), Kumar (2000) and Singh & Rawat, 2000.

Centella Asiatica (Brahmi)

Centella asiatica is locally called as 'Brahmi' in District Kangra of Himachal Pradesh. In Indian system of medicine it is medicinal plant used as a nerve tonic to promote and improve memory, mental health, intellect, youthful vitality and longevity since 5000 BCE. It has been extensively utilized as a nootropic, digestive aid and to improve learning, memory and respiratory function (Kirtikar and Basu, 1918; Nadkarni, 1988). My grandmother during childhood used to give us five leaves of this plant along with a spoon of sugar early in the morning. It is bitter, pungent, heating, emetic, laxative and useful in bad ulcers, tumours, ascites, enlargement of spleen, indigestion, inflammations, leprosy, anaemia, biliousness etc. Also, according to Unani system of medicine it is bitter, aphrodisiac, good in scabies,

222

leucoderma, syphilis etc. It is promising blood purifier and useful in diarrhea and fevers. Brahmi is also thought to significantly improve the speed of visual information processing, learning rate and memory consolidation. It has been reported to reduce oxidation of fats in the blood stream, which is a risk factor for cardiovascular diseases. It has been used for centuries to help benefit epilepsy, memory capacity, increase concentration, and reduce stress-induced anxiety. Thus, the entire plant is used medicinally (Satyavati et al., 1976).

Carrisa Spinarum (Garana)

This shrub is found in wild in District Kangra of Himachal Pradesh and is locally called as 'Garna'. Its small black fruits are sweet and fairly good quality valued for its taste and also sold in local Maelas (Fair) sometimes. As it is evident from the chemical composition of the fruit, it is highly nutritious and is a very good source of protein. The bushes of this wild plant are thorny and are very effective as a fence and are mainly used in the villages for protecting their animals from wild animals such as leopard. These bushes are very hardy and drought-resistant and can grow even on very poor and rocky soils. Therefore they can be used for a forestation in soil conservation. The leaves are fairly rich in tannins and wood is used for making combs, ladles and other useful household articles along with it being used as fuel. Now this plant is under threat due to the plantation of Pinus roxburghii in jungles of District Kangra (H.P.) by the Department of Forest Govt. of Himachal Pradesh (India) whose needles fallen on the ground are not allowing it to grow at the ground level.

Dioscorea belophylla (Tarari)

Dioscorea have been named after the ancient Greek physician and botanist, Dioscorides. It is a climber and known as 'Tarari' in District Kangra of Himachal Pradesh. It is valued for its underground tubers and is cooked in our homes in different forms like eaten as boiled or fried and as vegetable in dinner menu. Earlier genus has turned to be a famine food during tight time. Although root are deep and therefore return are little to those seeking and getting them; but the root tubers when got are very palatable. It is also used in Indian medicine system as tuber powder is given in sexual diseases or in sex linked diseases, as a poultice applied on whitlow, tubers boiled in water made into paste is also applied in abdominal pain.

Ficus roxburghii (Tremal)

In district Kangra of Himachal Pradesh it is a very common plant growing at elevations up to 1,500 m amsl. It is one of the very popular fruits bearing tree found growing wild in the forests, cultivated fields and in the grasslands. The fruits are very good for eating and the jelly-like substance contained in them makes them very tasty and special. We used to like fruits very much for the jelly-like substance contained in them which used to be much sweeter than the pulp during my childhood. The whole fruit used to taste fairly sweet. Fruit gathering from Ficus roxburghii (a multipurpose tree) hinders its regeneration through seed (Rana and sood, 2012). Also, the leaves of Ficus roxburghii are used as a fodder during the winter season and are very much liked by cattle. The leaves are also used as plates by stitching 3-4 leaves together for serving food in the village sometimes.

Murraya Koenigii (Gandhala)

It is a shrub common in occurrence in outer Himalayas in areas lying between 800-1400 m amsl. Almost every part of this plant has a strong characteristic odor. In our homes the leaves of this plant are used as a spice in curry (a local dish) preparations. We as children's have been using its branches for cleaning the teeth as tooth brush and it was said to strengthen the gums and teeth. The branches of Murrya koenigii are used to strengthen gums, popularly used to clean teeth as datum (Gupta et al. (2011). The leaves, the bark and the roots could be used as a tonic and a stomachic. The bark and the roots are used as a stimulant by the physicians. They are also used externally to cure eruptions and the bites of poisonous animals. The green leaves are stated to be eaten raw for curing dysentery, and the infusion of the washed leaves stops vomiting. Chevalier (1996) also reported curry leaf has medicinal value as tree. The fruits are very sweet and are eaten fresh. They have a characteristic odor and overall fruit quality is fair. This plant is quite ornamental due to its compound leaves and can therefore be used as a hedge and as an ornamental shrub. Leaves of Murrya koenigii constitute on important ingredient in the Indian diet to improve appetite and digestion additionally used in eastern Asia (Bhandari, 2014).

Phoenix sylvestris (Khajoor)

The word Phoenix sylvestris have been derived from two separate Greek words Phoenix means purple and Sylvestris means wild and is locally called as 'Khajoor'. It is found throughout the state of Himachal Pradesh upto a height of 1,300 m amsl. For thousands of years it was the staple food of the Middle East and Indus valley civilization. During my childhood days the leaves of this tree were used for making mats and bags in our village. The fruits were harvested unripe by removing the whole bunches and are then kept covered within rags of some older clothes or wheat straw and used to be ready to eat within 2-5 days. The fruits are sweet in taste and seedy which occupies more than half of the fruit. The, overall fruit quality is fairly good which provides a wide range of essential nutrients. The sugar content of ripe dates is more than 75% and the remainder consists of protein, fiber and trace elements. It is also believed that consumption of dates by women during pregnancy positively affect labor. The fruit is useful as cardio-tonic, oleaginous, abdominal complaints, fevers, vomiting and loss of consciousness. But I want to put here on record that this plant was not valued for above mentioned characteristics by us during childhood but for its sweet inner white fibrous and juicy part which we used to take out after playing hockey matches by cutting the plant into two have with the help of an axe. The central white portion of the plant used to be very delicate, fibrous, juicy and tasty which was very helpful in relieving our tiredness after hectic hockey matches and used to have a very cooling effect. The juice obtained from the tree is considered to be a cooling beverage. The central tender part of the plant is also used in gonorrhoea. The roots are used to stop toothache. In India, sugar and alcohol are made from wild date palm flowers and jelly is made from the fruit (Robert et al., 2010).

Vitex negundo (Bana)

Locally called as Bana and its extract, has been used in Ayurvedic medicine as a rejuvenative tonic for promoting virility. In Unani system of medicine the seeds are recommended for controlling premature ejaculation. The Ayurvedic Pharmacopoeia of India has documented the use of the leaf and the root to treat excessive vaginal discharge, edema, skin diseases, pruritus, helminthiasis, rheumatism and puerperal fever (Khare, 2007). In our village I still can recollect older ladies using a part of this plant as a protection shield against some sort of evil (locally called as 'chora') to young children's or Jams and Pickles and farmers to their seedlings. The research results of Vitex negundu indicated antibacterial activity of the extract (Verma et al., 2001). Also, during childhood whenever we have foot injuries (external swelling) while playing hockey matches, grandmother used to boil branches of this plant in water and used to place our injured feet in that for some time. It was really very relaxing.

Zanthoxylum alatum (Tirmira)

Toothache tree is native to North America and is also found in the subtropical parts of Kangra valleys of Himachal Pradesh and was used as tooth brush during our childhood. It is also referred to as 'Tingle Tongue' for the numbing effect on the gums and teeth. The fruit, bark and stem have all been used in traditional medicine to relieve toothache. The roots, stem and bark of this tree contain the alkaloid magnoflorine, which gives the tree its pharmacological benefits. Fruit of this plant are carminative, stomachic and seeds are used to cure dyspepsia & cholera (Das et al., 2012).

Zizyphus maurtiana (Ber)

Locally called as 'Ber' and is mostly found in arid conditions in district Kangra of Himachal Pradesh. In childhood sometimes during recess we used to eat 'ber' from nearby bushes. Its fruits are rich in Vitamin A, B and C. Its leaves are used as fodder for goats and sheep by local villagers. Fruits can also be processed to prepare murabba, candy, dehydrated ber, pulp, jam and beverage etc.

Fish Poisoning

During summers of those days there used to be a spurt in destructive fishing activities in the village 'Khads' local water channels as the water levels used to decrease and it was easier to catch fishes. Elderly farmers practiced frequent fishing within periphery of our village. We as children's some time used go to see these fish catching activities. The intensity of fishing used to increase during summers as the low flow used to force the fishes to stay confined into small crevices, which makes them more vulnerable. The commonly used plant species for preparing fish poison included Euphorbia royleiana, Casearia tomentosa, Zanthoxylum armatum, Agave americana, Yacca spp. and Randia dumentorium. Indiscriminate fishing was also done during some community based festivals. These are however, an integral part of the socio-religious fabric of people. Albeit the Fisheries Department was also soft on villagers who used nets and other traditional methods for their daily needs and used to took strong exception to the usage of dynamite and poison (Thapliyal, 2009).

Thus, it is very much clear that earlier wild plants used to play a very important role in the socio-economic life of rural population. The native people are the guardians of indigenous traditional knowledge associated with their surrounding biological resources (Rani et al., 2013). They have been using these resources for various purposes in their daily life for ages. As we have been advancing this traditional and very valuable knowledge about plants and their uses is very rapidly fading away from our minds. One of the reasons why we are losing interest in this could be agriculture intensification and our economic success ensuring our nutritional security. This has been proven in several ecology, conservation and restoration studies. However since wild plants fulfill a meager need and occupy barren lands and forests, both have been openly accessed and poorly managed and thus have been underestimated. Therefore, the decline of traditional ways of life and decreased use of wild edible plants are interlinked.

Also, in recent years the vegetation is under extreme stress due to climate change and of the several natural processes of evolution along with human activities at gigantic scale are responsible to the degradation of quality and quantity of plant life and communities in the Western Himalaya. Some opportunist plants like Lantana camara, Ageratum conyzoides, Eupatorium adenophorum and Parthenium hysterophorus have been found to have very rapidly replacing the native plants in the region. Furthermore, the situation has been worsened by plantation of trees such as Pinus roxburghii and Eucalyptus especially by Forest Department Govt. of Himachal Pradesh and people for quick gains which has caused more damage to the already deteriorated situation. Moreover, the native plants are innately resistant and adaptive to micro climatic changes such as low rainfall, high temperature etc., especially in comparison to exotic plant species. Therefore, preserving this very valuable traditional knowledge is very important before it is lost forever, moreover as an academicians also, it becomes our social responsibility to preserve and conserve it for our future generation. Photographs of some wild plants have been shown in Fig. 2. Let's put our hand and head together, so that

227

collectively we can make a world of difference. The documentation of the traditional knowledge through ethnobotanical studies is very important for the conservation and utilization of biological resources (Muthu et al., 2006).

References

1. Bhandari, P. R., 2014. Curry leaf (Murraya koenigii) or Cure leaf: Review of its curative properties. Journal of Medical Nutrition and Nutraceuticals, Vol 1 : 92-97.
2. Chauhan N. S. 1999. Medicinal and Aromatic Plants of Himachal Pradesh. Indus Publishing Company, New Delhi, India.
3. Chauhan, N. S. 1988. Ethnobotanical study of medicinal plants of Himachal Pradesh, In: Indigenous Medicinal Plants: Today & Tomorrow, edited by Kaushik P, Printers & Publishers, New Delhi: 187-198.
4. Chevallier, A. 1996. The encyclopedia of medicinal plants. Darling Kindersley, London, UK.
5. Chowdhery, H. J. and Wadhwa, B. M. 1984. Flora of Himachal Pradesh, Vol 1-3, Botanical Survey of India, Calcutta. 860 pages.
6. Collett, H. 1921. Flora Simlensis: A handbook of flowering plants of Shimla and the neighborhood. Thacker, Spink & Co. London.652 pages.
7. Das, T., Bhushan S., Mishra, Saha, D. and Agarwal, S., 2012. Ethnobotanical Survey of Medicinal Plants Used by Ethnic and Rural People in Eastern Sikkim Himalayan Region. African Journal of Basic & Applied Sciences 4 (1): 16-20.
8. Gaur, R. D. 1999. Flora of the District Garhwal Northwest Himalaya (With Ethnobotanical Notes) Transmedia Srinagar Garhwal, India. 811 pages.
9. Gupta P, Nahata A, Dixit V. K., 2011. An update on Murraya koenigii spreng: A multifunctional Ayurvedic herb. Zhong Xi Yi Jie He Xue Bao, 9:824-33.
10. Khare, C.P. 2007. Indian Medicinal Plants: An Illustrated Dictionary. 709 pages
11. Kirtikar, K.R. and Basu, B.D. 1918. Indian medicinal plants part II. Allahabad: Indian Press: 930-931.
12. Kumar, S. 2000. Revised working Plan for the Dharmshala Forest Division. Department of Forest Govt. of Himachal Pradesh. 349-356.

13. Muthu C, Ayyanar M, Raja N, Ignacimuthu S. 2006. Medicinal plants used by traditional healers in Kancheepuram District of Tamil Nadu, India. Journal of Ethnobiol. Ethnomed 2:43.

14. Nadkarni, K. M. 1988 . The Indian Materia Medica. Columbia, MO: South Asia Books: 624-25.

15. Polunin, O. and Stainton, A. 1997. Flowers of the Himalaya. Oxford University Press, New Delhi. 740 pages.

16. Rana, R. S. and Sood K. K., 2012.Effect of cutting diameter and hormonal application on the propagation of Ficus roxburghii through branch cuttings. Annals of Forest Research 55(1): 69-84.

17. Rani Savita, Rana J. C. and Rana P. K. 2013. Ethno medicinal plants of Chamba district, Himachal Pradesh, India. Journal of Medical Plants Research: 3151-3161.

18. Robert J. Northrop, Michael G. Andreu, Melissa H. Friedman, Mary McKenzie, and Heather V. Quintana, 2010. Phoenix sylvestris, Wild Date Palm in one of a series of the School of Forest Resources and Conservation, Florida Cooperative Extension Service, Institute of Food and Agricultural Sciences, University of Florida. University of Florida, IFAS extension 246: 1-2.

19. Satyavati, G.V., Raina, M. K. and Sharama, M. 1976. Medicinal plants of India. Vol. 1. New Delhi: Indian Council of Medical Research: 112-18.

20. Singh, M.P. 1996. Revised working Plan of Dharmshala & Part Dehra Vol-I. Department of Forest Govt. of Himachal Pradesh, 31-37.

21. Singh, S. K. and Rawat, G. S. 2000. Flora of Great Himalayan National Park, Himachal Pradesh, (Bishen Singh Mahendra Pal Singh, Dehradun).

22. Thapliyal, J. 2009. Fish in troubled waters. The Tribune, Chandigarh India.

23. Verma S. M., Ramchandran, P. and Verma R. K., 2001. Phtochemical characterization and anti-microbial activity of vitex negundu leaves. Ancient science Life. 21(2): 96–98.

Chapter-XVII

Environmental Legislations and Practical Disorientations

Vibhav Mishra*

Abstract

After increasing international pressure caused by the Stockholm resulting in the International Obligation to enact environment related laws, The Water (Prevention & Control of Pollution) Act, 1974 was enacted, which came as the first environmental legislation of free India. Followed by it, several legislations were enacted for protection of other wings of environment, but nothing positive is achieved, though to a little extent, only situations somehow got a bit regulated. But, on the practical examples, if deplorable state of Ganga, Yamuna and other rivers are observed, noise in the metropolitan cities, increasing deforestation, decreasing air quality throughout, increasing chemical imbalances in soils, loss of flora and fauna are observed, we are not gaining but loosing, by just filling the statute books by 'n' number of enactments and spending millions on dreamy implementation by appointing commissions on commissions, panels on panels and just waiting and watching whether actually anything could really happen. Sustainable Development is becoming 'utopian development'. The practical thing which actually is happening is that, there is a disorientation regarding the environmental legislations due to lack of general accountability , proper enforcement mechanism and faulty environmental impact assessment sometimes grounded on the ill considerations or undue influences of any nature.

Keywords: Deforestation, Enforcement Mechanism, Environmental Impact Assessment, Sustainable Development, Utopian Development

*B.A. LL.B. (Hons.) 5th Year- Five Year Integrated Law Course, Faculty of Law, University of Allahabad, Uttar Pradesh, India

Introduction

In the age of post modernism where only economy has its say, the materialistic tendencies such as industrial growth and rapid urbanization are a serious threat for environment. As a consequence, water pollution, soil erosion, land degradation, deforestation etc. are continuously applying brakes over development henceforth worsening the economic development of agrarian India, while the rapid industrialization and urbanization in India is causing serious environmental problems in cities. If all such activities of economic liberalization and increased urbanization are being carried out at the same rate, with the same overlooking of the environment, the damage to environment and health could be enormous. The challenge, therefore, is to maintain the quality of air, water and the land and protect the environment by reconciling environmental, social and economic imperatives.

For the protection of environment, the real concern started after the Stockholm conference. The Water (Prevention and Control of Pollution) Act, 1974 was enacted and similarly The Air (Prevention and Control of Pollution) Act, 1981 was enacted. After both these enactments an umbrella legislation the Environment (Protection) Act was enacted in 1986 to check those corners which were not covered by specific legislations. But it is pertinent to note that vide section 24 sub-section 2 of the EPA, 1986 the specific legislations shall have overriding effect over itself. Also, the concept of sustainable development is being followed by the industries or commercial setups on papers only with complete overlooking to the consequences of it over the future generations. The theme of Inter- Generational Equity, though secured a good pace in late 1980s, but is being now followed in the text books and the prescribed forms which are deposited to PCBs for consent to run the setup.

The paper apart from analysing the legal framework existing in India relating to environment, the judicial trends etc. also enumerate various disorientations existing in the present legal system and possible solutions thereof, for averting the damage which is being caused by such disorientation.

232

Legal Frameworks within India: Constitutional Scheme Relating To Environment

First express provision with respect to environment under the constitutional setup is Art. 48A and thereafter Art.51-A (g). Though first express provision in the constitution was made by The 42nd Constitution Amendment Act of 1976, but it shall be pertinent to discuss the constitutional framework also because of its being the grand-norm of the nation.

The Constitution provides for a federal structure within the framework of parliamentary form of government. Part XI of the Constitution lays down legislative and administrative relations between the centre and states. Article 246 system, viz, The Union List, State List and the Concurrent List. Therefore in critical perusal of the 3- list system, the jurisdictional extent as to subject matters are herein mentioned as under: provides for the jurisdictional extent of the federal separation with three lists

The Union List

Entry No.	Subject Matter	Entry No.	Subject Matter
6	Atomic energy and mineral resources necessary for its production	52	Industries, the control of which by the Union is declared by Parliament by law to be expedient in the public interest
24	Shipping and navigation on inland waterways	53	Regulation and development of oil fields and mineral oil resources
	Maritime shipping and navigation, including shipping and navigation on tidal waters	54	Regulation of mines and mineral development to the extent to which such regulation and development under the control of the Union is declared by Parliament by law to be expedient in the public interest
29	Airways, regulation and organisations of air traffic and of aerodromes	56	Regulation and development of inter-state rivers and river valleys
		57	Fishing and fisheries beyond territorial waters

233

The State List

Entry No.	Subject Matter
6	Public health and sanitation, hospitals and dispensaries
10	Burials and burial grounds, cremations and cremation grounds
14	Agriculture
15	Preservation, protection and improvement of stock and prevention of animal diseases
17	Water, that is to stay, water supplies, irrigation and canals, drainage and embankment, water storage and water power subject to the provisions of Entry 56 of Union List.
18	Land
21	Fisheries

The Concurrent List

Under the Concurrent List, both Parliament and State legislatures are empowered to legislate, subject to certain conditions. Article 248 empowers the centre to legislate upon any of the subject matters not covered under any of the three lists of seventh Schedule to the Constitution.1 This also makes a departure of Indian constitution with other federal constitutions of the world, with special reference to USA. Article 253 empowers the Parliament 'to make any law for the whole or any part of the territory of India for implementing any treaty, agreement or convention with any other country or countries or any decision made at any international conference, association or other body'. These provisions of the Constitution of India give a dominant role for the central government on matters relating to environmental

---

[1] Art. 248: Residuary powers of legislation.—(1) Parliament has exclusive power to make any law with respect to any matter not enumerated in the Concurrent List or State List.
(2) Such power shall include the power of making any law imposing a tax not mentioned in either of those Lists.

protection and giving effect to any environmental obligation undertaken.

Statutory Efforts Regarding Environmental Protection

Though the constitutional efforts have been made after Stockholm Conference, but statutory efforts are days old in India. Statutory efforts can be classified under 3 heads:

- Pre- Constitutional Efforts
- Post Constitutional Efforts (up to Stockholm)
- Post Constitutional Efforts (From Stockholm to now)

Year	Environmental Regulations
1860	Some provisions of Indian Penal Code
1927	Indian Forest Act
1948	The Factories Act
1956	The River Boards Act
1957	The Mines and Minerals (Regulation and Development) Act
1962	The Atomic Energy Act
1968	The Insecticides Act
1972	The Wildlife (Protection) Act
1974	The Water (Prevention And Control Of Pollution) Act, 1974
1974	Water (Prevention & Control of Pollution Act) Amendments, 1988
1975	The Water (Prevention & Control of Pollution) Rules
1977	The Water (Prevention & Control of Pollution) Cess Act
1978	The Water (Prevention & Control of Pollution) Cess Rules
1980	Forest (Conservation) Act
1981	The Air (Prevention & Control Of Pollution) Act, 1981
1981	The Air (Prevention & Control of Pollution) Act, Amendments, 1987
1982/ 1983	The Air (Prevention & Control of Pollution) Rules
1986	The Environment (Protection) Act. Amendments (1989,1990,1993,1996,1997,1998,1999,2000,2001)
1986	The Environmental (Protection) Rules
1992	E (P) Act Notification – "Environment Statement"

235

1994	E (P) Act Notification – "Environmental Clearance"
1997	Amendments in the Environment Clearance, Notification – "Public Hearing" made mandatory
1989	The Hazardous Wastes (Management and Handling) Rules, Amendments, 2000, Draft Amendments 2002
1989	Manufacture, Storage and Import of Hazardous Chemical Rules, Amendments, 1994, 2000
1991	The Public Liability Insurance Act/Rules, 1992
1995	The National Environment Tribunal Act
1997	Prohibition on the Handling of Azo dyes
1997	The National Environment Appellate Authority Act
1998	The Bio-Medical Waste (M&H), Rules
1999	Notification for making 100% Utilization of Fly-ash made mandatory
2000	Municipal Solid Waste (M&H) Rules
2000	Ozone Depleting Substance (R&C) Rules
1999	Regulation on recycling of Waste Oil and Non-ferrous scrape
2000	Noise Pollution (Regulations and Control)
2001	Batteries (M&H) Rules
2010	National Green Tribunal Act

Brief Introduction of Legislative Efforts

Out of the various statutes as mentioned above and the constitutional scheme as provided, the most important is the discussion over specific legislations for water, air and the umbrella legislation viz. the Environment (Protection) Act, 1986 The following is the brief introduction for the legislations enacted for air and water respectively.

Water

The Water (Prevention and Control of Pollution) Act, 1974 is the primary legislation regarding water pollution. It empowers access to the State Pollution Control Boards (in short SPCB) for taking samples, entry of SPCB to ascertain that the provisions of the Act are being compiled with, providing information to the SPCB. It also outlines for the various responsibilities casted upon the person establishing any setup. It enumerates as: Pay Water Cess as indicated in the assessment order, Obtain "Consent to Establish", Obtain "Consent to Operate"

236

Out of the various responsibilities casted upon the state pollution control boards, there are also responsibilities casted upon the operators, out of which, the following are the major ones:

Apply for renewal of the "Consent to Operate" before the expiry of validity period Consent to be deemed as granted automatically and unconditionally after four months from the date of application already given or refused before this period Refusal of "Consent" to be recorded in writing Affix water meters of the prescribed standards Provide access to SPCB Pay interest in case of delay in paying the Water Cess Pay penalty for non-payment of Cess Industry is entitled to 25% rebate if meeting certain conditions.

Air

The Air (Prevention and Control of Pollution) Act, 1981 was also enacted to carry out the international obligations incurred by the Government of India at the Stockholm conference in the year 1972. It also casts responsibility to the State Pollution Control Board for the protection and prevention of environment in a very similar manner to that of the water prevention and control of pollution act, 1972. SPCBs give "Consent to Establish", "Consent to Operate".

Out of the various responsibilities casted upon the state pollution control boards, there are also responsibilities casted upon the operators, out of which, the following are the major ones:

- Comply with the conditions in the "Consent to Establish" or "Consent to Operate"
- Not to discharge air pollutant (s) in excess of the prescribed standards
- Furnish information to the SPCB of any accident or unforeseen act or event
- Allow entry to the SPCB to ascertain that provisions of the Act are being complied with
- Provide information to enable SPCB to implement the Act
- Provide access to the SPCB for taking samples
- Comply with the directions issued in writing by the SPCB
- Obtain Apply for the renewal of "Consent to Operate" before expiry of the validity period
- Industry to ensure that specified emission sampling procedure is being followed by the SPCB

237

The Environment Protection Act, 1986

The key features of Environment Protection Act, 1986 are as under:

Setup to comply with the directions issued by the Central Government. The direction may include:

- closure, prohibition or regulation of any industry, or
- stoppage or regulation of the supply of electricity, water or any other service
- Prevent discharges or emissions excess of the prescribed standards
- Furnish information of any accidental or unforeseen event
- Allow entry and inspection to ascertain compliance
- Allow samples to be taken
- Submit an "Environmental Statement" every year before 30th September to the SPCB
- Obtain prior "Environmental Clearances" from Ministry of Environment and Forests (in short MoEF)

In case of a new project or for modernization/expansion of the existing project. The 186th Report of Law Commission of India recommended for the establishment of "Environmental Tribunals" with exclusive jurisdiction with regard to environmental cases. The report stated that environment courts must be established to reduce the pressure and burden on the High Court and the Supreme Court. Such environmental tribunals would exercise all powers of a civil court in its original jurisdiction. Therefore in adherence to the recommendation of the Law Commission, The National Green Tribunal (in short NGT) has been established on 18.10.2010 under the National Green Tribunal Act, 2010 for effective and expeditious disposal of cases relating to environmental protection and conservation of forests and other natural resources including enforcement of any legal right relating to environment and giving relief and compensation for damages to persons and property and for matters connected therewith or incidental thereto. It is a specialized body equipped with the necessary expertise to handle environmental disputes involving multi-disciplinary issues. The Tribunal shall not be bound by the procedure laid down under the Code of Civil Procedure, 1908, but shall be guided by principles of natural justice.

The Tribunal's dedicated jurisdiction in environmental matters shall provide speedy environmental justice and help to reduce the burden of litigation in the higher courts. The Tribunal is mandated to make and endeavor for disposal of applications or appeals finally within 6 months of filing of the same. Initially, the NGT is proposed to be set up at five places of sittings and will follow circuit procedure for making itself more accessible. New Delhi is the Principal Place of Sitting of the Tribunal and Bhopal, Pune, Kolkata and Chennai shall be the other four place of sitting of the Tribunal. It is worth mention here that by Feb. 28, 2013, out of 644 cases filed in the tribunal, 378 have been disposed off.[2]

Indian Law, Judiciary and International Scenario

It was believed that Indian legal framework was not open for international scenario with immediate effect because international treaties and obligations can only be adopted through Art. 253 of the Construction of India via legislative means, but, judiciary has overdone this concept by invoking Art. 32 and 226 of the Constitution of India and assumed in itself the power to enforce the international obligations via guidelines laid down in judicial pronouncements. Through "judicial activism" the Indian judiciary has played a proactive role in implementing India's international obligations under International treaties, especially in the field of human rights and environmental law. India follows the dualist theory for the implementation of international law at domestic level. 3 Judiciary, though not empowered to make legislations, is free to interpret India's obligations under international law into the municipal laws of the country in pronouncing its decision in a case concerning issues of international law.4 In Vishaka v. State of Rajasthan5, the court said, "…Any international convention not

---

[2] Report to the People, 2012-2013, Government of the United Progressive Alliance.
[3] Jolly George Vs. Bank of Cochin, AIR 1980 SC 470:- Implementation Of International Law In India: Role Of Judiciary- Dr. Sunil Kumar Agarwal
[4] Relying upon the Article 51, Sikri, C.J. in Kesavananda Bharathi vs. State of Kerala, (1973) Supp. SCR 1,observed as under:
> "It seems to me that, in view of Article 51 of the directive principles, this Court must interpret language of the Constitution, if not intractable, which is after all a intractable law, in the light of the United Nations Charter and the solemn declaration subscribed to by India."
[5] AIR 1997 SC 3011

239

inconsistent with the fundamental rights and in harmony with its spirit must be read into those provisions to enlarge the meaning and content thereof, to promote the object of the Constitutional guarantee." The origin of this tendency, relating to environment, may be seen in cases such as in Vardhichand 6, Olga Tellis7, R.L.E.K8. and Vellore.9

International law as a rule signifies the law of nations that states feel themselves bound to observe. In simple understanding, and international environmental law comprises of those substantive, procedural and institutional rules of international law which have as your primary objective the protection of environment.

The principles of Indian environmental laws are amalgamation in the judicial interpretation and the Constitution encompassing several intentionally recognized principles, thereby providing some semblance of consistency between domestic and global environmental standards.10 As stated above, the reason for judicial intervention in legislative area is firstly because of the constitutional setup we have and secondly, but more pertinently, because of overburdened legislature. The ratification or enactment of environmental statues in India, without real commitment to implement the same by the executive, has resulted into judicial interventions and activism in the field of environmental law. It is pertinent to point out that in India such ratification or enactment has often been done either without necessary national preparation or under compulsion to conform to the conditionalities of international financial institutions like World Bank.11 The Stockholm Declaration, 1972 and the Rio Declaration, 1992 have been considered milestones in the development of international environmental law. Though these two declarations have often been characterized as 'soft' law but their impacts both at international and domestic levels, have been profound.12

---

[6] AIR 1980 SC 1622

[7] AIR 1986 SC 180

[8] [1986] RD-SC 272

[9] (1996) 5 SCC 647

[10] Mumbai Kamgar Sabha v. Abdulbhai, AIR 1976 SC 1455

[11] M.K. Ramesh, 'Environmental Justice Delivery in India: In Context', Indian Journal of Environmental Law, December 2002, 9 at 12.

[12] Principles of International Environmental Law and Judicial Response in India: Dr. Shailendra Kumar Gupta, Sr. Lecturer, Faculty of Law, B.H.U., Varanasi, India

Though it was difficult, but its not so that India has not adopted any international convention or treaty filling all procedural requirements. Following is a small list of enactments enacted in the light of international obligations and treaties:

Sr. No.	International Environmental Laws	Relevant Indian Environmental Statutes
1.	The Stockholm Conference, 1972	The Air Act, 1981
2.	The Stockholm Conference, 1972	The Environmental Protection Act, 1986
3.	The Rio Conference, 1992	The Public Liability Insurance Act, 1991
4.	The Rio Conference, 1992	The National Environmental Tribunal Act, 1995
5.	Convention of Biological Diversity, 1992.	The Biological Diversity Act, 2002
6.	Convention of International Trade in Endangered Species of Wild Fauna and Flora, 1973.	The Wild Life Protection (Amendment) Act, 2002

The role of the Indian Supreme Court may be explained quoting views of Prof. S.P. Sathe and Prof. Upendra Baxi, two leading academics who have extensively written on the role of judiciary in India. Prof. Sathe has analyzed the transformation of the Indian Supreme Court "from a positivist court into an activist court". Prof. Upendra Baxi, who has often supported the judicial activism in India, has also said that the "Supreme Court of India" has often become "Supreme Court for Indians".13 Many observers of the Indian Supreme Court including Professor Sathe and Baxi have rightly opined that the Indian Supreme Court is one of the strongest courts of the world.14

---

[13] Upendra Baxi, 'The Avatars of Indian Judicial Activitism: Explorations in the Geography of (In) justice', in S.K. Verma and Kusum (eds.), Fifty Years of the Supreme Court of India : It's Grasp and Reach (Delhi, Oxford University Press, 2000) pp. 156-209 at 157.
[14] S.P. Sathe, Judicial Activism in India (New Delhi, Oxford University Press, 2000). See, 'Preface' of this work written by Prof. Upendra Baxi, pp. ix-xxi.

As said by Justice Oliver Wendell Holmes of United States Supreme Court, law is not which is written in the law books, rather it is what the judge says. Therefore it shall be of utmost necessity to discuss the judicial approach as regards to environment for Indian context. But law is not a static concept, rather it is of flux. Therefore judicial approach cannot be scrutinised in one go, the proper approach would be, bifurcations of the judicial approach in relation to the changing judicial trends and times. The following is the critical division of the judicial approaches as derived:

1) Phase- I (1950 to 1984)

2) Phase-II (1985 to 1995)

3) Phase-III (1996 onwards)

Phase- I

Indian litigation system is an adversarial one. His dogmatic spouse of adversarial litigation system has also affected the environmental litigation regime. From 1950 to 1984 Indian courts have adopted a traditional dualist approach that treaties have no effect unless specifically incorporated into domestic law by legislation. This was done by Indian courts due to strict and literal interpretation of the Constitution and believing that international law cannot be suo motto be the part of domestic law. In Jolly George Verghese v. Bank of Cochin15 the Supreme Court upheld the traditional dualist approach and gave overriding effect to the Civil Procedure Code over International Covenant on Civil and Political Rights. However, the court in this case, minimizes the conflict between the Covenant and domestic statue by narrowly interpreting the Civil Procedure Code. During this regime there was hardly any legislative exercise in the name of customary international law.

Phase- II

In India, the post Bhopal Gas Tragedy (1984) era was a creative period for environmental jurisprudence. Phase 2 started after Gramophone Company's case.16 In this case the court relied upon the English

---

15 (1980) 2 SCJ 358.
16 Gramophone Company Of India Ltd vs Birendra Bahadur Pandey & Ors., 1984 SCR (2) 664

decisions and endorsed the doctrine of incorporation. According to this doctrine rules of international law are incorporated into national law and considered to be part of national law unless they are in conflict with an Act of the parliament. Supreme Court in Doon Valley case17, dealt with the impact of mining in the Doon Valley region and through its orders impliedly generated a new fundamental "right of the people to live in healthy environment with minimal disturbance of ecological balance."18 In this case there were series of orders and in one of its orders the court recognized the influence of the Stockholm Conference by accepting that this "conference and the follow-up action thereafter is spreading the awareness".19 Considering this problem of overburdened legislature Supreme Court evolved the principle that by providing the guidelines it shall make into force the international obligations incurred by the Government of India. During this period, court began to interpret not only other provisions of the Constitution but also Directive Principles of State Policy in light of Article 21.20 The courts have invoked Article 48-A (duty of the state to protect environment) to develop a fundamental right to environment as part of the right to life under Article 21.21 In Calcutta Wetland Case22 the Calcutta High Court stated that India being a party to the Ramsar Convention on Wetland, 1971, is bound to promote conservation of wetlands. Again, in Kanpur Tanneries Case23 the Supreme Court extensively quoted the Stockholm Declarations and strengthened the

---

[17] R.L.E.K. Dehradun, v. State of U.P. AIR 1985 SC 652. Three judges bench order of March 12, 1985
[18] *Ibid,* 656 (Para 12).
[19] AIR 1987 SC 359, 363 (Para 19) order of Dec. 18, 1986.
[20] See Vishaka v. State Of Rajasthan & Ors, (1997) 6 SCC 253; M. C. Mehta v. Union of India, 1987 SCR (1) 819.
[21] In several leading cases the Indian courts have been guided and inspired by Article 48-A and developed a general fundamental right to environment under Article 21. See, M.C. Mehta v. Union of India (Kanpur Tanneries Matter) AIR 1988 SC 1037 at 1038; Rural Litigation and Entitlement Kendra v. State of U.P. AIR 1988 SC 2187 at 2199: Kinkari Devi v. State of H.P., AIR 1988 4 at 8; Bichhri Village Case, AIR 1996 SC 1446 at 1459, Sachindanda Pandey, v. State of W.B,. AIR 1987 SC 1109 at 1114-1115; T. Damodar Rao v. Municipal Corp., Hyderabad,, AIR 1987 A.P. 171 at 181 etc.
[22] People United for Better Living in Calcutta v. State of W.B., AIR 1993 Cal. 215.
[23] M.C. Mehta, v. Union of India, AIR 1988 SC 1037. See Para 4 (pp. 1038-1040) for detailed discussion of Stockholm Declarations by Justice Venkataramiah.

environmental fundamental rights and environmental jurisprudence in India, giving preference to 'environment' over 'employment' and 'revenue generation'. During this period the Rio Declarations, 1992 was also cited in the Law Society of India case.24

In nutshell, it may be stated that a field was being prepared during this era by judiciary for proper application and implementation of environmental thought and jurisprudence in practical fields. Whatever the field by judicial activism was prepared by court of records, its reflection is seen in the third phase starting from 1995.

Phase - III

The pitch was being prepared in Phase -II and practical application of that field began in Phase- III. It was the Vellore case25 from which the phase begins. India was moving forward and entering into many international obligations. It was the high time and the millennium was going to end the green Judge Mr. Justice Kuldeep Singh in his leadership established well settled principle under environmental jurisprudence. The Court in this case had considered Stockholm Conference 1972, Burndtland Commission Report, 1987, Caring of the Earth Report, 1991, Rio Conference, 1992, Convention on Climate Change, 1992, Convention on Biological Diversity, 1992 and Agenda - 21 (A programme of Action for Twenty-first Century) and many other relevant important environmental principles.

Disorientations

The current corpus of environmental law in India and its application thereof suffers multiple disability. The Environment (Protection) Act, 1986, for instance, was designed as an umbrella legislation to deal with the general environmental positions and to deal with every conceivable aspect of environment but has remained a law relating to problem of pollution. There has been a persistent lack of vision regarding environmental problems, either it may be at the stage of policy framework or the quality environmental impact assessment. It is not that environment was not in issue in India, but it has been subjected to adversarial litigation system prevailing from years in India. The

---

[24] Law Society of India v. Fertilizer & Chemical Travancore Ltd. AIR 1994 Ker. 308.
[25] (1996) 5 SCC 647

approach adopted by pollution control bodies are somewhat as "command and control" where law exhibits of preventive rather proactive role. The command includes laying down of standards and pollution limits, while the control includes the power to withdraw water or power supply of erring units, the imposition of penalties and fines, or even insignificant duration of imprisonment.

Here disorientation not only refers to the inadequacy of the laws regarding harsh penal provisions but also refers to mismanagement relating to laws. From the years altogether, a lot of money is being spent on the name of environmental protection, but nothing much has been achieved. The statement is not arising out of any personal experience or undue criticism of the opposition over the governmental policies but government itself in many reports of its own has stated the failure, though not in words but through the statistics.

Also, problem which is generally encountered is in the compliance, monitoring and enforcement done by the state pollution control boards. These boards carry out various activities such as sampling, inspection of facilities, impose corrective actions, issue and relocation of consent to operate etc. There is a difference in the enforcement mechanism as laid down under the Water Act, Air Act and the Environmental Protection Act. Where both the Water and Air Act provides for lesser penalties in case of violation of the rules mentioned there under, EPA provides for the steeper punishment. The problem arises because of section 24(2) of the EPA which excludes the liability under the EPA when there is a confrontation between The Water Act, The Air Act and in itself and lays down, in that case, the respective special legislation would apply, which means, specific legislation would prevail over the general one. This is a situation, when because of confrontation between two statutes such statute is given preference which has lesser penalty and that too in cases of such an important subject matter.26 Moreover, it has been observed that there is a vast difference in the conviction rate regarding the cases related to environmental pollution among various states.

According to the U.S. EPA (2005), there were 1551 initially non-complying facilities, of which 1351 facilities complied with SPCB orders for the check and regulation of drain generated pollution and 178 were shut down, with 22 units defaulting. This actually shows a

---

26 S. 24(2) of Environment (Protection) Act, 1986.

negative compliance trend in large industry in India in recent decade. In addition, the real compliance rates are likely to be lower, since inspections usually do not evaluate compliance with all environmental requirements (e.g., stack tests are rarely conducted to check air emissions for compliance). The situation with small and medium-sized enterprises (SMEs) is much worse. According to the MOEF, SMEs account for 40 percent of industrial production employ limited pollution control technologies and are responsible for an estimated 70 percent of the total industrial pollution load nationwide.27

Another problem which is of great concern is that of inadequacy of the technical staff and the man force employed in the pollution control boards, either at the Central or the state level. Due to this inadequacy of manpower many technical works and the quality suffer. Due to the absence of qualified technical staff, the work is entrusted upon the non-qualified one which degrades the quality. This also becomes one of the pertinent reasons why most of the serious treatment plants are functioning in either poor or very poor condition. The sanctioned staff strength in CPCB as in 2012 was over all 603. In the scientist Cadre itself many vacancies were ad hoc filled and out of 603 total vacancies under CPCB, 79 were either not filled or were quashed and 62 were filled ad hoc. After the notification of CPCB regulations out of 66 posts as approved by CPCB, 39 vacancies were unfilled and 8 were filled ad hoc. Due to the absence of technical staff the other problem which is faced is that of overburdened employees. Every year the annual report is required to be prepared and for that, the collection of data is necessary. For this, the inspections are carried out in a haphazard manner sometimes complying and many a times there is noncompliance of strict inspections. The infrastructural incompetence also plays a significant role. Because of the absence of laboratories and proper machineries for the testing of samples, it is many times referred to either other state laboratory or to a private body, which causes unnecessary expenditure.

Also, there is an old saying "one bad general is better than two good generals". State Pollution Control Boards are responsible to Central Pollution Control Board because it is an umbrella body. On the other hand, SPCBs receives some of its fund from state government, but are

---

27 Environmental Compliance and Enforcement in India: Rapid Assessment, *presented at the AECEN annual forum in Hanoi, Vietnam on 4-5 December 2006.*

technically dependent on state government for the functioning. Now, there emerges a problematic situation because each and every state has its own perspective relating to environment (because of various regional political parties in existence and also due to other regional circumstances). The functioning of the State Pollution Control Boards is dominated over by the political whims of the ruling party. The situation becomes worse when the regional party is in opposition to the party at centre. Practically what happens is that in order to criticise Central Government and the realise the selfish political aims the tasks entrusted upon State Pollution Control Boards are overlooked and the blame is put on Central Government either on the name of inadequacy of fund or improper management. Also, amongst different State Pollution Control Boards there lacks proper coordination in between them. The thought of subjecting State Pollution Control Boards under a State Governments was theoretically a good one because of the administrative convenience, but practically a bad one because of the existence of multi-party system in India. Therefore State Pollution Control Boards should be subjected all in all to the Central Pollution Control Board for better results.

The other biggest problem which we all see is at district level. The municipal authorities are reluctant over the disposal of wastes and it is being thrown on the side of the roads open, untreated and ready for causing infections. There is legislation for water, for air and overall an umbrella legislation named Environment Protection Act. Although there is a legislation for the disposal of the hazardous waste, but this too is under criticism because of the willful neglect of the administrative authorities performing the actions. There emerges a question as to how can there be proper protection of water and air from pollution when the nearby vicinity itself is not clean. In whatsoever number the water and sewage treatment plants are established, the water which falls on the road will ultimately either falls into river or a nearby pond or field. If either biological or non-biological wastes are present on the roads, or they are dumped by the municipal authorities without getting it treated and separated in accordance to their nature, it will ultimately contaminate the river or at whatsoever place it falls. Also such littered waste will cause a blockage to the drainage system resulting in water logging. Even if the perspective of rain is not considered, then too the littered waste of municipal authority will cause foul smell and ultimately cause air pollution.

Water Pollution

Comprehensive report was published by Central pollution control board in the year 2007 which was regarding the analysis of treatment plants. In this report, the observation made by the board was astonishing which laid down that out of 175 identified sewage treatment plants the report only dealt with 84 plants. Surprisingly five states have not submitted even a single data. Uttar Pradesh gave data only for 4 sewage treatment plants out of 23 existing in the prescribed format [28]

The study brought out large number of technological & managerial problems in operation of these 84 STPs of 13 different technologies spread over 9 States of India out of 15 sanctioned. The situation becomes more considerable when the report itself says that total scenario of STPs performance is dismal as 46 STPs have been found poor or very poor. Only 8 STPs have been rated as good would while remaining 30 are was only satisfactory.

Capacity utilization of the STPs observed is in general inadequate. Information on capacity utilization was collected from 55 STPs. Out of 55 STPs only 18 STPs (i.e 33%) were operating at normal flow (90 to 110% design flow) whereas rest 37 (i.e.67%) were either under-loaded or over-loaded. Sludge removal / treatment / handling appears to be the most neglected area in STPs operation.

The following are the extracts from the report of CPCB in 2007 which substantiate the reality:

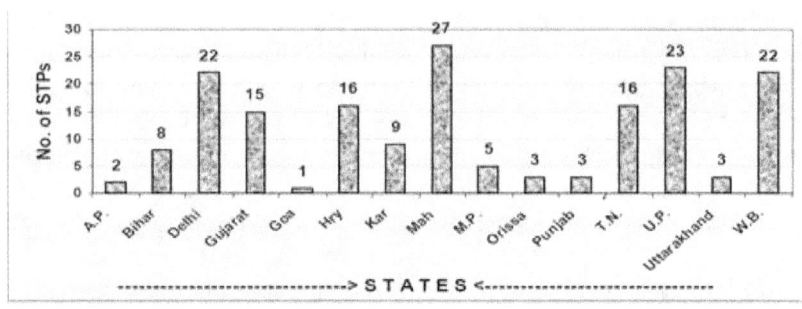

---

[28] Table 3.2 and 3.3, page. 14 & 15: Evaluation Of Operation And Maintenance Of Sewage Treatment Plants In India-2007 : by CPCB- SERIES : CUPS/68/2007

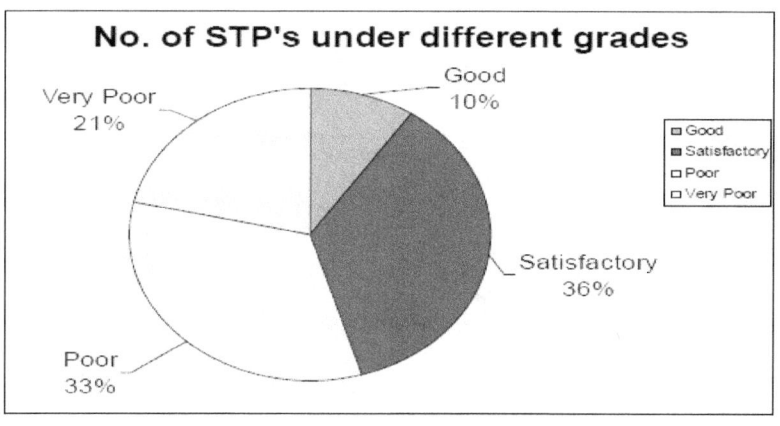

No. of STP's under different grades

Very Poor 21%
Good 10%
Satisfactory 36%
Poor 33%

- Good
- Satisfactory
- Poor
- Very Poor

S. No.	State	Evaluated	Very Good	Good	Satisfactory	Poor	Very Poor
1.	Bihar	4	-	-	-	-	4
2.	Delhi	16	-	-	7	7	2
3.	Goa	1	-	1	-	-	-
4.	Haryana	6	-	1	1	4	-
5.	Maharashtra	13	-	6	5	1	1
6.	Tamil Nadu	5	-	-	3	-	2
7.	Uttar Pradesh	17	-	-	1	9	7
8.	Uttarakhand	2	-	-	1	1	-
9.	West Bengal	8	-	-	3	3	2

In 2013, a new report was published29, which gives the newer data and institutional efforts:

---

[29] Performance Evaluation of Sewage Treatment Plants under NRCD, 2013, CPCB.

(a)

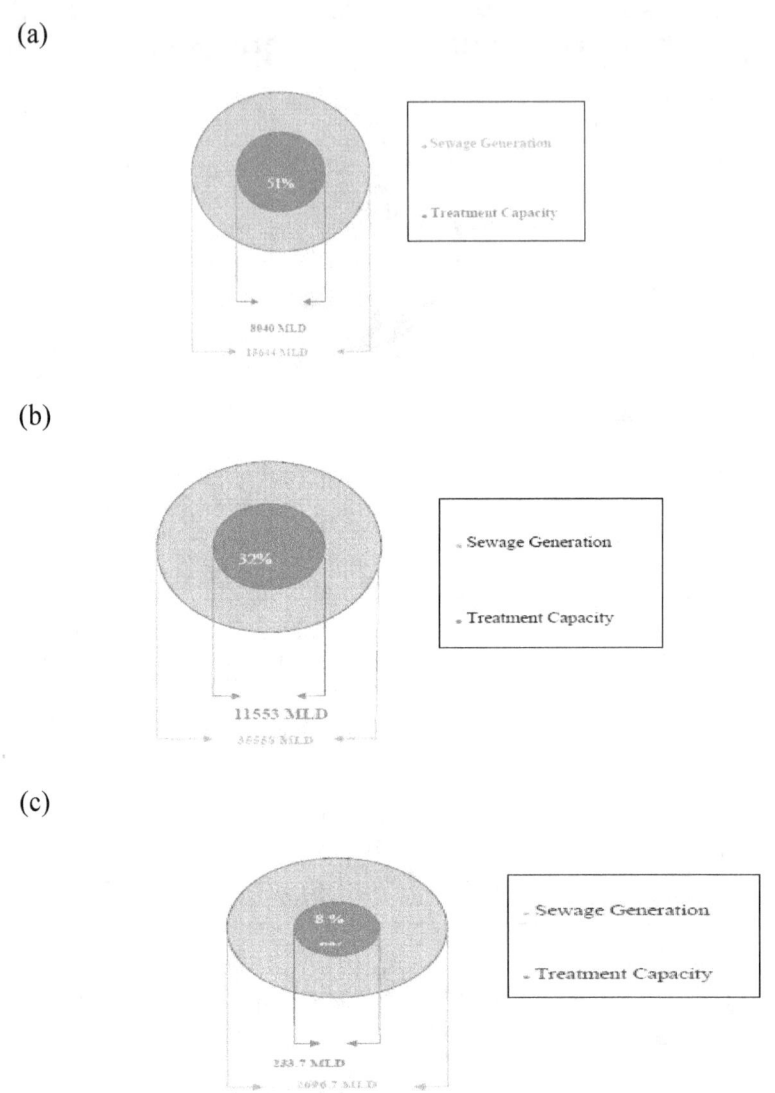

(b)

(c)

Fig. (a) refers to the Sewage generation and treatment capacity in Metropolitan Cities, whereas Fig. (b) refers to Sewage generation and treatment capacity in Class-I Cities and Fig. (c) refers to Sewage generation and treatment capacity in Class-II Towns.

All sewages finally culminate into rivers. If this is the situation of the sewages, how can we infer that there are to be clean rivers. With the perusal of the recent data, it can be said that not much efforts have been entrusted by the competent authorities in relation to the population growth, sewage generation and its treatment. Where in the Metropolitan areas the sewage generation to treatment capacity ratio is 51%, this ratio decreases to 32% in the class I cities and astonishingly 8% for the class II cities. It is to be noted that this is government generated data. The reality may be far beyond it.

India's rivers and streams suffer from high levels of pollution from waste generated primarily from industrial processes and municipal activities. Untreated sewage and non-industrial wastes account for four times as much pollution as industrial effluents. While it is estimated that 75 percent of the wastewater generated is from municipal sources, industrial waste from large and medium-sized plants contributes to over 50 percent of the total pollution loads. In major cities, less than five percent of the total waste is collected and less than 25 percent of this treated. In cases of rivers, where Indus catchment shows little deterioration whereas all major rivers like Ganga, Alaknanda, Mandakini, Bhagirathi, Yamuna, Brahmaputra (inclusive of all its tributaries), Tapi,Mahanadi, Brahmini, Baitarni, Godavari, Krishna(except insofar as pH, faecal coliform and Total Coliform criteria), Cauveri did not meet the water quality. Only few rivers in India had conformed the water quality standards, which are, River Mahi (except at two locations), Narmada mainstream with all its tributaries (meeting all criteria except that of pH at certain locations), River Subarnrekha, River Pennar. Out of all the major rivers of India, only Narmada conforms broadly criteria for beneficial uses.30

Air Pollution

Central Pollution Control Board in association with State Pollution Control Boards established National Ambient Air Quality Monitoring Network in the country. The beginning of ambient air quality monitoring was made in year 1982 initiating monitoring of three criteria pollutants i.e. Suspended Particulate Matter (SPM), Sulphur Dioxide (SO2) and Nitrogen Dioxide (NO2). National Ambient Air Quality Monitoring network was established during year 1984–85 with 9 stations in Agra, Anpara & Delhi and gradually additional stations have been established over the years. The National Ambient Air Quality Standards (NAAQS) notified in 1984 and revised in 1994 wherein three pollutants namely Carbon Monoxide (CO), Lead (Pb),

---

30 Annual Report, CPCB 2011-2012.

and Respirable Suspended Particulate Matter (RSPM/PM10) were added the parameter Ammonia (NH3) was added in year 1996. The NAAQS were revisited and revised in November 2009 including PM10 (Particulate Matter less than 10 micron), PM2.5 (Particulate Matter less than 2.5 micron), SO2 (Sulphur Dioxide), NO2 (Nitrogen Dioxide), CO (Carbon Monoxide), O3 (Ozone), NH3 (Ammonia), Benzene (C6H6), Benz-o-pyrene (BaP), Lead (Pb), Arsenic (As), and Nickel (Ni). The revised Standards have done away with area classification based on land-use so that industrial areas shall also confirm to the same standards as residential areas. The standards are applicable uniformly with the exception of NO2 and SO2 in the Ecologically Sensitive Areas while suspended particulate matter (SPM) as air quality parameter has been replaced with fine particulate matter (PM2.5).The Programme (NAMP) network presently comprises 700 sanctioned manual monitoring stations located in 300 cities/towns and industrial areas across the country out of which 523 manual monitoring stations located in 215 cities/towns and industrial areas across the country are operational.

Air quality data in India's major cities indicate that ambient levels of air pollutants exceed both the World Health Organization and Indian standards, particularly for particulate matter. Of the total air pollution load nationwide, vehicular sources contribute 64 percent, thermal power plants 16 percent, industries 13 percent, and the domestic sector 7 percent. Environmental effects from growing fossil fuel use can only worsen as India seeks to meet the energy needs of its growing economy. It is estimated that over 96 percent of India's total demand for commercial energy is met by fossil fuel with coal contributing 60 percent and petroleum products providing the remaining 36 percent.

Based on the statistics collected under the programme, CPCB in its annual report published the statistics which shows the outcomes of the efforts made. Out of the comprehensive annual report, a chart depicting Air Quality is as follows31:

---

[31] Annual Report, CPCB 2011-2012.

Air Quality in Major Metropolitan Areas

State	City	Total No. of Operating Stations	Annual Average in µg/m³					
			SO_2	Air Quality	NO_2	Air Quality	PM_{10}	SO_2
Andhra Pradesh	Hyderabad	9	5	L	28	M	74*	H
	Visakhapatnam	8	13	L	21	M	80*	H
	Vijayawada	2	6	L	11	L	90*	H
Bihar	Patna	2	4	L	36	M	158*	C
Chandigarh	Chandigarh	5	2	L	16	L	102*	C
Chattisgarh	Raipur	3	15	L	42*	H	310*	C
	Durg-Bhilainagar	4	8	L	22	M	104*	C
Delhi	Delhi	11	6	L	61*	C	222*	C

In most of the cases, the air quality is either subject to high pollution, because in most of the cases the level of Sulphur-di-oxide is at critical. This ultimately results into acid rain and then soil pollution and harm to vegetation. All the above data are the compilations with the help of the data is released by concerned ministry. Since all the above data are the data released by government itself, notwithstanding anything it can be stated that the reality may be far away from what it is actually reflected from the statistics. The real picture of pollution is that seem by a common man in his daily clean of life.

Conclusion and Suggestion

Whatsoever technology may be developed but nothing can replace the natural one. The natural purifier, our trees, are the foremost source of the environmental protection. They are required to be maintained, preserved, and increased the number. The concept of sustainable development viz. synthesizing technology with ecology is being disregarded for the realization of material needs. It is true that the efforts to increase social forestry are at great pace, but the violators are also not getting rid of the stubborn attitude possessed by them.

Although a lot of efforts are being put by the government for making the concept of sustainable development reality, environmental protection whatever today is being done is done under compulsion of law and not under affection. It is a legal thought that in a country if there are various legislations then the social conditions prevailing in that nation's state is not enough civilised and responsible, on the other hand, it is also said that if a nation's state is not having adequate laws then the legal awareness of the nation lags behind. We have enacted various legislations for the protection and prevention of environment, created many administrative authorities for supervision, have spent billions, but, the thing which is of utmost importance is that whether we are able to realise the aim for which we have done all this? In India, it is generally observed that people follow the laws not because the law is the code of conduct emerged after attaining statehood and because of the civilised society, but it is the command of sovereign backed by sanctions. The same attitude is towards environmental protection. The way environment is treated is that it is a public asset and not a private one, making the people or private individual neglectful towards its protection. Environment is not treated as a private property which requires utmost care and protection. The owners of the industrial organisations are set up keep the environmental protection mechanism on the last hand, though it should be the first one because environment is the public property and not of any private individual.

From the aforesaid discussions and after perusal of data released by concerned departments it is suggested that:

- A lot of effort is needed for achieving the minimum prescribed standards for the protection of environment

- The inadequacy of staff, especially the technical one, is needed to be filled with utmost priority for efficiently carrying out of work by the concerned departments.

- The dual line of command should be abolished and State Pollution Control Boards should be made subordinate to Central Pollution Control Board both financially and administratively.

- The penalties as mentioned in The Air Act and The Water Act should be enhanced so that it may create a deterrent effect for the prospective offenders.

- After 2010, National Green Tribunal Act was passed which aimed at the establishment of National Green Tribunals. The number of benches of this tribunal should be increased so that there is speedier disposal of cases.

- Both Central and state government should initiate widespread programs relating to environmental protection we should aim that it is also spread in the most remote corner of the country.

- Law doesn't create impact unless it is set into motion. In India, the worst thing is that Law is only set into motion when there is a personal cause. There is a great lack of administrative accountability in India. This creates a hindrance between the policies framed out by the government and the practical implementation. When for not implementing policies in full go the administration will become accountable, the practical implementation will become efficient and speedier.

Last but not the least, it is the individual himself being the smallest unit of society who should become vigilant for the environmental action and treat environment as personal assets and not a general one. The day when people themselves will become conscious about safeguarding the environment, majority of the task will itself be done.

References

1. Indian Journal of Environmental Law, December 2002
2. Report to the People, 2012-2013, Government of the United Progressive Alliance
3. Environmental Compliance and Enforcement in India: Rapid Assessment, presented at the AECEN annual forum in Hanoi, Vietnam on 4-5 December 2006
4. Evaluation of Operation and Maintenance of Sewage Treatment Plants In India-2007: CPCB, SERIES: CUPS/68/2007
5. Performance Evaluation of Sewage Treatment Plants under NRCD, 2013, CPCB
6. Annual Report, CPCB 2008-2009
7. Annual Report, CPCB 2011-2012
8. Dr. Sunil Kumar Agarwal- "Implementation of International Law in India: Role Of Judiciary"
9. Dr. Shailendra Kumar Gupta, Sr. Lecturer, Faculty of Law, B.H.U., Varanasi, India, "Principles of International
10. Environmental Law and Judicial Response in India" U. Shankar, "Laws and Institutions relating to Environmental Protection in India" Fifty Years of the Supreme Court of India: It's Grasp and Reach (Delhi, Oxford University Press, 2000)
11. S.P. Sathe, Judicial Activism in India, (New Delhi, Oxford University Press, 2000)
12. Ministry of Law and Justice, Legislative Department, "Constitution of India."

Chapter-XVIII

Discourses of Cultural landscape and Water: An understanding of the nexus through the lens of Anthropology in the Ravi valley of Chamba district

Chandan Kaushal & Sarmistha Pattanaik*

Abstract

Cultural landscape provides a historical and ethnographic background describing changing social and spatial arrangements in the region which is both product and producer of the material culture through which human agency is enacted. It can be used to describe important shifts in water ownership, management and use over time. The study focuses on water resource in the Chamba district in general and Ravi valley in specific. The objective has been to relocate the nexus through a cultural lens and to apply it in the understanding of narratives through ethnographic research. Chamba has historically unique relationship with water that is reflected in various artifacts like fountain stone slab, legends of sacrifices, folklore of the region etc. In the past, the local communities were more dependent on 'traditional' sources of water such as springs or 'Panihar' and small streams called "kuhls".

The paper describes that how cultural landscapes in a particular region are shaped by their culture and history. The idea is to describe changing social and spatial arrangement in Chamba region with respect to water resource. The ethnographic study focuses on the water resource how it is perceived, treated and controlled and changes over a period of time. Study conducted in the Ravi valley in Mehla Panchayat shows changes various changes values of water. Usages of 'traditional' resources have declined and preferences for piped water have made resource placeless and scale less.

Keywords- Cultural landscape, water resource, cultural values, ethnography, anthropology

---

*Department of Humanities and Social Sciences, IIT Bombay

Introduction

Cultural landscape is both the producer and product of the material culture through which human agency is enacted [1]. So 'cultural landscapes' can provide a historical and ethnographic background which describes changing social and spatial arrangements in the region. In case of water it can used to describe various important shifts in terms of water ownership, management and use over time. Much can be known about water resource by understanding the meaning assigned to it and by considering the artifacts and technology through which it is contained, controlled, moved around, treated, and made decorative or sacred [2]. From this account of study focuses on the district Chamba in Himachal Pradesh in general and Ravi valley in specific. The purpose of doing ethnographic study is to look the discourse of water from both historical perspective and in the present context how of everyday people interact with their environment in general and water resource in specific. The other aspect in this paper is about water in the context of climate change and vulnerability. Decrease in the availability and usage of 'traditional' sources can be associated with the climatic change, the less dependence of the community on these sources and shifts in the cultural values. Based on these backdrops, the present study is undertaken. The paper is divided into various sections

The first section discusses about the cultural landscape in general and Chamba landscape specifically focusing water resource in Ravi valley. This section describes the value of water in a particular cultural landscape that can be deciphered from artifacts, myths, folklore associated with water. Second section deals with the recent development in the cultural landscape with respect to water resource. Third and last section throws light on the climate change and its impact on water resource.

'Landscapes' are the symbolic environment created by humans by giving environment particular definition and form from a standpoint which is filtered through values and beliefs of people. People transform their natural environment into cultural landscape through the use of different symbols that bestow different meanings on the same physical object. Paper describes Chamba landscape with respect to water resource and how it is being shaped by various symbols [3].

Cultural landscape of Chamba has unique relationship with water that is reflected in of various artifacts like stone slab associated with water, legends of sacrifices, folklore of the region etc. Cultural value attached to the water will be used to understand this unique relationship with water resource. Water resources are harnessed in the locality depending on the availability to fulfill their everyday needs. In the past people depended more on 'traditional' sources for both drinking and for irrigation purpose. This paper tries to understand the values attached to water resource in a particular cultural landscape in historical as well as in the present context and the response of the people towards changes in the environment.

Fieldwork was conducted in Mehla Panchayat in the month of April and May in 2014, a unique place surrounded by water on all sides in the form of river, rivulets and springs. Decrease in the availability and usage of 'Panihar'32and 'kuhl33' can be associated with climatic change, less dependence on them for procuring resources for fulfilling their needs and shifts in the cultural values.

Cultural landscape and Water Resource

Landscape refers both to a way of viewing the environment surrounding us. Landscapes provide the setting for our daily lives whether it is of aesthetic value or not and the concept of landscape recognizes people interaction with the environments so links people to nature [4]. The very notion of landscape is highly cultural but the term 'cultural' has been added to stress on the fact of the human interaction with the environment and the presence of tangible and intangible cultural values in the landscape [ibid].The human geographers define a cultural landscape as "a concrete and characteristic product of the interplay between a given human community, embodying certain cultural preferences and potentials, and a particular set of natural circumstances. It is a heritage of many eras of natural evolution and of many generations of human effort." [4]

Ingold (2000) proposes that engagement with the land and its human and non-human components continuously generates both cultural knowledge and bodily substance. The landscape is thus constituted as

---

32 *Panihar-* it is term generally referred to a spring of water source in the local dialect
33 *Kuhl-* the traditional irrigation system of the region

"an enduring record of – and testimony to – the lives and works of part generations who have dwelt within it and in so doing, have left there something of themselves." Ingold's approach attempts to bridge the "the sterile opposition between the naturalistic view of the landscape as a neutral, external backdrop to human activities and the culturalistic view that every landscape is a particular cognitive or symbolic ordering of space" [5].

There are two frameworks to understand the cultural landscape. The first objective framework of cultural landscape focuses on person in a defined area. The second subjective framework focuses on "imputed meaning" that is how people interact with; perceive or understand their local cultural and natural environment [6]. Objective framework is described from a "scientific standpoint, detailing the geographical, biological, and geological features of the landscape." These data become a crucial part of cultural landscape studies, for changes in these features reflect the tangible interaction of a cultural group with their environment. The meaning of the subjective framework can be understood by references made to landscape perception, the symbolic nature of objects in the landscape, and landscape cognition [6].

From this stand we analyze the discourses in Cultural landscape of Chamba. This landscape is rich with religious associations, rituals, meanings and places associated with mythological and past events, people, and their history of evolution. Chamba is culturally rich area known for its temples, its antiquities and ancient ruling dynasty of Vermans with a well-documented history from circa 500 A.D. Its high mountain ranges have given it a sheltered position and helped in preserving its centuries old relics and numerous inscriptions. In circa 500 A.D. a legendry hero called Maru migrated to north-west from Kalpagrama and founded Brahamputra (Bharmour) in the valley of the Budhil River, 65 kilometer to the east of present Chamba town. For over three hundred years his successors continued to rule over the country from that capital city until Sahil Verman shifted his capital from Brahamputra to Chamba the more centrally located plateau in the lower Ravi Valley [7] There are different opinions about why the town was called Chamba but the popular belief is that Sahil Verman named the town after his beloved daughter Champa [8]. There are various opinions on why capital was shifted to from Bharmour to Chamba [9].

Historically Chamba landscape is one of rare place which escaped from the successive waves of Muslim rule a result of natural mountain barriers [10]. Chamba is part of Himachal Pradesh in the political sense, but the province has had long links with Kashmir to its west and North-west. There is similarity in art, architecture of the region which is the strong evidence of cultural exchange between the two regions. For significant amount of time Chamba was under the control of Kashmir [11].

There are two types of temples in Chamba district: the hill type and the plain type of temples. The Spired or Shikhara style temple dates back to 10th century belongs to plain type of temple shows the strong influence of Vaishnavism culture in the region that came along with the Varman dynasty. The hill type of temple structure which consists of single cell in which image is placed; these temple of Devi and Nag are considered as original cults of hill region [9]. Many temples of Devi and Nag cult are associated with water resource in the landscape.

The typical feature of the Ravi valley is that the most of the habitation is situated in between 50 to 100m above the river level generally on the terraces. Though the rapid flowing water of Ravi through gorges with huge boulders was natural barrier which prevented anyone approach near them and it was not feasible to carry water up for the irrigation where habitats are located [10]. Thus, the early settlers in the region might not have considered Ravi River as a potential source for the daily needs. The existing and some of the spring sources and rivulets were the considered as the main source of water for the all the purposes.

The characteristic feature of Chamba landscape there is particular value that is associated with their natural resource. The concept of natural resource is also an expression of social and cultural structure of a community, it is necessary to understand how human beings are responsible for maintaining or damaging the ecosystem. Since humans are considered as agents responsible for change so there is need to understand their perceptions, ecological understanding and strategies to cope with environmental crisis [12]. Focus of this paper will be on water resource how it gets shaped and shapes cultural landscape.

Characteristic features Chamba landscape is its association with water resource either in the form of snow or in the form of river, rivulets, lakes and spring water. The snow clad mountains fills some of these the lakes and is also the source of perennial rivers flowing throw the district. The other major source of drinking water in the locality is spring water available at the various places which is locally known as 'Nada'[34] or 'Panihar'. The number and distance between the two spring sources can vary from place to place. 'Panihar' may or may not be a natural spring source but some of the designated 'Panihar' is actually water was transported by Kuhl or mud baked pipes to that place. Scholars have made distinction between 'Panihar' and 'naun Panihar' [10]. Some of the respondents make difference between 'nada' which literally means a steak of water falling down but in case of 'Panihar,' it also constitutes a social place where there is proper place for sitting which earlier meeting place for villagers.

Mehla is located 16 kilometer from Chamba on Bharmour road is present in the foot of Dhauladhar range. The name of the place Mehla comes from palace (Mehal) of Jagirdars who were staying at this place. The place is surrounded by water form three sides some of the respondent call it as Sri Lanka of the region. There are two perennial rivulets flowing down along the sides of Mehla, along with Ravi flowing below it. Once flourishing with fruit orchard on one side of the panchayat with famous spring water made this place very famous tourist spot especially during summer season. People usually visited the place during Jalpa mata[35] Jatra[36]. In past people use to come to stay at this place for week or more to enjoy their holidays. Most of them stay at the place around Lohri nada, one of the very famous spring sources once located in the ambience of orchard. It was considered to be one of the coldest spring sources where people usually had parties. Folk song re-iterates the story "mehle di jatra lodi da pani."

During 1950 cloud burst resulted in a flash flood thus modification of physical and cultural landscape. The orchards and many houses were washed away in the flood. The enormous and famous three loin headed outlet of Lohri nada was lost though later comparatively smaller spring started flowing out of the same place but the quantity and quality of water was lost as per respondents. The size and the amount of water flowing through rivulet around Lohri nada increased drastically after the event. Similar event happened recently in mid 90s bi-furcating the rivulet and washing some more land. This explains how can shape the

---

[34] *Nada*- a streak of water falling on the ground through a outlet
[35] *Jalpa mata*- local deity, a form of goddess incarnated form water henceforth the name
[36] *Jatra*- religious fare in the local dialect

cultural landscape giving it all together a different meaning. Some of the respondents still have remembrance with the old landscape that existed once.

Presently reminiscent of this event can be seen in the form of big enormous boulders that are present in the middle of the village. Over the period of time Mehla has grown in terms of population and extent of habitation. With the big market that has extended downside of the two temples of Jalpa and Hadimba devi 37temple facing each other now in the middle of Mehla.

Two rivulets is the major source of water for irrigation via kuhl system. Almost all the fields come under irrigated land but only wheat and corn are two crops most preferably cultivated in the region. There are few villages at higher reaches in Panchayat where kuhl are not functional permanently and in some villages non-functional in particular season because of less availability of water.

Cultural value associated with water resource

In this paper the term 'culture' is understood and adopted in a dynamic sense. Some of the scholar's current interpretations of culture as dynamic processes are being viewed as where there is active engagement of people in constructing group life and its products [13]. There are three overlapping ways in which 'culture' is used today—in an anthropological sense as the whole way of life of a people; as a functional means of ascribing identity to a group; and to refer to particular social processes [14]. People are considered to live culturally rather than in cultures, with the generative source of culture being human practices rather than in representations of the world [15].

The concept of 'value' was once considered as an intrinsic and universal state. It is now considered to be a social construction which arises from the cultural contexts of a time and place [16]. According to Brown et al. (2002) not only people hold certain 'values' but also express 'value' for certain objects. So, understanding landscape in this sense involves understanding both the nature of the valued 'object' that is aspect of landscape, and the nature of the expressed values for that object. These values do not speak for themselves: they can only be identified when they are expressed by those who are part of the cultural

---

37 *Hadimba Devi*- form of goddess

context, or by those who are in a position to observe and understand [17]. Thus, cultural values are those values that are shared by a group or community, or are given legitimacy through a socially accepted way of assigning value. In the sense it is used here, 'cultural values' are inclusive not only of attributes traditionally considered to be part of 'culture' such as stories and myths, but also of attributes that might be considered to be part of 'nature' yet which are valued by a culture (....).

The cultural element of the environment that is different for people is a reflection of value embodied in culture [18]. Cultural values are fundamental in the understanding importance of natural resources for different people such as spiritually enriching values attached to land and natural resources [19]. The indigenous knowledge of resource management ranging from taboos, myths, belief system etc. often encoded in cultural practice [20]. In Chamba landscape one of the resources that had unique relationship and value in the life of people was water resource. This association can be observed and understood through various means such as history, artifacts, myths and stories associated with water.

Some part of the history about landscape has already been discussed earlier but the other historical facts have close relationship with the artifacts, folklores associated with water resource. Fountain and memorial slab is one of the artifacts that draw attention here.

The fountain stone slabs are the artifacts unique and peculiar to the Chamba region. In the local dialect stone slabs of Chamba are known as Naga, Varun, Panihar, Naun, Autra. These Fountain slabs hold a great significance and are very important aspects of historical events. These are pictorial representations of history which plays a vital role in studying progressiveness as well as spiritual development of human society. These are symbols of sacrifices, offering and name and fame. The excellent carving on these historical works shows well developed architecture skills of laborers of that very period. It throws a light on the minute and skilled art and craft of Chamba in past [10].

There are various religious myths associated with fountain stone slabs. Most of slabs have been constructed as offerings to different deities which reveal that these deities have a great influence on the life of the people. A fountain stone slab not only depicts the religious, political and social aspects of Chamba but also cultural and traditional aspect.

Pictorial representations show the manner and style of Chamba of that era. It sheds light on the fact the importance of the water as a site of worship and recording history in written from or through pictorial representation [10].

In Chamba region there are very few fountain slabs but there are small stone tablets represented with lone figure with folded hands is known as Autra in the local dialect. These tablets are Autra means without son (Aputra), so these figures represent those people who died without sons. This represents the social and religious life of hill area where there is belief and faith in worshipping of water gods and ancestors which are represented in these fountain slabs and memorial stones [10]. These figurines are found lying on the fountain spring or lying under the banyan or peepal tree near the water source or in temples. People generally visit these places frequently so the idea of keeping these tablets in such places were that they regularly worshipped by the people who will visit these places. There are very few Autra tablets in the field area, which belong to older time so one hardly finds a new figurine indicating the decreasing trend in this belief.

There are various religious myths and legends associated with water in this cultural landscape. In the hills water is associated with the Nag cult which is one of the oldest customs of the hills. Nags are considered as water spirits [21]. In Chamba, Birbatal are the water spirits that live in every water source such as river, streams or lakes. Their female counterparts are Jaljogan. These spirits are malevolent but they prevent man from spoiling the water [21].

Varun is the god of water. The Minjar fair of Chamba is also considered to be a part of Varun worship and Minjar has historical and mythological significance as it organized to please Varun devta. In older times the king use to participate in the ceremony of pushing a he-buffalo in the river Ravi. If the buffalo reached the other shore, it was portentous of good fortune; if he turns about and reaches back it was not considered good. This practice no longer exists and now instead a red cloth and coconut is offered to river. It is to please Khawaja, a Muslim appellation is Varun [21]. Varun is also worshipped during marriage ceremonies in the locality.

There are various legends of sacrifices associated with water in this cultural landscape. The most famous and well known is the Sacrifice by Nenna devi wife of king Sahil Varman. According to the story after all the efforts failed to bring water to Chamba town by the King, one day Nenna devi got a dream that in order to bring water successfully to the town they will have to give either of broom stick or someone from royal family will have to give the sacrifice. So the queen willingly decided to give her life in order to bring water to the town. In the memory of her devotion a small shrine was erected afterwards by her husband on the spot where she sat for the last time at the hill top to have last look at the Chamba before she sacrificed her life at the place called 'Salotha'. That shrine is now known as 'Sui mata38' temple and every year 'jatra' or fair is organized from 15 Chait to 1 Baisakh called as "Sui jatra or Sui mela." During this fair only women and children were allowed to visit the shrine in the past but now everyone visits shrines during fair. Gaddi women have special importance in this fair. On the first day when Sui mata is taken to the shrine, these women lead the procession singing "Ghurayi39" and on the last day journey from the shrine back to the palace these women sing "Sukrat40".

There are sacrifices made for pleasing local deities and goddess for either bringing rain or stop the excessive rain. One such temple in field area is Jalpa mata temple. According to the legend Goddess incarnated in the nearby village from the pot of curd that was kept on the side river for fermentation. Since goddess origin was from water that is why she came to be known as Jalpa (jal= water). Sacrifices are given to please goddess in order to get rain or stop it.

Concept of purity and pollution is applied by people to the water and water source. Water is believed to be pure and responsible for the all form of life existing in the world by many respondents. There is a belief that if the polluted women visit water source, water quantity decreases and it may also dry up in the course of time so anyone from the village will perform a small ritual ceremony to appease water god. But this is not universally applicable rule for all the spring sources in the region.

Kuhl which is traditional interconnected rivulets system used mainly for the irrigation purposes. But in the past these also a source for drinking, bathing, washing and for animals use. Earlier quality of kuhl

---

[38] *Sui mata*- queen who sacrificed her life for water is worshiped as goddess
[39] *Ghurayi*- local folk combination of folk songs and dance that is performed generally by Gaddi women in circle
[40] *Sukrat*- local folk song sung on last day of Sui fair

was maintained as it was used sometimes even for drinking water. According to respondents because of population increase these kuhl water is not in condition to be used even for washing purpose or for animal use. In past water used for domestication of animals from kuhl or khud water was used. But now tap water has taken over all these sources and most of the daily usage is being satisfied by tap water. There is shift from 'traditional' water system to almost complete dependence on piped water in the field of study.

Recent developments in the cultural landscape

Cultural Landscapes can provide a historical and ethnographic background which describes changing social and spatial arrangements in region. In case of water it can used to describe important shifts in water ownership, management and use over time. In the present context Chamba is witnessing a change in the way its water resources was perceived, managed and used in the past. Introduction to the water pipelines at large scale in the region by IPH department that was established in the year 1977 is significant point which is responsible for the shift in the way water resource is perceived in the Chamba. Though it has changed scenarios in some water scarce regions where people were spending hours for fetching water but on the other hand it has changed the way water resource was perceived, controlled and treated.

Robert (1994) suggests that water in the modern age is promised with potentially infinite supply and yet it is scarce; it is piped indiscriminately from one basin to the other, and is therefore scale-less and place-less. On the other hand, if there is a constant relation between water and man in history up to modem times that is, water was always in place within a scale [22]. This same phenomenon can be witnessed in the Ravi valley in general and Mehla Panchayat in specific. It was only in mid-1960s that first water pipeline came in to being under block development schemes serving water only to few households. Public Works Department (PWD) was in-charge of water supply and distribution before IPH came as separate department to take care of water sector. There are still some old public taps are there in the field which belong to the time of PWD. Before 1977 with limited resources there were not many schemes in water sector for dinking or irrigation purpose but post 1977 new water supply schemes were launched and is increasing with fast pace according to respondents.

To meet the increasing demand for drinking water, IPH department tapped of the spring sources at higher reaches with small storage tanks, so from this tank water was directly supplied to the villages in the Panchayat. In the field filter tanks are built on one pipeline which is non-functional, rest all the pipelines supply water directly from the source without any filtration process.

Quality of the water according to some respondents is the major issue in the region as there are no functional filter tanks. During the heavy rains muddy water comes in the taps because the source of the water is either directly from the rivulet or the spring source near rivulet. So mud gets mixed up with the water. According to the respondents water quality is only issue during rains though some reports earthworms in the water but not many have seen it with their eyes. Work of Van Wijk-Sijbesma (1985) and Mukherjee (1990) in African and Indian context respectively shows local communities, the concepts of water quality are reportedly based on sensory perceptions like clearness, colour, taste and temperature and special significance is attached to cooking water quality. Similar concepts about the water quality based on sensory perception are present in the field [23].

Recently, increase in water demand which is generally associated with increase in the population area as perceived by respondents, water scarcity was perceived by local people as supply of water to households were time bound and water supply would come in shifts in the mornings and evenings. To overcome this problem department planned for new pipelines from new sources out which one has spring source and other two pipelines supply water directly from 'khad' or rivulets as the source of water. So, according to the respondents new pipelines has solved the problem in such a way that for coming 10-15 years there will be no scarcity of water in that area. The water is available in the village for 24 hours with enormous pressure to such an extent that water controls are used by people to save water taps from breaking. With no assurance of water quality without water filter tanks and direct supply from rivulets, respondents are still satisfied with present water supply.

There are several spring sources of water but the usage of these sources depends on the distance that is how far it is located and season as it is generally preferred in the summer season. If located in proximity most of the people to use spring water for drinking purposes.

Impacts of Climate change and vulnerability on water source in the region

Himalayan ecosystems are predominantly sensitive to climate change. The conservation, sustenance of these ecologically fragile regions is the biggest challenge faced at the moment which can get further aggravated due to financial and resource constraint [24]. Climate change induced weather extremes such as unprecedented drought, frequent floods, cloud burst, erratic and changing pattern of rain and snowfall. Higher temperature and milder and late winters have affected the availability of natural resources in general and water in particular. Over the years, the water availability in all towns of the state has declined and majority of them are facing scarcity situation. The traditional water sources are either on the verge of extinction or dried [24]. Changes in climate over the period of time have affected the water availability and usage pattern. Some of the spring sources which were perennial in nature have started drying up during the summer season.

Climate and weather are understood as part of a universe associated with spiritual significance in many communities. Changes are often interpreted as a violation of religious, moral, and social norms [25]. This is evident in the field area where goddesses, Nag devta are worshipped for rains etc.

Kuhl are interconnected water rivulets which run across and downstream through village. Earlier it was used for various purposes so the water quality was taken care of as people on the downstream would use the same water; it represented collectiveness and interdependence within the village. But in present situation water pipes has lead to more personal use of water and kuhls have become of limited usage so not taken care of as it was done in the past. However some erratic rainfall pattern has been observed in the recent past in the region. The problems of water scarcity are due to population growth, increase in per capita demand, urbanization, agricultural use and industrial demand. Baories, dug wells, step wells, khatries and springs are the traditional water harvesting structures that have been used as source of drinking water in this region over the centuries. In many villages these systems are not used with the spread of piped water supply. The size of catchments limits the quantity of water collected. The water demand has risen many times. Mostly it is sometime not possible to meet the demand of the villagers from the local sources [26].

Conclusion

The paper describes the nexus between the cultures; landscape and available resource in a region especially water. The cultural construction of the environment has a strong historical linkage in Chamba which determines how people develop the sense of their surrounding which shapes their understanding of cultural landscape with respect to water. The artifacts, myths, folklore associated with water shows the cultural and religious values assigned to water in Chamba landscape. This understanding has changed in past and is changing in the present. The understanding of culture values in a cultural landscape which effects and gets affected by water resource in Chamba will help to understand how people cope up in their daily life with challenges faced with respect to water like Climate change.

References

[1] A. Appadurai, The Social Life of Things (Cambridge: Cambridge University, 1986).

[2] V. Strang, Meaning of water (Berg, New York, 2004)

[3] T. Grieder and L. Garkovich, Landscape and social construction of environment, Rural Sociology, 59 (1), 1994, 1-24.

[4] N. Mitchell, Mechtild Rössler, Pierre-Marie Tricaud, World Heritage Cultural Landscapes: A Handbook for Conservation and Management (World Heritage Center, Paris, 2009)

[5] T. Ingold, The Perception of the Environment: Essays on Livelihood, Dwelling and Skill (Routledge, London, New York, 2000.)

[6] K. Fleming, Cultural landscape: A theoretical perspective (Forthcoming)

[7] Chamba official website http://hpchamba.nic.in/. Accessed on 10- June-2014.

[8] K.R. Bharti, Chamba Himalaya: Amazing land and unique culture (Indus publishing company, New Delhi, 2001)

[9] Thakur Sen Negi. Himachal Pradesh district gazetteers Chamba (Standard printing Press, 1963).

[10] S.M. Sethi and H. Chauhan. Fountain stone slab of Chamba (Literary circle, Jaipur, 2006).

[11] H. Goetz, The early wooden temples of Chamba: Memoirs of the Kern Institute; No. 1 (Netherland, 1995)

[12] S. Sharma, The Himalayan eco-crisis and the people of the Himalayas, in N.K. Rustomjee and Charles Rambe (Ed.) Himalayan environment and culture (IIAS, 1990).

[13] R. Johnston, D. Gregory, G. Pratt, M. Watts, (Eds.), The Dictionary of Human Geography (Blackwell, Oxford, MA, 2000)

[14] N. Thrift, S. Whatmore, (Eds.), Cultural Geography: Critical Concepts in the Social Sciences (Routledge, London, New York, 2004).

[15] T. Ingold, (Ed.), Companion Encyclopedia of Anthropology (Routledge, London, New York, 1994).

[16] E. Avrami, R. Mason, M. de la Torre, Values and Heritage Conservation—Research Report (The Getty Conservation Institute, Los Angeles,2000).

[17] G. Brown, P. Reed, C.Harris, Testing a place-based theory for environmental evaluation: An Alaska case study. Applied Geography 22, 2002, 49–76.

[18] Byers et al., Linking the Conservation of Culture and Nature: A Case Study of Sacred Forests in Zimbabwe. Human Ecology, Vol. 29(2), 2001.

[19] M. Cocks, Biocultural diversity: moving beyond the realm of indigenous and local people, Human Ecology, 34 (2), 2006, 185–200.

[20] A. Mandondo, Trees and spaces as emotion and norm laden components of local ecosystems in Nyamaropa communal land, Nyanga District, Zimbabwe, Agriculture and Human Values, 14 (4), 1997, 353–372.

[21] U. Bande, Folk tradition and ecology in Himachal Pradesh, (Indus Publisher in association with Institute of Integrated Himalayan studies HP University Shimla, 2006).

[22] J. Robert, Water is a common, (Mexico: Habitat International coalition, 1994).

[23] Nadita Singh, P. Bhattacharya, G. Jacks and Jan-Erik Gustafsson, Women and Modern Domestic Water Supply Systems: Need for a Holistic Perspective, Water Resources Management 18, 2004, 237–248.

[24] State strategy and action plan on climate change, (Himachal Pradesh, 2012)

[25] C. Roncoli, T. Crane, B. Orlove, Fielding Climate Change in Cultural Anthropology http://cred.columbia.edu/files/2012/05/Roncoli-Crane-Orlove_2008_ AnthroCC.pdf.

[26] Hari Pal Singh, M.R. Sharma, Q. Hassan, N. Ahsan, Impact of drought on drinking water resources of Himachal Pradesh, Biological Forum - An International Journal, 2 (1), 2010, 73-77